Seven Pillars Volume One: Anti-Knowledge
As the Cause of Human Suffering

Copyright 2012
by Anthony Shkreli

ISBN: 978-0985135300

All Rights Reserved

Published by:
Seven Pillars House Publishing
www.sevenpillarsonline.com

TABLE OF CONTENTS

Preface: The Cause of Suffering   *1*
Introduction: Paradox Gained   *10*

Chapter One   *24*
History Pillar: We are Losers

Chapter Two   *54*
Science Pillar: Et Tu, Scientia?

Chapter Three   *82*
Politics/Economics Pillar: That Which is Unseen

Chapter Four   *120*
Fortean Pillar: UFO's are Suppressed Technology
Part One 19th Century Beginnings

Chapter Five   *166*
General Philosophy Pillar: The Poison Fountain
of Education

Chapter Six   *213*
Health Pillar: For Those Who Have Eyes to See

Chapter Seven   *253*
Theology/Metaphysics Pillar: A New Argument
For Murder

Select Bibliography   *275*

PREFACE: THE CAUSE OF SUFFERING

There is something about the image of a crossroads.

The image inspires poems, legends, and oratory; even ancient prophets and prophecies make references to a crossroads. One example from our modern era is from the poet Robert Frost. In his poem, *The Road Not Taken*, Frost depicts himself as a traveler confronting the two divergent roads. The problem of the traveler, what Frost goes on to explain in poetic terms, is the epistemological problem—it is the problem that every person faces when they stand at a crossroads. It is a problem of knowledge; whether the traveler should take one or the other road is not really clear because there is *limited information*. The full weight of it all hits him when he stands where the two roads begin to divagate. As Frost tells us,

long I stood
And looked down one as far as I could
To where it bent in the undergrowth . . .

A reasonable and prudent thing to do, to look down as far as one can before taking that road but difficult at the

1

same time as one can not see the end from the beginning. It is the one thing that gnaws away at a weary traveler— 'Is this really the right way?' Because at the outset, nothing seems to distinguish one path from the other— they both seem to have the same wear at the beginning although after he has made his choice, he realizes at some point that the path he chose *was* less traveled.

How did he know this? Perhaps as he was traveling on his chosen road he noticed abrupt u-turns from the tracks left in the ground. But if you are noticing these sudden reversals of direction, why on earth would you want to stay on that path? I mean, there must be some reason why everyone is turning back. I believe this particular traveler stays on this path because he knows something— this traveler has some inside knowledge. He chooses the path less traveled because what is implicit in this poem is that the traveler has a certain epistemological view of reality and it is this: Frost, or the traveler, *does not buy the argument from numbers*. To this traveler, if no one is going down his path, so much for the better. With a sigh, at the end of the poem, Frost tells us that his journey based on this criteria turned out Okay— that his choice was a correct one. But this goes against the conventional wisdom of the world. When you see all those tracks of previous travelers going back, the natural inclination is to follow the majority. It is quite an audacious and strange move to keep going forward. Yet I feel this fact of everyone turning back, except for Frost the traveler, is *exactly what gave him comfort and assurance that it was the best path*— in other words this traveler is surveying the path and making the gutsy assertion to himself, "If the world is not going down this path, if it is unpopular, then it must be the correct choice!"

A PICNIC WITH GRAVITY

This book adheres to two tenets. First, dear reader, it is the contention of this book that almost all of your beliefs, whatever they are, are popular beliefs . . . Now, you may take issue with this but what you must understand is that we are not talking about issues in which there is clearly division such as political philosophies of right and left or global warming versus no global warming. What I am talking about is the *belief behind the belief* — a primary belief. This is the core or root belief that is prior to and cause of many of our commonly held beliefs. This prior belief sort of lurks in the shadows and is not recognized especially whenever two seemingly opposing philosophies clash. In many cases this prior or primary belief is shared between the opposites in an argument so that the odd result is that those who think they disagree, really are in agreement. What these primary beliefs are sometimes called in philosophy are *presuppositions*. Again, as we will see, when you apply this presuppositional apparatus to a topic, for example, such as political dissension (right and left, marxist and capitalist etc.) surprisingly, you will see that there is a *primary belief* that both parties adhere to and *agree* upon— therefore, it is a popular belief. This will be found in many subjects where it is thought that there is disagreement in an issue.

The second tenet and overarching principle of this book is that most of these primary beliefs or popular beliefs are unremittingly *wrong*. How do I know this? Because there is suffering in the world . . .

A primary belief hovers over *and governs* our every waking moment— it is the shadow behind you, unnoticed and overlooked. Yet no action can be taken by a human unless he has an assumption or belief that governs that act. Every person alive on the planet has primary foundational beliefs, or presuppositions, that govern their actions, even if they are not fully conscious of this. Now, what is important to grasp here is that these unseen, non-physical beliefs eventually *materialize,* because a primary belief is the cradle *from which* human action emanates.

To demonstrate this let us use a simple example from the realm of Science. A principle from Science that governs much of our actions and decisions is gravity. We have both been taught this and actually experienced it for ourselves and so we hold this principle as a primary belief. Therefore, this particular primary belief of ours has the power to govern our actions and decisions. Though we are not always consciously aware of it, we somehow manage to incorporate this primary belief into our subconsciousness— this is the nature of a primary belief— we don't consciously dwell on it but it somehow lurks just beneath the level of consciousness *while influencing our decisions.*

For instance, if we are picnicking by a cliffside, on a windy day, we stay comfortably away from the edge because we know what can happen if we venture too close. But as we are sitting there eating and drinking and making merry, we do not discuss or think about the concept of gravity, yet it governs our actions powerfully yet unobtrusively just below the level of consciousness. Interestingly, even though we may not be scientifically minded, we give heed to a principle that we may care less about studying intellectually. The concept of gravity is not talked about at this gathering but it looms behind our *actions* at this gathering when we make sure that the children stay safely away from the cliff. The belief, which is a nonphysical entity, really, has materialized in the physical world through our actions— *it has borne fruit so to speak.* Whether for good or bad, the primary beliefs stand over us, dictating our behavior.

I think if we understand the above then we can readily see how a primary belief can cause suffering. For instance, if the primary belief we hold is 'bad', that is, incorrect— then it follows that the eventual outcome or the action will be 'bad' or incorrect. Let us again use as an example our cliffside picnic. What if we have an incorrect conception of gravity at this picnic? We may suffer pain . . .

If a person carries on about how he can fly and *believes* that gravity does not have the same effect upon him as it does to the general population, by simply flapping his arms, it is obvious he will undoubtedly experience pain at some point. What is not so obvious is that the suffering he will eventually experience is not due to him jumping off a cliff and testing his new found powers. It is due to a *wrong belief.* If he had the right conception about the the physical world, the pain in his body would not be there.

So let us magnify this principle and apply it to a larger and more general context by asking the question: Could it be that the pain and the suffering in the world is due to wrong beliefs? It is an old contention of ancient philosophers and of the ancient literature of the world that this is in fact so. It is also the contention of *Seven Pillars.* In fact, *suffering in general may be a clue that our knowledge is distorted.* It may not be so easy to see that pain can be caused by a wrong understanding of history or say, the wrong understanding of biology, but it is my conviction and the goal of *Seven Pillars* to show that this is in fact the case. But, likewise, to also show that when we have the right beliefs— the truth about history, science, economics and other such topics— good things follow because they are immutable laws . . . like gravity. Again, how do I know that the seven areas of knowledge spoken of in this book are misguided and have incorrect foundational principles? Because there is suffering in the world . . .

WEB OF LIES

But what must be understood is that these primary beliefs have children. These offspring are the secondary beliefs or assumptions which flow out from the primal belief *by necessity*. Take our primal belief in gravity. If we were to hear about someone falling off of a very tall building we would not have to be told about the outcome. Our knowledge of gravity has given us the conclusion (further knowledge) without us having to hear about it— the individual surely is dead. But here is the problem if our primary beliefs are wrong— every secondary assumption we make will also be inaccurate. This will create a web of beliefs which rest on a false foundation. The primal belief constrains us into following a certain course that we can not get out of because the web now has become so intricate and convoluted because these secondary beliefs give birth and attract further beliefs that must be in line with the foundation of primal beliefs even though the foundation is shaky. This goes on and on for ever until we die. Now this construction or *this web of beliefs then becomes an interpretive apparatus for all of reality.*

In other words, because of the continual accumulation of 'facts' that align with the web, the web begins to act as a tightly packed filter that only accumulates 'facts' that are in alignment with the overall web. Any facts that are contrary to this 'web' are simply dismissed as ludicrous or fringe. Overall, this construct is what is known as a *world view*. But the disturbing thing about all this is that because of the primal belief being incorrect the whole structure which is intricately designed . . . is wrong. This is a humbling thought that one could think they 'have' knowledge when if fact they don't— it is a false knowledge. It is anti-knowledge.

As will be shown in this book, this anti-knowledge can not possibly breed freedom or prosperity. The ancient literature of the world bears testimony to anti-knowledge as being in direct relation to suffering.

IGNORANCE IS NOT BLISS

In Platonic thought, there is a direct relation between anti-knowledge and suffering. Plato, through Socrates, tells us that a person who does wrong only does so because he is conceptually blinded as to what he is actually doing— he doesn't *know* what he is doing because if he did he wouldn't do it. The wrongdoer is ignorant— there is missing knowledge in the wrongdoers mind, so to speak. But it is not a complete ignorance. It is just an ignorance of the truth— correct knowledge. For example, as we will see, a thief does have knowledge but it is false knowledge. He believes that stealing from others is right but how do we know that this is false knowledge? Because it is self-stultifying or self-negating. The philosopher C.S Lewis has pointed this out throughout his writings (especially in Mere Christianity), that a wrongdoer does not like to suffer wrong. Lewis would have put it like this: 'Thieves do not like being stolen from.' This implies that their philosophy is self-negating. In light of this we could say that the thief may gain the missing knowledge by having his possessions stolen— he then suffers pain. At this point he may come to the realization that this is what he is causing in others. Like gravity is brought home to us when we fall, so the primary belief of the thief changes when his goods are stolen from him— by now understanding that those whom he steals from are subjects just like him and not objects that have no feelings. Before, he thought that he was the only subject, the only being with feelings— this was his primary belief or the *belief behind the belief*. Because of this incorrect conception the thief no doubt caused suffering in the world because it was anti-knowledge. I have only gone to this length to show that the wrongdoer is not in complete ignorance— he has knowledge but it is not the right kind. We could say that ignorance really implies knowledge of a sort but of the false or wrong kind— anti-knowledge.

In the 8th century B.C., Isaiah the prophet pointed out that the primary beliefs of his fellow Israelites were of a false nature and that their suffering was directly related to this. The people of Israel were being threatened by invasion from the cruel Assyrian empire who planned to take them into captivity. But Isaiah says a strange thing to the people of Israel; he says that Assyria, the cause of their suffering, is not their real problem. Instead he points to something else as being the cause of their suffering and he says that the message is straight from the mouth of God: "Therefore my people go into exile for lack of knowledge; their honored men go hungry, and their multitude is parched with thirst."(Is. 5:13) Around the same time period Hosea the prophet warns Israel about the same thing: "My people are destroyed for lack of knowledge; because you have rejected knowledge, I reject you . . ."(Hosea 4:6) The job of these prophets was to warn the Israelites that they were at a crossroads, that they were considering the popular path that all the nations around them had chosen but this popular path would end in suffering— "Therefore Sheol has enlarged its throat and opened its mouth without measure . . ."(Is. 5:14) Isaiah is making the connection between ignorance and suffering. But again, as with Plato, it is not a complete ignorance. The Israelites do have knowledge but it is *wrong* knowledge— anti-knowledge. Isaiah blames the people for believing that this false knowledge is the truth and that they should instead confess that, " . . .we have made falsehood our refuge and we have concealed ourselves with deception."(Isaiah 28:15)

There is suffering in the world and it is because, regarding knowledge, mankind has followed the path well trodden. It is time to retrace our steps, if we can, and go down that other path so that possibly at some point in time we can say with the poet:

" . . . *that has made all the difference* . . ."

INTRODUCTION: PARADOX GAINED

In the Preface we have introduced the idea that suffering is caused by something known as anti-knowledge. The fact that there is suffering requires no proof. What we will answer in this chapter is how anti-knowledge comes about. What are the origins of anti-knowledge which is the cause of human suffering?

THE BEGINNING OF SORROWS

As Jeremy Campbell points out in his book, *Grammatical Man*, something happens to information before it comes to our consciousness. This seems to be a universal phenomenon. Information, as it leaves its source, does not degrade by virtue of itself. Instead, it succumbs to the forces of entropy which are innate in the medium; these forces disorganize that which was once organized. In other words when information reaches us it is contaminated by a thing called *noise* and therefore, becomes either somewhat or completely incomprehensible to us. Noise is the death of information.

Now, noise is an important concept in information theory but it will also be an important tool in understanding the overarching, all-embracing principle of this book—which is that *truth and suffering are inextricable from each other*. It can be simplified by putting it in these terms— to the degree that there is suffering is the degree to which there is truth or lack of it. In other words, more truth equals less suffering. Less truth equals more suffering..

So we will borrow from information theory and proceed by saying that noise is disorganization, it has no *specificity*. When information is first transmitted in a medium, one of its properties is that it has *specificity*. In other words, there is something that distinguishes it from the medium or its surroundings. If I say to you on the phone, 'It is raining here', I have accomplished this. Before this, all you heard was silence; the words I spoke 'stuck out' from the medium. But this same message can get contaminated or corrupted by something known as 'noise.' It is possible the phone is not working well and you hear this, 'It is . . .ing here.'

This corruption by this externality called noise does an interesting thing because now the possibilities for *interpretation* are endless. For after all, it could be 'snowing here' or 'boring here'. So noise, or entropy, introduces a concept called *interpretation*, which would not be needed in a pristine environment unencumbered by noise. Entropy or noise has interfered with the transmittal and the end result is corrupted information which must now call in the function of interpretation. But has the information vanished forever? That is, can the message be restored?

Remarkably, Campbell believes that lost information can become disentangled, so to speak, from the morass of noise. It is always there and available but it must be extricated or decoded in some manner. Noam Chomsky has elaborated on this topic as it pertains to human language. There are two worlds in language— the *deep structure* and the *surface structure*, according to Chomsky. The deep structure contains that which the surface structure only hints at. We could liken surface structure to noise. As Campbell puts it while explaining Chomsky, "Deep structure is closest to the meaning intended by the speaker, and the least affected by distortions and ambiguity. It is the structure to which all other structures can be reduced." Deep structure would be "Boy loves girl." However, as this essence becomes surface structure it transforms into an utterance that is vaguely related to the deep structure: "Upon hearing about Carol's flirtation in class with Harry, Carl decided to take a walk." This is the surface structure of 'Boy loves girl' and we can see a little of what has happened in the transformation from deep to surface structure. Many changes have taken place from 'Boy loves girl' to get to this surface structure which barely hints at the truth. How does one recover 'Boy loves girl'? Chomsky believes that the deep structure, that the original message, can be reached because it follows certain rules on its way to becoming surface structure. These are called *rules of transformation*. The original message (deep structure) becomes transformed by certain techniques into something, at times, which barely resembles it. However, these changes that occur to original information are not a good thing, for as the authors Kress and Hodge point out in their book *Language as Ideology*, "The typical function of transformations is distortion and mystification, through the characteristic disjunction between surface form and implicit meanings."

But it is not only in language that this distortion takes

place. The burden of this book is to show how noise, or corruption of information, has been injected into every field of knowledge. It is also the goal to show that the original message can be retrieved; the corruption of knowledge can be lifted and cleared. But to bring the concept into focus a little more, we will use a template for our further investigation into what noise is . . . .

EVE TELLS THE SERPENT A STRANGE THING

We must keep in mind what happened to the deep structure as it became transformed into surface structure: The original message is distorted through various means or trans formations— this is noise. The picture may become a little clearer if we look to the origins of when noise was introduced. The Serpent, in the Garden of Eden, introduced the possibility of noise in his showdown with Eve, the mother of mankind. The original message from the Creator had *specificity* and clarity; it was information without any interference. When the Serpent confronted Eve he *attacked the specificity* of the message from the Creator thereby introducing Eve to the concept of noise and chaos. But this is all he does at first. Once Eve is introduced to the concept of noise she takes it and runs with it. She does two things at once— she affirms the original message while at the same time pulling off a most stunning move: She says that the original message does not have *enough* specificity when she says to the Serpent, "God has said, 'You shall not eat from it or *touch it* . . .'"

Now here is an interesting thing: When did God ever say not to touch the fruit? There was no such injunction ever given to Adam about touching the fruit, only about not eating it. Here is Eve introducing an unnecessary layer to that which was the original message. She took what was simple and intelligible and complicated it by adding— noise. There was nothing said about touching the fruit in the original transmittal of information yet Eve seems to want to add onto the original message by saying proudly to the Serpent, 'Yeah and by the way we can't touch it either.' By doing this she has transformed the deep structure, the original message, and she has now introduced what Chomsky calls surface structure and hence, as a by-product, interpretation. So we see here that this concept of noise takes on a certain shading of color of having something added unnecessarily. We can call this an unnecessary addition or an accretion or whatever you like but the message should be clear that it complicates something that was simple. But also, this noise that Eve has added has the danger of being confused with the truth because it is in the form of information though it is needless and unnecessary information. It never occurred to Eve that what she was doing was unfruitful.

THE WEIGHT

It seems to be an inveterate, innate characteristic of humanity to create noise in any endeavor it undertakes, especially in the various fields of knowledge. In fact, *every* field of knowledge known to man is corrupted by this influence. This book will explore the various corruptions in the various fields of knowledge but for now we will establish and confirm the *template* by looking at an example from New Testament times, circa 30 A.D.

The scribal sect in Judea, around the time of Christ, were the teachers and interpreters of Mosaic law. They were usually associated with the religious order of the Pharisees but had a higher standing in the eyes of Jewish society—

for to become a pharisee did not require the rigors that attaining scribal status did. Teacher or Master (rabbi) were the names given to this group which in the Hebrew carries the sense of 'great' or 'revered'. To become a Rabbi or Teacher of the Law one had to go through rigorous training and preparation. One of the reasons for this intensive training was because these rabbis also served as lawyers and judges in penal cases. The memorization alone of all the oral tradition was astounding. Their authority was great for according to the New Testament they " . . . sat in the chair of Moses."

Actually, what they did to the Law or Torah (information) was compound or complicate it with their interpretations; these additional laws and restrictions transformed a simple injunction like *Honor the Sabbath,* into something nightmarish. Hundreds of bylaws and injunctions were incorporated into this one commandment. According to the Old Testament, Honoring the Sabbath simply meant to rest from any kind of work. But this was not enough for the scribes; work had to be defined. So scrupulous were they in defining work and its concomitants that they lost sight of the original intent of the commandment. The scribes defined work by creating 39 categories of what could be categorized as work. Then all these categories had to have interpretation and these interpretations then became lawful injunctions.

This madness led to such declarations as: "The school of Shamai teaches: 'Bones and husks may be removed from the table.' The school of Hillel, however, teaches: 'One may only lift the whole table board (or cloth), and shake off what is left over.' All crumbs smaller than an olive may be removed from the table . . ." — and this,

"MISHNA VI. Whether a light may be extinguished on Sabbath either for fear of accident or to afford rest for the sick . . . . .

Is it allowed to place a pitcher of cold water into one filled with hot water in order to heat the water; or, vice versa, in order to heat the water?"

Or this, "One may lift up a (petted) child, that has a stone in its hand, also a basket in which there is a stone; one may also handle unclean Therumah (heave-offerings), together with clean and with ordinary grain." These are all quotes from the *Tractate Shabbat* which is a book of 24 chapters wherein the Sabbath law is reinterpreted into these strange declamations.

This led Jesus, their opponent, to say that they were, "Neglecting the commandment of God (truthful information)..." by adding on to it unnecessary layers that complicated the matter and thereby putting the subject out of reach for most others. Instead they would " . . . hold to the tradition of men" — which we know as noise.(Mark 7:8) These needless accretions of the Law affected the lives of those who received their teachings: "They tie up heavy burdens and lay them on men's shoulders . . ." (Mat. 23:4) Again, we can see from this verse that noise carries the connotation of a *needless addition*, from the picture we get of a weight (heavy burdens) affecting mankind (on men's shoulders). Very much the same thing is happening here as in the Garden with Eve.

With hundreds and hundreds of unnecessary additions to a simple commandment, the Law of the Pentateuch takes on a different appearance. It now seems daunting and intimidating to the average person thereby insulating what is simple from being accessed and approachable.

Their opponent (to them), Jesus, seemed to think that they missed the boat on what the Law (information/truth) really meant. He pointed out their tendency to becloud an issue with noise at almost every confrontation. He believed that the Truth was simple and intelligible and that it was not beyond the grasp of ordinary people to understand, that the truth was able to be understood by those who were 'childlike' in distinction to those who had degrees and were 'learned'. (Matt 11:25) This threat of breaking the monopolistic power of the scribes galvanized them to such a point that they became instrumental in obtaining a death sentence for Jesus (Matt. 26:57; 27:41 Luke 22:66; 23:10). 'Power over the people' rather than 'power in the hands of the people' was their mantra.

The mystery, the arcane aura that surrounded this field of knowledge that Jesus felt was simple was now an intimidating structure to the man on the street. So much so, that we could probably guess the reply of a typical individual Jewish person living at that time if we were to ask him or her the following: Do you feel you have a good understanding of the Law of the Pentateuch? The answer would be undoubtedly: "I am not a Rabbi . . ."

As we stated at the beginning, truth, when it is encumbered with noise, now must call in the aid of *interpretation*. Because of the now convoluted nature of the field we must call in the interpreter, the *professional*, whom we entrust to unravel the opaque knowledge. We don't blame that citizen of Judaea for being hesitant about saying 'Yes, I understand the Law of Moses . . . ' Anyone would be reluctant, for the

Law of Moses was the province of the trained professionals—yet Jesus said that anyone could understand it.

But if we brood over that reply of that Judaean citizen for a moment, there seems to be something in it that sounds familiar. There is a timbre to the reply that is reminiscent of something that is happening today. For example, let us take the typical citizen of today and ask him or her the same question— not about the Law of Moses, obviously. Let us ask the average person who works an average job and has an average life the following:

Question: Do you feel you have a good understanding of the field of Economics?

Answer: I am not an Economist . . .

Different time period, different field of knowledge— but it is the same scribal pattern as at the time of Jesus and as in the Garden with Eve. The highly specialized form of knowledge the scribes had is a characteristic of the modern fields of knowledge. Who can wend their way through all the data and opposing view points? It is an intimidating monolith and just as with the scribes, those who hold claim to being the interpreters, or professors, are held in reverence by the populace— that someone could know so much about such arcane and convoluted matters is highly esteemed.

The thesis that this book unveils is that *all fields of knowledge follow this scribal pattern of unnecessary additions, omissions and distortions, creating opaqueness and confusion when there should be clarity and simplicity. The end result is annoyance and avoidance by the general populace, when each field, in reality, is simple and understandable.*

Could it be that the same thing is being done to all these

fields of knowledge as what was being done by the scribes to the Torah? And, if the same thing is happening, could it also be that it is possible to understand the essence of these fields of knowledge so that we could be on an even greater footing than the so-called professors in those fields? Keep in mind, Jesus repeatedly made the point that the scribes, though they had great training, were missing the whole picture— the general idea of the Torah. According to Jesus, the so-called professionals missed the boat and had what amounted to as useless knowledge. Is it possible that by understanding the essence of a field of knowledge, understanding the whole rather than the Talmudic-like, obscurantist ways of the modern interpreters, that we could gain an even greater understanding than those who are the so-called experts of those fields?

SOCRATES AND THE WEIGHT

Many who have pointed this out about truth, i.e. that it is graspable and simple, in whatever field of knowledge, have suffered persecutions that range from public ostracism to professional excommunication and even to extremes of corporal punishment. Socrates was another example of one who suffered from the latter. He made light of his primary accusers when they said it was because of atheism (not believing in the Athenian gods) that Socrates was being put on trial. Socrates pointed out the real reason; that it was in fact because he challenged the *information monopolists* and their veracity, pointing out that all they were spouting was noise. These professions, (priests, poets, scribes, political orators and officeholders) had the monopoly on all information, therefore they had the truth. But Socrates pointed out that noise was all they were spouting— that information does not by necessity equal truth. Because of his innovative teaching style he gathered to himself followers that eventually learned his style of dialectic. These followers, most of them young, then challenged those in the above mentioned authority positions about their respective fields of knowledge and it turned out they were successful: "A number of young men . . . often take me as their model, and go on to try to question other persons . . . they find an unlimited amount of people who think that they know something, but really know little or nothing. Consequently, their victims become annoyed, not with themselves but with me, and they complain that there is a pestilential busybody called Socrates who fills young people's heads with wrong ideas."(all quotes from the *Apology*)Through the special reasoning process (dialectic) taught by Socrates, they found out and proved Socrates's life-long conviction about people in general and those in the professions mentioned above specifically— *"they are being convicted of pretending to knowledge when they are entirely ignorant."*(emphasis mine)

Socrates sealed his fate, however, when he found out that these monopolists of information would not sit still for this exposure of their ignorance: "So, jealous, for their own reputation, and also energetic and numerically strong . . . these people have been dinning into your ears for a long time past their violent denunciations of myself." The three main accusers he mentions happen to be in professions that deal with information about the most important fields of knowledge: "Meletus being aggrieved on behalf of the poets, Anytus on behalf of the professional men and politicians, and Lycon on behalf of the orators." This covered the gamut as far as knowledge for that time period. If he were alive today he might have had a longer list but the point is this: The truth about *reality* was defined by these groups; the general populace had their worldview shaped by these groups with their *opinions until Socrates came along.* He recognized, even then, what the intent of this group was against anyone who dares oppose them: *"They have been fatal to a great many other innocent men, and I suppose will continue to be so; there is no likelihood they will stop at me."* More true words could not be spoken as many after Socrates found out.

RECOVERY

Can the message be recovered? That is, can the noise and distortion be whittled away in science and history and religion and politics until the kernel or essence is revealed? The goal is to reach that essence, to come to a place where Socrates himself would be satisfied— to come away with a special kind of knowledge, an understanding that is able to pierce through the dense maelstrom. Having reached it, we will know that what we have is . . . . *wisdom.* This is in distinction to what the world perceives as knowledge but *the world never makes a distinction between information and truth.* Knowledge, as this world thinks it, is concerned with information but we must keep in mind, however,— it seems strange to say this but it is not readily apparent, especially to the Western mind,— that information does not equal truth as we have seen above. In fact, here is a rule to remember: The more information there is available, the less truth will be available.

This is, in essence, the paradox of this world and it is that which will be unraveled in this and further volumes.

The fact that, in this culture of information access and excess, *the truth is not available*. From the examples we have used above we have gained a little insight into the mechanics of this phenomena in human knowledge but the full length and breadth of it will be explored in the coming pages. As we tackle the subjects of knowledge in this book we must keep in mind how the scribes claimed the truth but the fact was, the truth was being veiled— hidden. The same thing will be seen in the various fields of knowledge which we will soon take on.

But the choice lies with mankind as it did with Eve . . . . . Information or Truth? Understanding and wisdom or memorization and inundation with 'facts'?

The dichotomy of knowledge is illustrated in the Proverbs of King Solomon where he describes wisdom as a woman who prepares a feast for 'whoever is naive'. What stands out about this description is how wisdom is concerned for the proper nutrition of her guests. To him who lacks understanding she says, 'Come, eat of my food and drink of the wine I have mixed."

Immediately after this Solomon paints us a picture of that which is in contrast to Wisdom and he illustrates it by means of the *woman of folly*. What is interesting is that she also, like wisdom, issues an invitation to 'whoever is naive'— the same exact overture that wisdom makes but there is a difference. Whereas wisdom prepared a feast for those who would come to her table, the woman of folly does not care about the nourishment of her conquests; she does not prepare any food for her guests at all, leaving them hungry. As Proverbs 9:18 says, "Her guests are in the depths of Sheol", that is, they are dead from malnutrition. Much of the 'information' in this modern age has that quality of leaving one malnourished to the point of death. Does anyone feel they are nourished when they come away from a newscast or reading a newspaper? Wisdom in contrast, at least to the wise King Solomon, has a satisfying, appeasing affect. But there are many other ways in which wisdom differs from the bulimic knowledge of this world . . . .

Wisdom or understanding is a way of looking at things and being able to see all possibilities, all potentialities without having to go through all the roads and pathways to find out what is there.

It is looking at a seed and *seeing the tree or plant*.

It is about distilling an essence that escapes everyone else.

It is about knowing where to look when everyone else is looking at the wrong hand in a magicians trick.

It is the big picture . . . .

The children of the scribes and the children of those who persecuted Socrates lurk in every field of knowledge known to man. Whether it is history, economics or science, they have added noise to the terrain, and the noise needs to be eradicated if one desires understanding— wisdom. Once the noise is removed, we can hear the message without interference. For these layers of distortion, as we will see, are the primary hurdle to solving the problem of human suffering. Once we remove the noise we will see the clarity and pristine character of truth— for truth and only truth is the enemy of all human suffering. Now we shall see the interplay between these two in the fields of human knowledge . . .

HISTORY PILLAR: WE ARE LOSERS

1

The trains would probably still run. The sun would rise the next day and people would still buy and trade and make wedding plans and divorce and commit crime and make love. In short the world would keep turning. I venture to guess there would be no great mourning by most of the world.

It is just a thought experiment but what inspires it is the book, *Childhood's End,* by Arthur C. Clarke, specifically one scene in the book that will serve us as a sort of parable. In the book, the Galactic Overlords have arrived and among many of the things that happen as a result of this historic meeting between the two races, the Supervisor assigned to Earth, Karellen, has decided upon a way to settle disputes between historians on matters of history. He hands over a device to the World History Foundation that is able to dial in on space and time co-ordinates; once this is done, a television screen displays exactly what happened at that point in time in history. Needless to say, most of history, when dialed up, turns out to be false; the historians are in shock and disillusionment but life goes on . . . the trains still run.

Let us just suppose, for a moment, that the world has been given a device like the one in Clarke's book and historians the world over gather together and audit history— all of it. After carefully going over each time period they make an official announcement that, yes, 90 percent of history is completely wrong. Who would care? Would this affect daily life and trade and commerce? Would people be jumping out of windows? Finding out untruths about the Revolutionary War or that Napoleon never existed wouldn't really jeopardize commerce or stop trade on Wall Street. Except for academic historians there would be no great disillusionment or grief. So the question is, why even bother with history?

However, this question gets swallowed up by an even bigger question that looms over this whole episode written by Clarke which he leaves unanswered and it is this—why was history false in the first place? In other words, what were the historians doing wrong? How could there be such a divergence from what the historians reported and what was showing up on Karellen's video screen? Maybe, if Clarke were allowed to answer, the excuse would be that historians were working with incomplete information. On the surface this sounds valid but upon examination falls apart. Even when all the facts are present to an individual, he still must *interpret* the data and . . . *interpretations, even with all the facts, have been wrong.* Information that is missing or incomplete is not the problem with history. The problem is that the information that is available to historians is not allowed entrance— it is either minimized or left out altogether. However, a good place to begin to study this phenomenon would be Howard Zinn's, *A People's History of the United States* for examples of American history gone wrong. It is a compendium of these 'inconvenient facts'— information and facts that have always been available to historians but have been skipped over because this realization would change something . . . it would change history. In fact we don't need to use Karellen's machine of truth to see that something strange is happening with history; all we have to do is survey this ploy of historians briefly and then examine a particular occurrence of this in depth— because there very well may be a reason why people are indifferent to history, as we have illustrated in the thought experiment above— it is because they smell a rat . . .

MYTH(i)STORY

The British writer and historian Clive Ponting is known for shattering the myth of Winston Churchill and also for recasting World War 2, known fondly as 'the good war', in a much more unfavorable light. When he was researching Britain's involvement in the Second World War he was quite surprised when he ran into certain documents relating to that war in the Public Record Office, a branch of the National Archives, in the United Kingdom. He was well acquainted with Winston Churchill's book, *The Second World War*, but as he was going through the archives, he was surprised at how much was omitted from Churchill's book. It led him to characterize the work as " a politician's memoir designed to relate his version of events and to present the story as he wanted." Churchill, for 'his version of events', won the Nobel prize for Literature in 1953.

Another idol of historians, Abraham Lincoln, has fallen off his throne due to the work of Thomas J. Dilorenzo. In his book, *The Real Lincoln,* a new picture comes into focus and appellations like 'Honest Abe' are completely eviscerated under DiLorenzo's examination. The litany of crimes and transgressions by Lincoln and his administration against the populace were staggering. Arrest and imprisonment of newspaper publishers and editors; suspension of Constitutional freedoms such as habeas corpus. DiLorenzo writes, "Northern citizens were subjected to the threat of arbitrary arrest by the military for the duration of the Lincoln administration." In fact thousands of protesters *were* arrested by Secretary of State William Seward's secret police force. Seward boasted that he could "ring a bell" and have any man arrested in any state. To protect himself and his administration from legal reprisals he orchestrated the passing of the "indemnity act" in 1863; in effect putting himself and the administration above the law. There were more than 13,000 political inmates in Lincoln's military prisons. The arrest of the duly elected members of the Maryland legislature in 1861 would top it off if it wasn't for the mass execution of the Santee Sioux Indians of Minnesota in 1862. By not paying the Indians what they were owed, the federal government broke another treaty. The Indians revolted and General John Pope, whose purpose was "to utterly exterminate the Sioux" (his words), was put in charge by Lincoln. Women and children were put into prisons at military forts and the 303 male Indians captured were to be put to death. Lincoln came to his senses somehow, and decided that it wouldn't be good marketing to do that and hence, in his grace, *only* allowed the execution of 39 Indians. This is all there for every one to see, but somehow it has been 'omitted' from popular accounts. Even professional historians gloss over these warts, and the justifications they make are outrageous; such as calling the mass arbitrary arrests as "unfortunate" and done with the "best of motives" or that Lincoln, despite his faults, was a "benevolent dictator".

Recently, Gavin Menzies has kindled consternation in the hearts of professional historians due to the claims in his book, *1421: The Year China Discovered America*. Strangely, the facts that he brings up have been circulating and documented for quite some time, especially in China, but they have been ignored by western scholars who were hoping the din would become a little more low-pitched. To their dismay, it didn't; and it took Mr. Menzies, a retired submarine commander, to 'right the ship', so to speak. In his book he gathers evidence that shows that a vast fleet of the early Ming dynasty with their 400 plus ft ships circumnavigated the globe one hundred years before Magellan; all the while establishing outposts of trade along the route– with some being in North America. This took place decades before Columbus.

CREATORS OF THE MATRIX

What are we seeing here? Historians like to say, "let the documents speak for themselves"; instead it seems like the historians are acting like editors and censors. In all three cases above we are dealing with people from outside the profession of history who are only doing what the historians should have been doing all along, 'letting the documents speak for themselves'.

History that is edited by leaving out pertinent facts is not history. The redaction of history by the 'professionals' is particularly ominous because it seems to be whole-scale; it's everywhere you turn. The three examples above are three different time periods; this is just a sample, for the length and breadth of the obfuscation is mind numbing.

The subject has a dark pall hanging over it. John Gager, professor of religion at Princeton university has a quote that sums it up quite well, "Our sense of the past is created for us largely by history's winners. The voices of the losers, when heard at all, are transmitted through *a carefully tuned network of filters.*" (emphasis mine)

Gager craftily words his objection to how history is done, especially his last phrase. He is implying that the dissemination of false history is highly organized and even more foreboding . . . it is intentional. Who is responsible for the propagation of lies and half truths that pass for history?

Michael Parenti has an excellent roundup of the usual suspects in the first chapter of his book, *History as Mystery.* What he concludes is probably not that surprising . . . the disseminators and propagators of incomplete history are all *AUTOBIOGRAPHERS.* It will become more clear as we proceed . . . .

In the first century A.D. we have Josephus with his chronicle of the Jewish rebellion, in which he *served both sides.* First as a Jewish military commander in Galilee then after his capture and subsequent release we see him serving the Romans. Upon receiving a generous pension from the Romans, he commenced his work of history. Ranging further back in time we see Thucydides, who wrote a history of the Peloponnesian war; he happened to be a military leader in this war. Polybius, circa 150 b.c., seems to have shared a similar fate as Josephus; serving both sides and then commencing his Histories. We have Caesar with his Gallic wars, Cicero, Sallust, and Dio Cassius. All of them historians who were also active participants in the events they wrote about. You may recall the phrase above used by

Gager that, 'History is written by the winners' ?

The pattern is not limited to ancient history. In more modern times we have Francois Guizot, Edward Gibbon, Theodore Roosevelt, Adolphe Thiers. Thiers, for example, was a prime minister of France and then a leader in the suppression of the Paris Commune revolt which involved mass executions of the rebels. He then went on to write a history of the event and therein is our official report in the matter.

Lest one think that the histories written by professors in universities are unbiased, one must look again. Universities are government funded and the main professional organization that the historians belong to, the American Historical Association (AHA), maintains a dogmatic stance on 'official' history. The AHA was officially incorporated by an act of Congress in the late 19th century and since then it has been the watchdog of official history. Ask historian Howard Zinn when he challenged the AHA at an Association business meeting in 1969; he physically had the microphone wrestled away from him by a former AHA president while bringing up inconvenient facts concerning the Vietnam war. Perhaps the most influential historian of the first half of the Twentieth century was the prolific Charles Beard. He was also president of the AHA at one point and well respected by all. Then a strange thing happened. He broke ranks with his colleagues concerning World War 2 and as one historian stated, attacking Beard was an 'industry'. His sin was bringing up facts that were being routinely omitted concerning Roosevelt and his administration in regard to the second world war.

If an individual writes an auto-biography of himself we

can hardly expect that it will give us the truth about that individual. What we see in historical writing is the same bias working. Since most of history is really political history we see an interesting phenomenon. Individuals that are politically affiliated and identified with the State, the political power, are writing about the State. In effect, because of this identity of the historian with the political, we have this absurdity: *the State writing histories of the State.* How can this ever be objective? Also, how are we to know when something is true?

WARTS

In *Childhood's End* all of history was shown to be false by Karellen's device. Why was it false? Karellen would have helped us a great deal if he pointed out that it was false because of the historian's patent omission of material. False because those who are reporting, filter and gloss over facts that would be deleterious to their cause, whatever that may be.

The disposition to disregard data that is inconvenient for the historian has been the norm throughout history except, possibly, in one place - - - ancient Israel. The transmittal of history in Hebrew culture was different in kind. There are two things in this culture, which stand out in regard to history. First, there was to be an attitude of reverence for the past because it was God acting in history and, like breathing, this history was to be a part of every moment in everyday life: "And these words, which I am commanding you today, shall be on your heart; and you shall teach them diligently to your sons and shall talk of them when you sit in your house and when you walk by the way and when you lie down and when you rise up." (Deuteronomy 6:6,7)

Secondly, as a result of this respect and reverence for the past, an attitude of integrity and incorruptibility was naturally engendered. To ensure integrity in the transmission of history to the next generation there were certain principles that needed to be followed. These were to guide against errors that could creep in and sully the information: "You shall not add to the word which I am commanding you, nor take away from it...." (Deuteronomy 4:2) Interestingly this injunction is repeated throughout the Old and New Testaments in various places and sometimes with a harsh penalty affixed to it: "...the words of the prophecy of this book; if anyone adds to them, God shall add to him the plagues which are written in this book." (Rev. 22:18) In the book of Proverbs in the Old Testament the injunction is also there to respect the transmittal of history: "Add thou not unto his word , lest he reprove thee..."(Proverbs 30:6) In other words, do not distort the material in any way by addition or omission.

If we dare to apply the latter principle to much of historical writing, it will receive a failing grade. But in the Old Testament we have an interesting thing happening— embarrassing material that, maybe, your typical historian would think of leaving out, is kept in. We can see this principle demonstrated throughout the narrative of the Old Testament. Representative of this principal is how the narrative, regardless of the individual's position in the Hebrew hierarchy of importance, spares no one. Whether prophet, king, priest or founding father of one of the twelve tribes, no one is granted clemency in regard to their actions. Nothing is concealed, there is no respect of persons or position. There is no attempt to camouflage an individuals foibles.

For instance, Abraham, the founder of the Jewish nation, is a habitual liar. Jacob, his grand-son, has a penchant for duplicity. Moses, the deliverer of the Jews from bondage, has an ego trip that results in him being barred by Yahweh from entering the promised land. Judah, the founding father of the tribe from which the Messiah was to come, exhibits moral weaknesses in the extreme. He seeks out prostitutes and one of them ends up being his daughter-in-law. King David recklessly commits adultery with Bathsheba and then plots to kill her husband. Solomon, his son, collects wives like some teens used to collect baseball cards. The interesting thing about all this is that these are all important people in Jewish history . . . warts and all. This is in marked contrast with much of history that is written. How about Honest Abe and Washington never telling a lie? It may be that this is a good tip off that *if* the history we are reading does not include warts and all— it should be branded for what it is: *propaganda*.

WARTS IN PLYMOUTH COLONY

A ritual tradition in America is Thanksgiving Day. Young people are taught the so called history behind this day from very early on in school systems throughout the land. It is all very much sleight of hand however, for upon investigation there is something of great importance that is omitted from the account given in the schools and standard texts in high schools. As we will see, the distortion in the reporting of this event is blatant.

The primary source we will be using is William Bradford's, *Of Plymouth Plantation*. Bradford became governor after John Carver died in the first winter that the colonists endured. The version of Thanksgiving in textbooks of today bears no resemblance to that reported by Bradford. As we will see, there is very little correspondence, as a whole, between Bradford's text and the conventional reporting of this event by historians, especially in school textbooks.

We begin with the Pilgrims arriving in November of 1620. About five months later, in the spring of 1621, they are introduced to Massasoit, the sachem of the Wampanoag tribe. The winter of 1620-1621 is devastating. Half of the original 102 passengers of the Mayflower are dead. The conditions were so bad that Bradford said, " there died sometimes two or three of a day in the foresaid time". On top of this, "all this while the Indians came skulking about them," stealing their goods and causing general consternation. Massasoit was well aware of their vulnerable situation and with an eye to his own interests, offered to help the ravaged Pilgrims, hoping to eventually enlist their aid as an ally against his enemies. He happens to have an English speaking Indian in his service, Tisquantum. Here is one of those interesting coincidences of history which, by the way, upon investigation are not really coincidental. We will leave this for another time however. . .

As a result of this fortuitous meeting, a treaty is agreed upon between Massasoit and the Pilgrims with the help of the interpreter Tisquantum or Squanto. Seeing their plight, Massasoit offers them the services of Squanto. In Bradford's words, this is what that consisted of; "Squanto continued with them and was their interpreter and was a special instrument sent of God for their good beyond their expectation. He directed them how to set their corn, where to take fish, and to procure other commodities, and was also their pilot to bring them to unknown places for their profit, and never left them till he died."

With their new found guide and teacher they had hope of becoming self sustaining, "As many as were able began to plant their corn, in which service Squanto stood them in great stead, showing them both the manner how to set it, and after how to dress and tend it. This new technical knowledge enabled them to revive "the old grounds" with fish as fertilizer lest " it would come to nothing". This, "they found true by trial and experience." So far we have a correspondence between high school texts and Bradford's account. But it does not last long . . . .

THE GREAT DIVERGENCE

So what was the result of Squanto helping them? Would their problem of want and scarcity go away? "All that summer there was no want; and now began to come in store of fowl, as winter approached." This, as a result of Squantos tutelage. The corn harvest along with their hunting of fowl, "made many write so largely of their plenty to their friends in England." Edward Winslow, one of the pilgrims, relates in a letter to a friend in England that a feast followed their harvest of corn, " after we had gathered the fruit of our labors ...at which time...many of Indians coming amongst us, and among the rest their greatest king, Massasoit with some 90 men, when for three days we entertained and feasted."

That November of 1621, a ship arrived from England, the Fortune, in which 35 persons came, "to remain and live in the plantation; which did not a little rejoice them." Everything seems to be going well as a result of Squanto's guardianship; if there was scarcity they would not be rejoicing about welcoming 35 new settlers who, "found all well and saw plenty of victuals in every house...the plantation was glad of this addition of strength." And they all lived happily ever after. This is what as known popularly as the first thanksgiving. Children in school learn this and everyone 'knows' this. The truth is, this is not the end of the story but the very beginning. Instead, this is where the great divergence begins from Bradford's account, and it is consigned to oblivion. In fact, Bradford, writing thirty years after the fact, did not call this the first thanksgiving— it was actually the beginning of sorrows. In light of what occurs after this first harvest he would have felt it abhorrent to call this the first thanksgiving. He does name the first thanksgiving but it doesn't happen until some time later in 1623— two years after this alleged thanksgiving and *only after a very significant and strange event*. So significant and strange, that historians are afraid to contravene convention and elaborate on it. And it had nothing to do with Squanto.

What is omitted after that so-called first thanksgiving is how they suffered to an even greater extent than before, even with Squanto's knowledge. They barely made it out of the winter of 1621-1622— this is after their celebration we mentioned above. The Pilgrims had an even worse winter after Squanto helped them? This is not the impression we get from the conventional story. So desperate were they that after this second winter in March of 1622 they set about to see if they could trade with the Indian tribe, Massachusett; all the while they were looking to the ocean in hope of a ship with supplies because of their plight. The trip to the Massachuset was risky because they heard rumours of a conspiracy against them among the tribes, but they had no choice. Barely a couple of months from their bountiful harvest, notwithstanding the wildlife they could hunt, Edward Winslow writes in *Good Newes* (1624) pg 6, that they had to undertake this risky maneuver, "because our store was almost empty and therefore must seek out our daily food, without which we could not long subsist." In desperation they had one eye trained upon the empty ocean, "their (the pilgrims) provisions were wholly spent, and they looked hard for supply but none came." Back to where they started. This is not the happy ending that everyone is told and assumes. It is a far cry from being the self sustaining Pilgrims that lived happily ever after because of Squanto's help. To be looking to the sea for help is surely not a good sign and it is a refrain that we will hear repeatedly from Bradford. According to conventional texts, the Pilgrims, after attaining a level of technical ability with the help of the Indians, were self sufficient. This is myth because the suffering went on . . .

BAD MANAGEMENT?

Perhaps it was just poor management by Bradford and company. For instance, we see texts, like the last ones where Bradford maintains that the harvest was 'plentiful' —but then another starving winter? Maybe it was a matter of poor calculation and they just needed to improve in this area of allocating food they had for storage after harvest. In light of the plenty from the previous harvest this might be a fair assumption. Bradford explicitly says that the allocation of goods was up to him and his assistant. There are several examples of him using his distribution method. It was a sobering and difficult duty. For instance after the departure of the Fortune in 1621, "the governor and his assistant...took an exact account of all their provisions in store and proportioned the same to the number of persons, and found it would not hold out above six months at half allowance, and hardly that; . . . So they were presently put to half allowance, one as well as another, which began to be hard, but they bore it patiently under hope of supply." We see here the careful dispersal of goods. There was no squandering; even when they did run into good fortune, for instance, he was very careful to distribute always with an eye to the future; for as he says in one place, "otherwise, had it been in their own custody, they would have ate it up and then starved." He was also allocating by the commonly accepted method of the colonists—*equal allocation from a common store*. The common store was the center piece of the Pilgrim economy. It was the first thing set up when they found the land in Plymouth. This was where all the food and provisions were to be placed and then distributed equally amongst all. This economy was acceptable to all. In fact, it was planned to be in this manner from the start as it was a stipulation in the contract between the colonists and the company which granted the patent. The tenth condition of the contract states, "That all such persons as are of this colony are to have their meat, drink, apparel, and all such provisions out of the common stock and goods of the said colony." That first harvest of 1621 with corn and 'fowl aplenty' was put into that common store. That same winter of 1621-1622 anything that was caught was treated the same. We can say that Bradford followed the commonly accepted rules and used the available methods to the best of his ability and also showed that in his dispersal of goods there was no waste. So we can dismiss bad management as a reason for the lack. Yet there was still hunger even after the bountiful harvest. The situation was as desperate as their first winter despite the advantage of Squanto's knowledge.

LOOKING TO THE SEA

In the spring of 1622 they were hard put and anxious for ships to pull into the harbor, and when one did in May there was great disappointment, for the ship, "brought seven passengers and some letters, but no victuals nor any hope of any." 'Thanksgiving' (according to the conventional texts) is over but the suffering goes on. The evidence that they were far from being self sustaining is brought home in the fact that they were always hoping that the next ship would carry items that they could trade with the Indians when their food supply ran out. For example after that ship came in May of 1622 we hear Bradford, "They were left destitute of help in their extreme wants, having neither victuals nor anything to trade with." As we will see even with the newly acquired farming skills they still needed to supplement their harvest with trade.

What's more, in one of the letters Bradford received from that ship, the investors informed him that he would not be receiving supplies until they "heard good news" from him; that is, they wanted to see a return on their investment. They were already in an uproar that the Mayflower returned to England 'without any lading', i.e., goods. The Fortune was sent back with good clapboard, beaver, and other skins but to the dismay of the colonists and the investors, that ship was captured by a French warship and was pillaged of its cargo. The walls were closing in for Bradford and company.

Somehow Bradford held it together in spite of the "60 lusty men" that came in June of 1622— more mouths to feed. They were short on supply as it was and the harvest was a couple months away. For the 60 men it was to be a temporary stay until they settled into their future home a little north of Plymouth in an area now known as Weymouth, they still left their sick behind as another burden to the already exasperated pilgrims. Because of these newcomers they were in desperate straits now. They were on the verge of famine when Captain John Huddleston stopped by, on his way to Maine on a fishing voyage. As Bradford puts it, "Amidst these straits, and the desertion of those from whom they had hoped for supply (the investors), and when famine began now to pinch them sore, they not knowing what to do, the Lord presents them with an occasion beyond all expectation." Huddleston provided them with bread which no doubt was a delicacy for them but they were running out of options, "But what was got.....came to a little; yet by God's blessing it upheld them."

Finally, the much anticipated harvest of 1622 comes, "Now the welcome time of harvest approached in which all had their hungry bellies filled." This harvest was not only for immediate consumption, however; it had to pull them through the winter also. When Bradford estimated its yield, he came to this dire conclusion, the harvest, "arose but to a little...so as it well appeared that famine must still ensue, the next year also if not some way prevented." You can feel his desperation. The situation was made more bleak because they also had nothing with which to trade for corn. "Markets there was none to go to, but only the Indians, and they (the Pilgrims) had no trading commodities." With no where to turn, heaven smiled once again. "Behold now, another providence of God. A ship comes into the harbor, one Captain Jones being chief therein."There was no food but

Jones did have items the Pilgrims bought with beaver skins. The ship had beads and knives and with these they "intended to buy what they could." With these items bought from Jones they were able to buy corn from Aspinet, the Nauset Indian chief, the harvest being so deficient. Even so the winter of 1622-1623 proved to be as bad as the previous two. Needless to say there was no 'Thanksgiving' that year.

PHILOSOPHY AND HUNGER

Three hard winters despite Squanto's instruction and help. This third winter of 1622-1623 was a little too much for them to bear and there were voices of dissent, particularly from the young men. It was an hour of desperation and it forced them to re-examine beliefs that were held close to their bosoms . . . but something, anything had to be done. Out of this desperation Bradford tells us how they solved their problem. He writes, "All this while no supply was heard of, neither knew they when they might expect any. So they began to think..." We will quote the passage in full but it is worthwhile to stop on this path to ruminate on this sentence by Bradford because it is illuminating and also a classic example of under-reporting. First of all, he is about to explain how they solved their problems and he prefaces it with this little phrase that means so much more than what it seems—*they began to think*. For three years they followed their beliefs which were the common assumptions of mankind— but they had tried everything, so maybe, just maybe it was a problem with their *beliefs*. How many years does it take most of us 'to think', to question our most basic assumptions, when something is just not working. This questioning, this *thinking* was the prelude to solving their problems —and having the bravery to confront their most basic assumptions. If you think about it, this is a very hard thing to do. The second thing that led them on the path to the truth and hence, self sufficiency was this: "At length, after *much debate* of things..." Bradford's prose is very sedate and composed. He's not given to much overstatement. For him to modify the word *debate* with the word *much* may give us a slight glimpse into the scene. The substance of the conclusions reached by the Pilgrims as a result of this 'much debate' also help us in reconstruction of the event. This was a serious argument involving everyone in the colony and in light of what he tells us later it must have gotten very heated. We know this from what Bradford will relate shortly; but the main thing is that they found an answer as a result of these two phrases: 'They began to think' and 'After much debate of thing's.'

What sparked the debate was a complaint from the young men of the colony, as we shall see, but it fell upon deaf ears because of a certain philosophy that the Pilgrims and most everyone else in the world were guilty of holding. It was a common primary assumption that was hardly ever questioned because it was backed by authority and tradition. As a result of 'thinking and 'debate, the complaint of the young men was finally listened to (there may be another lesson here too, I'm not sure) and the result was that a long revered and monolithic belief came crumbling down. The Pilgrims discovered themselves and a little about human nature also . . .

A COURSE FITTER FOR THEM

Ultimately, what Bradford and the Pilgrims were in search of was self-sufficiency— the ability to provide for themselves, to avoid the basic problem of hunger. The discovery of self sufficiency had nothing to do with agriculture techniques learned from English speaking Indians or management skills. The discovery of what was causing their scarcity is brilliantly put by Bradford himself. We'll let his words ring out in all their cogency and incisiveness.

"All this while no supply was heard of, neither knew they when they might expect any. So they began to think of how they might raise as much corn as they could, and obtain a better crop than they had done, that they might not still languish in misery. At length, after much debate of things, the Governor gave way that they should set corn every man for his own particular, and in that regard trust to themselves; in all other things to go on in the general way as before. And so assigned to every family a parcel of land, according to the proportion of their number....This had very good success, for it made all hands very industrious, so as much more corn was planted than otherwise would have been by any means the Governor or any other could use, and saved him great deal of trouble, and gave far better content. The women now went willingly into the field, and took their little ones with them to set corn; which before would allege weakness and inability; whom to have compelled would have been thought great tyranny and oppression.

The experience that was had in this common course and condition, tried sundry years and that amongst godly and sober men, may well evince that conceit of Plato's and other ancients applauded by some of later times; that the taking away of property and bringing in community into a commonwealth would make them happy and flourishing; as if they were wiser than God. For this community was found to breed much confusion and discontent and retard much employment that would have been to their benefit and comfort. For the young men, that were most able and fit for labour and service, did repine that they should spend their time and strength to work for other men's wives and children without any recompense. The strong, had no more in division of victuals and clothes than he that was weak and not able to do a quarter the other could; this was thought an injustice. The aged and graver men to be ranked and equalized in labours and victuals, clothes, etc, with the meaner and younger sort, thought it some indignity and disrespect unto them. And for men's wives to be commanded to do service for other men, as dressing their meat, washing their clothes, etc., they deemed it a kind of slavery, neither could many husbands well brook it. Upon the point all being to have alike, and all to do alike, they thought themselves in the like condition, and one as good as another; and so, if it did not cut off those relations that God hath set amongst men, yet it did at least much diminish and take off the mutual respects that should be preserved amongst them. And would have been worse if they had been men of another condition. Let none object this is men's corruption, and nothing to the course itself. I answer, seeing all men have this corruption in them, God in His wisdom saw another course fitter for them."

The answer was right in front of them but a primary belief can blind you. The young men and the strong, were working very hard for the common store of goods from which everyone was given an equal share. The problem was they were working more than the rest and getting the same amount back as everyone else, even those who were not working as hard. They found out rather quickly that there was no incentive to work harder than the rest so they began to curtail their production. The young and the strong saw that there was no correspondence between their labor and the fruits of that labor. More work did not mean more bounty for them. Here is where the whole cascade of ill effects begins in this 'community' system. Because there is no correspondence between labor and reward, the laborer, who was producing, now starts to conserve his output, seeing that there is no benefit. So as a result, the person that was bringing benefits to the group, begins to curtail production to the further detriment of the group. The downward spiral begins. Why should they work hard when others who were less vigorous began sloughing off seeing that they would not lose out in this community system. They would get the same as those who worked hard . . .

To break this pattern Bradford took a bold step. The answer was that everyone should have their own *particular*, their own plot of ground—no common store. This truly is a historical moment. He was going against the weight of tradition (conceit of Plato) and his culture. But the results were immediate as far as production. The women, now seeing that they would reap the fruits of their labor, were working, and working willingly. Whereas before they would make excuses or as Bradford puts it 'allege weakness and inability'. The effect that this new philosophy had was immediate as far as making all hands 'industrious'. But whether it was to solve the problem of being self sustaining was another question. But it was their hypothesis that this was the reason, otherwise they would not have struck out on this course. The Platonic ideal that Bradford alludes to is set forth in the Republic of Plato in which he had all children belonging to the community; same as for wives, for there were no marriages in this platonic ideal state. The Pilgrims did not take the philosophy to this extreme but we can see hints that they had gone far enough. For instance we see from his comments that women did chores for the community and not specifically for their husbands. Can you blame the women for not being enthusiastic about washing other mens clothes and not their own husbands? This caused dissension or as Bradford puts it, 'confusion'.

A rather incisive and interesting observation by Bradford, was the effect this communal philosophy had on human relationships. It degraded the dignity that each individual had. There is a uniqueness to each person that distinguishes them. The communal philosophy endangered this by blurring the distinctiveness of each individual. In Bradford's words, this type of philosophy, "to have alike and do alike, they thought themselves....one as good as another." It didn't allow a person to be who he was and the end result, what Bradford saw, was a loss of respect for a person and his individuality. Bradford puts it well, "Yet it did at least much diminish and take off the mutual respects that should be preserved among them." For instance out of respect, perhaps the eldest should have at least the first choice of food and perhaps more food than a young person, out of respect for his age and position. But in this system, that was disregarded; so you have Bradford saying 'they thought themselves one as good as another'. The uniformity of property blurred the lines as to a persons uniqueness and individuality.

The 'commonwealth' or commune-ism, was a disaster up until this point, so they dissolved it. Philosophically, they took a 'new course fitter for them'. But this new course or philosophy was only as good as its practicality; that is, was it going to work? This was the ultimate test. Instead of breeding confusion and causing general dissension and scarcity, would it bring plenty and would it beget peace? This would take some time for as Bradford reports "all their victuals were spent and they were only to rest on God's providence". They set their corn according to their new philosophy and waited.

THE TEST

That spring and summer of 1623 was a trying time. That June, another ship came and these passengers were not staying temporarily. About 60 were for the colony as some were wives and children of 'such as were here already'. The conditions these passengers saw caused great distress amongst them. They "were much daunted and dismayed...others fell aweeping. Some wished to be in England again. In a word all were full of sadness." This is interesting, because in spite of all this, they stuck to the agreement that they would pursue the 'fitter course'.

The hope for the coming harvest was almost crushed when they suffered a drought that lasted from the third week of June until the middle of July. With more mouths to feed and a severe drought on their hands Bradford, with compunction says, "The best dish they could present their friends with was a lobster or a piece of fish without bread or anything else but a cup of fair spring water....God fed them out of the sea for the most part."

PHILOSOPHY OF THANKSGIVING

The time period that Bradford covers in his chronicle of the colonists is from 1620-1647. We can see that some of it was written in hindsight as when he says at the end of chapter six that he has written this account so that progeny would "see with what difficulties their fathers wrestled in going through these things in their first beginnings; and how God brought them along." He also hoped that perhaps something in these accounts would teach or be of practical use to them, "As also that some use may be made hereof in after times by others in such like weighty employments." Certainly, this experiment would qualify. And thirty years later he could look back and judge whether the experiment failed or was a success.

In chapter fourteen, the outcome of their new philosophy, in which they chose a course fitter for them, is given, "By this time harvest was come, and instead of famine now God gave them plenty, and the face of things was changed, to the rejoicing of the hearts of many, for which they blessed God." Now, we've heard this story before. Their first harvest was a success under the tutelage of Squanto and we saw the squalor they soon fell into each winter. Is this harvest of 1623 different in any way? Will the new philosophy make the Pilgrims self sustaining? Bradford continues, "And the effect of their particular planting was well seen, for all had, one way and other, pretty well to bring the year about; and some of the abler sort and more industrious had to spare, and sell to others; *so as any general want or famine hath not been amongst them since to this day.*"

They had discovered self sufficiency and it was through discovering a vital fact about human nature. The new philosophy was about individuals and that through individuals a community can be helped— the individual is superior to the community, strange as it may sound to modern ears.

The former belief was that the community was superior to the individual. That the individual is primary was not lost on Bradford as he was led to write, "the face of things had changed." He didn't have to wait years to see the results of the new philosophy; it was already in the air, the release from bondage, the re-invigoration of the human spirit.

This dramatic change in attitude and spirit would normally compel a group to commemorate such a renewal of hope. And this they did, as Bradford says, "For which mercy, in time convenient, they also *set apart a day of thanksgiving.*" This was the *first* thanksgiving according to William Bradford.

According to Bradford they had suffered because they had followed a philosophy that was wrong. After 'thinking' and 'debate' they changed their course and things got better. Bradford doesn't cover it up; it's all there. He could have edited the places where he describes their bleak and hopeless condition; he could have attributed their eventual self sufficiency to something else . . . but he didn't. He admitted that following an ancient tradition, Plato's conceit, was wrong and harmful. He reported everything . . . warts and all.

A TALE OF TWO PHILOSOPHIES

There are two major systems of social philosophy in the world. The one that is the most popular and packaged in sundry and diverse ways to make it smell and look good is the one that holds the *community as primary over the individual.* This is in very broad terms but sometimes we can get a sense of direction when looking at the whole forest rather than one tree; today's philosophy has a very analytical bent that fails to bring the whole into view. In distinction to this, we have the philosophy that perhaps has never been tried out whole-scale and that is where the *individual is primary over the community*. The community as primary was the social philosophy of the Pilgrims until pain and suffering made them examine their primary beliefs. What Bradford did by instituting the particulars was a bold move considering the weight of tradition and not to mention their immediate surrounding culture which fully imbibed the philosophy of the community as primary. For instance less than ten years later in 1630 we hear John Winthrop governor of Massachusetts Bay Colony, uttering these words in his classic text of 17th century New England, *Model of Christian Charity:* "the care of the public must oversway all private respects, by which, not only conscience, but mere civil policy, doth bind us. For it is a true rule that particular estates cannot subsist in the ruin of the public . . . We must be willing to abridge ourselves of our superfluities, for the supply of others' necessities." This is definitely, if not more so, the same spirit the Pilgrims had when they first arrived nearly ten years earlier. I am sure that word had gotten out about the philosophy the Pilgrims adopted but no further development or elaboration of their philosophy is heard of. It is as if the whole episode was covered up with the dust of age and consigned to the relic bin.

At the beginning we used Karellen's device in a sort of parable to demonstrate why much of history was inaccurate. Hopefully, we understand now how this episode was distorted but the question lingers as to why this would not be reported— that is, why is this not common knowledge? We can safely guess it is because of the *philosophy* that permeates this particular event. It does not conform with our thinking. The philosophy of who or what is primary has been debated throughout history by philosophers, politicians and religions; we could definitely sit here and argue a philosophical position that the *Individual is Primary* but there really is no need to. Why? *We have an episode demonstrating a philosophical position historically.* This historical episode is saturated with philosophy. It is philosophy acted out. But yet this philosophy is hidden because the historical episode is hidden, concealed. In this case we have a historical event that speaks volumes about a *philosophical issue*. The Plymouth colonists were not philosophy students researching their PhD.'s on the superiority of Marxism or Capitalism. The struggle that these people underwent was remarkable; they weren't trying to prove a philosophical point. Most people reading this will not worry about where they are going to hunt for their dinner tonight; these people had to struggle for bare necessities . . . philosophy wasn't exactly on their minds. They unwittingly discovered a truth that evaded mankind for ages and still evades them. No amount of sophistry can wiggle out of the finding of the Pilgrims about human nature. Regardless of your belief system about society, this particular historical episode can't be reshaped into something else. History, when it is not concealed really can serve as a laboratory for philosophy, it can *demonstrate philosophical truth even more effectively than a philosophical argument*. This is why history is distorted. NO amount of arguing, rational debate or dispute would have changed William Bradford's mind about their communal philosophy, and this philosophy was actually hurting them. No amount of *philosophizing* would have changed Bradford's mind at the beginning. That emphasizing the individual over the community would bring plenty was not something they would have given assent to. Unfortunately it was adversity that brought them to a point of open mindedness. Perhaps we don't have to go through the adversity— maybe we can gain from their experience . . .

WE ARE LOSERS

We hear, much of the time from historians, that history gives us lessons, that it can, in fact, teach us. In the case of Bradford and this historical episode the lesson seems to have been lost. Over the next few hundred years many experimental communities popped up in various places around the United States having as their foundation the principle of emphasizing the community over the individual. Another thing that they had in common was that they all failed. No one seems to have paid attention to the Pilgrims and their plight. A study of the Pilgrims and their eventual resolution of their situation would have let anyone know that it was emphasizing the individual that was the key to prosperity and peace. If historians had emphasized this principle in Bradford's account it would have spared all this needless experimentation and waste. So we hear silly stories of these communities that believed that man could achieve a level of prosperity and peace previously unachieved. The reason this has not been achieved, according to the Utopians, is because man is 'always out for himself ' and once this unnatural inclination is educated and taught that the needs of the community are primary, then and only then do we have peace and prosperity.

Not only this, but the whole edifice of modern political thinking is against what the Plymouth colonists unearthed.

By putting their output into a common storehouse the theory was that everyone would benefit to a greater extent than keeping the output of each person for him or herself. The whole point of this article has been to show that, without utilizing philosophical arguments, we have a concrete historical example of this philosophy not working; in fact it is counter productive. But where else do we see this philosophy of putting things into a common storehouse? In every modern society we have communities putting their output into a common store. . . . . it's called taxation. The Pilgrims found that this philosophy caused lack and want. It makes you think of what the possibilities could be if we followed the Pilgrims in their approach. Do the Pilgrims have the answer? Would allowing individuals to keep the product of their labors be beneficial for society? Would it cure the ills of society? In embryo form, I believe that the Pilgrims point us in the direction of prosperity and growth because of their discovery. But we must seize this truth and meditate on it— perhaps it will spur us to 'think' and to 'debate' as they once did on that day long ago in 1623. A day that started out with hunger and squalor but gave rise to hope and a bright ending. The philosopher George Santayana has the famous quote, "Those who can not remember the past are condemned to repeat it." However, Mr. Santayana should have had the following question asked of him, "How can we remember the past when it is concealed?" When this happens, we are all losers . . .

SCIENCE PILLAR: ET TU, SCIENTIA?

2

As I write this, and very likely even as you read this, a branch of Science is stealing money from our pockets. The scale of this pilfering is not even calculable in its breadth and depth— it affects the entire world. How? It is all due to a wrong idea— an incorrect presupposition. Because of this wrong idea our current standard of living suffers to a great extent, as will be shown. However, this incorrect presupposition seems to have another belief attached to it that is a deeply held philosophical belief— one could say a primary belief that is held about human nature. This primary belief is even more dangerous to us as a human race because it is anti-human and hence, anti-life. So not only in the short run of day to day living but also in the long run, in terms of the aspirations and progress of human kind, this philosophy that is wedded to a science, is inimical to every man and woman and child. And you thought geology was harmless . . .

A BUBBLIN' CRUDE

Everyone has probably heard the term 'fossil fuel' tossed about simply because the refined product, petroleum, is the lifeblood of our modern civilization as we know it. It is an unquestioned assumption by scientists that crude oil or petroleum "is derived from ancient biomass" as one encyclopedia puts it, or to simplify— fossilized plant and animal life. Another encyclopedia corroborates this by saying that "the material that is the source of most oil has probably been derived from single celled planktonic plants." According to the theory, this ancient mass of vegetable and animal debris was deposited in the sedimentary layers of the earth where it decayed, due to pressure and heat, and changed into oil. So this theory is called the *biogenic* theory signifying the oil having its origin (genic-genesis) from life (bio).

Now, the sedimentary layer of rock forms the most upper part of the crust. It is really a thin veneer covering the deeper layers of igneous and metamorphic rock. This sedimentary rock happens to contain all the biomass that oil is supposedly made from. If this is our theory then we are only going to drill for oil in areas of sedimentary rock that have these biological markers of biomass deposition. We would be out of our minds drilling into non-sedimentary rock. The theory precludes us from doing this and anyway, it's been pretty successful. In other words this theory works for scientists. They see no reason to abandon it in light of its success and the evidence that supports it.

The main evidence is found in the oil itself. There is an abundance of molecules, called biomarkers, that resemble biological matter. Because of their association with oil, these signatures of life constitute proof that oil comes from ancient, reworked biological material. This sign of life indicates to those who believe in this theory that the oil came from life or at least a formerly living thing.

Also, there is a philosophic substructure that is implied

in this biogenic theory: there is, as with everything else, a limit to this resource— so the philosophy goes. If the world's oil comes from a limited source such as the biomass, then obviously the world's oil supply is limited. Regardless of newer technologies in finding oil there still is an upper limit that we are approaching. The greater the demand on this 'fossil fuel' the quicker we get to the bottom of the barrel, so to speak. This is a logical outcome of the biogenic theory.

But, as we will see, when a theory can't explain an anomalous circumstance satisfactorily, it may be time to let it go. Even better, if you can test the theory . . . But here is the first interesting fact to be found about the biogenic theory. No one has duplicated it in a laboratory. As the scientist, Thomas Gold says in his book *The Deep Hot Biosphere*, "Nobody has yet synthesized crude oil or coal in the lab from a beaker of algae or ferns."

OIL IS A RENEWABLE RESOURCE

Keeping in mind the general idea of the origins of oil, we should not be able to find oil in rock structures far below the sedimentary strata which is the area of the deposition of the biomass from ages past. In the Ukraine this corollary of the biogenic theory has been exploded. The Dnieper-Donetsk Basin is the principal oil producer in the Ukraine and it shouldn't be. This area had been explored before for oil but the speculators wouldn't drill deep enough. Their biogenic theory wouldn't allow them to; for how could oil exist in 'crystalline basement' rock? Biogenic theory says it is only in sedimentary layers, so it was never pursued. An interesting thing occurred however. In the early 1990's the area was explored again but this time with a different outlook, a *different theory*. It actually is a whole new way of looking at the earth. This theory completely repudiates the biogenic theory and its premises. This theory carries with it a whole different set of assumptions. Working on these different assumptions, drilling began anew in the Ukranian basin. This time they went deep and behold they struck gold, or rather oil. According to the US Dept of Energy the Ukraine has close to 400 million barrels of proven oil reserves and most of this is in the Dnieper Donetsk basin. But this should not be . . . . at least if you hold to the biogenic theory.

In the 1980's the Russians teamed up with the Vietnamese to form Vietsovpetro to drill in the South China sea. There was only one problem though— they were drilling into crystalline basement structure. This is not what typical western countries would be doing, for there is no sedimentary rock to signify oil. Amazingly, seven production oil fields were discovered. The largest field is known as White Tiger and it produces 280,000 barrels of oil a day. According to the US Dept of Energy, the Russians, in 2004, nearly outproduced the Saudi Arabians. The Russians produced 9.27 million barrels per day compared to the 10.4 million barrels of the Saudi Arabians. You might start noticing the theme here. The Russians seem to be doing something a little different. These actions are based on a knowledge, a theory that has proven itself to work, yet it is ignored by the rest of the world. What do the Russians know that is making them so successful?

Here we must introduce the Soviet scientist, Nikolai Kudryavtsev, the father of the a-biogenic or abiotic theory. Simply, the abiotic theory says oil does not come from life but rather it is due to a geological process deep within the earth.

The process involves primordial hydrocarbons which are an integral part of all planets in the solar system. Kudryavtsev, until his death in 1971, prospected areas for oil based on his abiogenic theory. Because of the success of the theory, Russian scientists during and after the time of Kudryavtsev, published thousands of scientific papers on the abiogenic approach to finding oil. With the mountain of evidence the Russians had gathered they saw that the opposing biogenic view was obsolete and did not support the evidence. According to the book *Black Gold Stranglehold* by Jerome Corsi, Kudryavtsev "ridiculed the idea that an ancient primeval morass of plant and animal remains was covered by sedimentary deposits over millions of years, compressed by millions of more years of heat and pressure." But if we allow for the abiogenic theory instead, we have some very interesting conclusions derived from its major premise, namely:

Since oil is a byproduct of hydrocarbons that are natural to and integral to the planet then all you have to do to get this oil is dig deep enough and you'll find it. In other words it is everywhere.

Since the earths vast reservoirs of hydrocarbons are practically inexhaustible it follows that oil is an inexhaustible resource.

A possible sign that a theory is true is that it has *explanatory POWER*. It is able to explain anomalous circumstances without resorting to an auxiliary assumption(s). No patchwork collection of epicycle theories or such mumbo jumbo. An example of an anomaly that fossil fuel adherents have a difficult time with is the phenomena of refilling. For instance, Eugene Island 330, in the Gulf of Mexico is causing problems for the fossil fuel crowd. Here is what the April 16,

1999 *Wall Street Journal* had to say: "Something mysterious is going on at Eugene Island 330. Production at the oil field, deep in the Gulf of Mexico off the coast of Louisiana, was supposed to have declined years ago. And for a while, it behaved like any normal field: Following its 1973 discovery, Eugene Island 330's output peaked at about 15,000 barrels per day (2,400 m3/d). By 1989, production had slowed to about 4,000 barrels per day (640 m3/d). Then suddenly – some say almost inexplicably – Eugene Island's fortunes reversed. The field, operated by PennzEnergy Co., is now producing 13,000 barrels per day (2,100 m3/d), and probable reserves have rocketed to more than 400 million barrels from 60 million." This is a general trend with the oil fields refilling that is difficult to explain with the biogenic theory. It is easily explainable with the abiotic theory, in that this oil is *continually being made* deep within the earth from primordial hydrocarbons. In time, it then seeps its way into the sedimentary layers. The fossil fuel theory has a little bit of creativity to resort to in order to explain this. The earths layers can be rearranged, they say, from their usual order. The sedimentary layer which is usually on top can actually be under the igneous rock layer in some areas due to what is known as subduction. A neat little theory for the biogenic people that says when two tectonic plates converge one of the plates becomes subsumed under the other plate. Hence, you may find sedimentary strata from one plate under the igneous rock of the other plate and this is where the oil is coming from, the subducted sedimentary layer beneath the igneous layer. Again, we must not fail to notice that an auxiliary theory is brought in to support the original biogenic theory which can't explain the anomaly primarily.

IT"S HARD TO LET GO

The philosopher of science, Imre Lakatos, describes a situation that enlightens us as to when a scientific belief should be jettisoned, in his book, *Criticism and the Growth of Knowledge* on pages 100-101: "The story is about an imaginary case of planetary misbehavior. A physicist of the pre-Einsteinian era takes Newton's mechanics and his law of gravitation, N, the accepted initial conditions, I, and calculates, with their help, the path of a newly discovered small planet, P. But the planet deviates from the calculated path. Does our Newtonian physicist consider that the deviation was forbidden by Newton's theory and therefore that, once established, it refutes the theory of gravitation, N? No. Instead, he suggests that there must be a hitherto unknown planet P2, which perturbs the path of P. He calculates the mass, orbit, etc of this hypothetical planet and then asks an experimental astronomer to test his hypothesis. The planet P2 is so small that even the biggest available telescopes cannot possibly observe it; the experimental astronomer applies for a research grant to build yet a bigger telescope to find planet P2. In three years time, the new telescope is ready. Were the unknown planet P2 to be discovered, it would be hailed as a new victory of Newtonian science. But it is not. Does our scientist abandon Newton's theory and his idea of a perturbing planet? No. Instead, he suggests that a cloud of cosmic dust hides the planet from us. He calculates the location and properties of this cloud and asks for a research grant to send up a satellite to test his calculations. Were the satellites instruments (possibly new ones, based on a little tested theory) to record the existence of the conjectural cloud, the result would be hailed as an outstanding victory for Newtonian science. But the cloud is not found. Does our scientist abandon Newton's theory, together with the idea of the perturbing planet and the idea of the cloud which hides it? No. He suggests that there is some magnetic field in that region of the universe which disturbed the instruments of the satellite. A new satellite is sent up. Were the magnetic field to be found, Newtonians would celebrate a sensational victory. But it is not. Is this regarded as a refutation of Newtonian science? No. Either yet another ingenious auxiliary hypothesis is proposed or.... the whole story is buried in the dusty volumes of periodicals and the story never mentioned again."

It would do us well to read the above again and consider the implications of holding onto a faulty theory; to ruminate a little on how much damage and waste a faulty explanation can cause. Auxiliary on top of auxiliary hypothesis is brought in to explain phenomena that the *original theory can not explain*. These addendums are supposed to buttress the original theory but in reality they extend the life of something that should be put to sleep.

When a theory relies on auxiliary theories then it may be a sign to let go of the theory. But the history of science shows us otherwise. It shows us the incredible stubbornness that scientists have in cleaving to something that has inconsistencies and contradictions. If you have to come up with an auxiliary theory to support the initial theory and you find that this is happening with regularity then the theory is in trouble. But scientists have been known to go down fighting to their graves in supporting balderdash. The risks arc great for those who challenge the prevailing theory but what isn't noticed is the existential suffering it causes in not allowing humanity to progress and thrive with the new found knowledge.

We hopefully now understand that phenomena can have two opposing theories of explanation that can explain equally well what is going on— to an extent. The warning sign of the wrong theory is when multiple explanations must be invoked to explain anomalies that keep popping up that the original theory can't account for. It would be irrational to keep making excuses for something that doesn't pan out whenever aberrational data is found, yet scientists do it with amazing consistency. This attitude of holding on to wrong theory no matter what, does not bode well for mankind. As we said earlier, tremendous waste of resources is involved when this occurs especially pertaining to our point that we made at the beginning about wrong thinking in geology.

To simplify this we can look again at a different paradigm in ancient Greece. Our farmer from ancient Greece has done everything right yet no bountiful harvest. He has done the right sacrifices, libations etc but still no harvest. The priests tell him that Demeter is having some problems with another god and to sacrifice to that god also. He does this and gets the same result. The priests then say that there is something wrong with the way the farmer is offering the sacrifices. So he gets instruction from the priests on how to offer sacrifices for a small fee and still no result. Auxiliary theory upon auxiliary theory are brought up and the farmer never notices his neighbor, who does not believe in the Athenian religion, utilizing certain techniques that he uses to treat the ground. This neighbor never prays to Demeter yet he gets a bountiful harvest every year. Of course, it may be dangerous to advertise his new found discovery since the priesthood would be threatened. Whether it is an old priesthood or the modern priesthood of scientists we can see a common thread between them— they both explain reality (or try to) and they both are given to making ancillary explanations *when their original theory is not comprehensive enough to explain new data.* Hence, an incorrect theory that is zealously maintained by scientists suppresses mankind from progressing.

There seems to be nothing that can mitigate against a view or theory that has been 'proven' like the biogenic theory. Any fact that is brought out against it will be re-explained to make it fit in. All swans are black. The moment a white swan is spotted it is reinterpreted as being actually black because, you see, some one came along and sprayed the animal with white spray paint. Karl Popper tried to point this inconsistency out in the middle of the 20th century with his theory of *falsifiability*. This basically says the same thing, there is no way the black swan believers will allow their theory to be falsified. They will keep coming up with something, anything, even if ludicrous, to save their theory. The biogenic theory relies on this technique to survive because the theory does not allow for oil in rock that is not sedimentary without resorting to an ancillary theory.

A NECESSARY TOOL

Without logic as a tool, any argument can seem right. Emotions can deceive us. So can our senses. Logic offers the one tool that can clarify an issue. It can illuminate and cut through the fog of contention.

In science, a common error lies in *attributing causality by association*. The most important evidence that the biogenic side has is the fact that there are what are known as *biomarkers* in the fuel. The biological material in the oil points to a biological origin, so say the biogeneticists. There seems to be two types of biomaterial in the oil coming up from the ground. First we have pollen and microbial spores that have been found in the oil. Then there are the molecular materials that are similar to molecules associated with life. This particular material, porphyrins, isoprenoids, pristane, phytane, cholestane, terpines, and clorins—are *related* to biological material; they are *not* biological matter. For instance the thinking goes, since cholestane is related to cholesterol (a hormone precursor in living beings) in its structure, this indicates biological origin.

But J.F. Kenney, an American scientist collaborating with the Russians in their successful drilling in the Dnieper basin in the Ukraine, states that this association of biomarkers with biological origin is a fallacy. This is from his website Gas Resources: "These molecules have often been given the spurious name "biomarkers." The scientific correction must be stated unequivocally: There have never been observed any specifically biological molecules in natural petroleum, except as contaminants. Petroleum is an excellent solvent for carbon compounds; and, in the sedimentary strata from which petroleum is often produced, natural petroleum takes into solution much carbon material, including biological detritus." Also, some of these molecules were *reproduced in a laboratory setting with no biological materials*. Kenney also points out that these molecules have been found in meteorites. Meteorites are abiotic i.e. non-life containing.

So, what is happening is that as the oil migrates toward the surface it becomes contaminated with biological material that is a part of each rock layer. In logic this is what is known as a variety of the *post hoc* fallacy. In the biogenic theory we can restate this as *Association Does Not Imply Causation*. This fallacy confuses coincidental relationships with causes. A simple example we can use is of the rooster crowing as the sun rises; does this association imply causation? Since the sun rises each time after the rooster crows we could draw the implication that the rooster *caused* the sun to rise. This may be an absurd illustration but the fallacy becomes easier to see. This is what commonly occurs in science. When observing a chain of events it is tempting to come to this type of conclusion but just because someone is at the scene of a crime does not imply guilt. This correlation with biomarkers as proof of causality from biomass is still printed in Western textbooks and held as proof of biological origin of oil.

It could just as well be pointed out that oil, as it comes to the surface, is 'contaminated' with biological materials that are part of a fascinatingly alien environment that one astronomer/scientist called the *deep hot biosphere* . . .

THE DEEP HOT BIOSPHERE

The scientist Thomas Gold points out in his book, *The Deep Hot Biosphere,* that there is a living community of organisms that flourish deep within the earth. These organisms are known as *extremophiles*. They generally thrive in harsh environments that have extremes of temperature, pressure or chemical composition such as acidity or alkalinity. Gold believed that the molecules that are found in the oil such as we have mentioned above are byproducts of these Archaea that live in these extreme habitats. For instance from pg 84 of *The Deep Hot Biosphere,* "Another interesting molecule (a terpenoid)...found to be common in hydrocarbons is also present in bacteria known to make their living by oxidizing methane." So here we have a possible explanation for a particular biomarker such as the terpenes. A particular extremophile that thrives in a methane environment actually contains this molecule. So when terpene is seen in oil it could be from these microbes known as Archaea. His conclusion is that, "The biogenic molecules discovered in natural hydrocarbons throughout the world can all be linked to constituents of bacteria or archaea...There is thus no evidence in these observations that anything other than a substantial microbiological contamination of oils is required to explain all the molecules observed." (page 84)

This is the same view of J.F. Kenney and the Russian-Ukrainian scientists. The abiotic group has been able to explain this with a provable assertion and not just some theory or hypothesis. Every point of contention from the biogenic theorists, in fact, has a simple explanation that is provable by the abiotic scientists. For instance the biogenic scientists contend that the ratio of carbon in the oil is an indicator of life. For our purposes all we need to know is that carbon12 is in greater proportion to carbon13 in oil. Carbon 13 is not associated with life. Carbon 12 is found in life and it is used in photosynthesis so therefore its presence in oil points to a biological origin. We have the association thing going on again here but nevertheless this has been proved to be false in a laboratory. JF Kenney states on his website that carbon, as it makes its way to the surface becomes lighter. So carbon 13 can lose weight and become carbon 12. From Gas Resources website, " Colombo, Gazzarini, and Gonfiantini demonstrated conclusively, by a simple experiment the results of which admitted no ambiguity, that the carbon isotope ratios of methane change continuously along its transport path, becoming progressively lighter with distance traveled. Colombo et al. took a sample of natural gas and passed it through a column of crushed rock, chosen to resemble as closely as possible the terrestrial environment. Their results were definitive: The greater the distance of rock through which the sample of methane passes, the lighter becomes its carbon isotope ratio."

THE HYDROCARBON HERESY

The proof is actually in the pudding. What is the actual success rate of the biogenic theory? Here again we'll quote JF Kenney from his Gas Resources website: "The statistics of exploration success for western petroleum companies, drilling while following the traditional British/American biological-origin-of-petroleum (BOOP) notion, and in absence of seismic information (which permits visual identification of oil in the ground) is no better than one (1) successful commercial well out of approximately twenty-eight (28) dry holes, - which statistical success rate is no better than random."

No better than random. But in contrast, according to the abiotic theory you could drill just about anywhere and find oil if you drilled deep enough. That is exactly what a company like Transocean (company website www.deepwater.com) is setting out to do with its 'super deep drilling'. They bill themselves as the worlds largest offshore drilling contractor and are set to drill to depths in excess of 40 thousand feet. This has never been done before and this is not something the biogenic theory espouses. They seem to know something that ordinary geologists don't.

That 'something' has been out there since 2004. It was reported in the Proceedings of the National Academy of Sciences in September of 2004. It was popularly written about in Harvard magazine with the title *Hydrocarbon Heresy–Rocks Into Gas*. What was reported on was the final nail in the coffin of the biogenic theory— methane was produced in a laboratory. Dudley Herschbach, nobel prize winner in chemistry 1986, coordinated a team of scientists in an experiment. He was inspired by a book about the Russian chemist Dmitri Mendelyev, *A Well Ordered Thing*, in which the abiotic theory was mentioned. This spurred his curiosity and further research led him to Thomas Gold's book, *The Deep Hot Biosphere*. Before he died Gold mentioned how unfortunate it was that the earth's pressures could not be duplicated in a laboratory because the equipment did not exist. Herschbach believed this could be done with a device called the diamond anvil cell. Using three abiotic materials–iron oxide, water and limestone---they then simulated the earth's pressures with the device and voila!— methane, the major component of natural gas, was created.

PROPHETS OF DOOM

Because of its basic premise of limitation, the biogenic theory is prone to prophetic mania by its adherents. Since there is only so much biomass, the stuff has to run out at some time and because this is so, we are at the mercy of the professional prophets of doom. In 1989, Colin Campbell, the petroleum geologist from Britain, predicted that 1989 was the peak year of oil production. After that year everything was supposed to decline in production. The demise of oil as the fuel that runs civilization has been predicted many times before by many who would seem to have the right credentials. But somehow the world's oil reserves always seem to be increasing. Perhaps they didn't have the right tools to do it with, as Colin Campbell complained when he made his wrong predictions. But even so, this lack of explanatory power for the biogenic theory should at least peek the interest of scientists to look into the alternative theory of the Russians. Yet we don't see this happening. The only trend that we see is that the biogenic theory has no predictive power. In the book *The Doomsday Myth* by Charles Maurice and Charles Smithson they document the predictive power of the prophets of doom concerning oil. These are just a few of the official pronouncements made in the past:

1891 The U.S. Geological Survey predicted that there was no chance of finding oil in Texas

1926 The Federal Oil Conservation Board predicted the United States had only a seven year supply of oil remaining. Senator LaFollette predicted that the price of oil would soon rise to a $1 dollar a gallon.

1939 The Interior Department predicted that U.S. petroleum supplies would last less than two decades.

1949 The Secretary of the Interior predicted that the end to U.S. oil supplies was in sight

There are others but it is too tedious to list— I think we can see a trend here. If the biogenic theory has difficulties in explaining supply and it relies on auxiliary theories why is the scientific community still latching on to this theory?

SEASON OF DISTRESS

The biogenic theory rides upon a covert belief system that is inimical to mankind. There is a higher belief that biogenic theorists hold that prevents them from 'seeing' any alternative like the abiotic theory. The philosophy that they hold, in turn, is supported by a wrong interpretation of man's nature. This incorrect view of man's nature has broad implications in our daily life for much policy is based on this false premise. First we will look at the philosophy that controls their scientific thinking.

The authors of *The Doomsday Book* touch upon it when they talk about the so called energy crisis of the 1970's. During this time the creed of the 'doom merchants' was the book *The Limits of Growth* by Donella Meadows et al. In this book the authors document the problem that mankind faces in the near future and that it can't be solved by technology or any kind of know-how. The basic premise of the book can be summed up in their assertion that "the application of technology to apparent problems of resource depletion . . . has no impact on the essential problem, which is exponential growth." The variable that is a given is the fact that resources are limited, this can not be changed. The variable that *can* be changed is the amount of people consuming those resources. The solution the authors present is " deliberate checks on growth."

The idea of limiting growth and/or limiting the population of man is not new. Thomas Malthus (1766-1834) was a British clergyman who wrote, *An Essay on the Principle of Population* in which he explicated his ideas on this topic. The Reverend believed, as many have and still do, that population can not be sustained beyond a certain number of people or what is known to Malthus's intellectual progeny as 'carrying capacity'. The earth can only hold so many people before supplies start running out. With Malthus, the situation has an inbuilt correcting mechanism. Whenever population starts getting out of control a correcting influence is spawned in order to reduce population numbers. From chapter 7, in his *Essay on the Principle of Popula-*

tion, "The power of population is so superior to the power in the earth to produce subsistence for man, that premature death must in some shape or other visit the human race." Of which he goes on to list the correctives of over population. Should the vices of mankind e.g war, murder, fail in reducing population then "sickly seasons, epidemics, pestilence and plague advance in terrific array, and sweep off their thousands and ten thousands." Since population is always ahead of subsistence resources it takes awhile before resources can catch up and meet the needs of the increased population. In that period of scarcity, called " this season of distress, the discouragements to marriage, and the difficulty of rearing a family are so great that population is at a stand."

The disciples of Thomas Malthus say the same thing. In each century since, and almost every decade there has been a 'watchman' so to speak, who alerts society to the scourge of . . . population. Yes, population is an evil to these folk; with terms like 'explosion' and 'bomb' in their rhetoric it seems there is an enemy at hand and the enemy is . . . 'people'. Paul Ehrlich, an American biologist, was one such watchman who 'gallantly' warned the world in his popular book, *Population Bomb.* In that book there were many claims that, to be kind, missed the mark. One such claim had Americans starving and dying by the millions by the early 1980's. Instead, by that time, there were millions of diet books and weight loss centers in America. But what is not so well known is the public debate between Ehrlich and an individual by the name of Julian L. Simon. This debate culminated in a showdown that proved once and for all the stupidity and ignorance of Malthusianism and put to death the 'scarcity of resources' theory. It was all due to the brilliant Mr. Simon and his unique but nevertheless correct view of the nature of man.

SEASON OF DISTRESS OR INFINITE MIND

Comparatively, Julian Simon was an unknown. As professor of business administration at Univ. of Illinois and Univ. of Maryland he wrote many books and articles on a variety of subjects. But it was his brilliant work, *Ultimate Resource*, which punctured holes in the balloons of the neo-malthusians. He single handedly eviscerated their arguments theoretically and, as we shall see, practically. Of course criticism came against his theoretical arguments so Professor Simon decided to put flesh on his arguments by challenging Mr. Ehrlich in a bet. He was confident that his theoretical destruction of Malthus and his adherents would be borne out practically also.

A premise of the doomsayers is that resources lag behind population growth. The growing population makes more use of an already limited supply so it follows that the price of these materials will go up due to their greater scarcity. In a public challenge Simon asked Ehrlich to pick any five hard commodities, i.e. metals, and over a period of time, Simon wagered that the price would go down. Ehrlich agreed to the bet and they picked 5 metals and set a date of 10 years after the initial bet, which was in 1980. By 1990 the worlds population had grown by 800 million people, the largest recorded increase in any one decade. The 5 metals chosen; copper, tungsten, chrome, tin and nickel had all fallen in price. Some, like tin, had fallen drastically. Mr. Simon had won the bet and proved a point. To understand how he knew, we must grasp the central tenet of Simon's thought which was hinted at many times before, but never expounded with such clarity and profundity as Simon in his work.

To the abhorrence of those who would like to mandate putting funny stuff in the drinking water to control population(ala Ehrlich in Population Bomb), Simon, in his book *Ultimate Resource*, postulated that, now pay attention,— *the greater the population, the greater will be the abundance of raw materials*. No, the previous clause was not an error; let's state it more simply. More people equals more resources. This is completely antithetical to the Malthusians. How can this possibly be and how was he so sure about the bet with Ehrlich?

To make it more unnerving for the Malthusians, Simon asserts that natural resources cannot be measured, so in chapter 2 of *Ultimate Resource* he states this bombshell, "Here I draw the logical conclusion: Natural resources are not finite." If this is the opening salvo in his attack against the doomsayers what could possibly come next? The premise of the other side has a peculiarity that is not commented on enough, "Over the course of history, up to this very moment, copper and other minerals have been getting less scarce, rather than more scarce as the depletion theory implies they should. In this respect copper follows the same historical trend as radios, undershirts, and other consumer goods." Something is happening that is not fitting the theory of the malthusians. Population growing and so-called 'scarce' items becoming more abundant? He also cites government prognostications such as the Paley commission which assessed raw materials in the United States shortly after World War 2. The commission predicted scarcity and hence a rise in price of raw materials for the next 25 years. They were wrong.

According to Simon, there is an endless supply because *the human mind is endless or rather infinite*. Every situation of scarcity has to do with knowledge, the mind. If you transplant an Eskimo into the middle of a wheat field he will not know what to do about his hunger although there is food all around him. He takes the wheat for granted having no idea what the potential is all around him. He lacks knowledge. At one time it was the same with this thing called 'rock oil' which was just lying around seeping onto the surface of the earth in places, looking so unseemly and vulgarizing the landscape— that is, until a use was found for it. This useless rock oil became petroleum— the impetus for civilization as we know it. Simon explains in chapter 4 of the *Ultimate Resource*, "The more we use, the better off we become—and there's no practical limit to improving our lot forever. Indeed throughout history, new tools and new knowledge have made resources easier and easier to obtain." The reason there is advancement in the first place is *because* of population growth. How about that for inverting the Malthusian argument? The ability of man to subdue nature is equivalent with his ability to focus the light of reason on nature. This occurs when their is scarcity or a threat of same. When population increases, man looks for answers and what inevitably happens is what is called improvement in mans conditions. When population does not increase man has no incentive to seek for answers which will improve his lot. The more people the better off we are!

As Buckminster Fuller put it in his book *Critical Path*, human knowledge "can be entered into the capital account ledgers." He recounts a story in which a prominent banker "was asked what commodities were involved in that bank's export-import dealings with the rest of the world on behalf of the Chinese government, he answered that know-how was the prime commodity being acquired by the Chinese for that bank." Fuller went so far as to say that the living standards for each person in the world far exceeds our imagination. He says that it is "eminently clear that we have four billion billionaires aboard our planet, as accounted by real wealth, which fact is obscured from public knowledge . . ." Fuller points out that our knowledge has become meta-physical, in the sense of beyond what our senses can register. We have discovered the chemical elements for instance, which we use and put to work and in the process making more out of less. This is all due to our knowledge that discovers things that we can't see just like the Eskimo could not see all that food in the field of grain.

What we have in Malthus and Simon are two opposing views of mans nature. What should be troubling is not what Malthus said about population but of his views of mans nature, the latter view is the origin of his philosophy. To Malthus, scarcity is a force outside, a thing impinging on man. In a Newtonian/Malthusian world view we are controlled by forces. Nature is a mechanism. This force of scarcity makes man inert and submissive for man is part of a machine, a bigger mechanism. In contrast, in Simon's view man actually becomes activated because of scarcity. He acts (with all that entails) *because* of scarcity and hence, because of this dynamic tension, we have what is known as progress. If there is no scarcity there is no progress. Malthus delimits man's nature while Simon's view actuates man—in essence fulfilling man's potential as *creator* and *subduer*. Malthus sees man as destroyer, as solely a consumer who, because of his consumptive voracity, must be kept in check. Since we know that hurricanes, earthquakes and plagues consume and destroy we have put man on the same footing as something that is destructive. Plagues are to be eradicated or to be avoided at the very least. Natural disasters are not welcome either. But Malthus puts man on the same footing as these things when he says that populations cause scarcity. The previous items mentioned cause scarcity just like man does. If those things are to be avoided or eradicated then so is man. And this is the crux. Every person who states that there is a scarcity problem *sees man as destroyer and not as creator*. If man is solely destroyer then he must be destroyed . . . or kept in check. Those who take up this line of thinking will be seduced by eugenics and population control and whatever these might entail.

The interesting thing that Simon found out though, was that the infinite ability of man was not the presupposition he started out with. It was only through looking exhaustively at historical trends that he saw this extraordinary phenomenon. It all seems counterintuitive that scarcity causes a human to act and innovate and invent but the conclusion was and is inescapable.

Our idea of scarcity is not complete without investigating it fully, however. This is the part of scarcity that is stunningly suppressed and it is this: Most scarcity is really only *an apparent scarcity*— in other words the scarcity is manufactured by forces in political power. The method of creating a scarcity is done through a lie. However, to create a lie that makes mass populations believe something requires a reputable, authoritative source to substantiate the claim/lie. Today, what else has the authority that science has?

CUI BONO?

In the book *Doomsday Myth: 10,000 Years of Economic Crisis* the authors point this out about oil and fuel: "Every ten or fifteen years since the late 1800's, 'experts' have predicted that oil reserves would last only ten more years. These experts have predicted nine out of the last zero oil-reserve exhaustions." This is well documented. If this game of scaring the public is true, and we can see it is historically, the question remains what is the agenda of the doomsayers especially in regard to black gold? Let us bring in an eyewitness to tell us . . .

It was 1970 and Lindsey Williams had been a pastor for 12 years already when he felt called to become a missionary in Alaska. The Alaskan pipeline was being built at the time and through a bit of persistence he was able to become chaplain to the men in the camps who were working on it. He was not being paid by the oil company but by his church. The personnel director took a liking to the fact that he didn't have to pay Mr. Williams and also that he saw that Williams could be helpful as an intermediary in employee/management relations. They suggested that the pastor convene with them at their board meetings and be granted executive status. Because of this status he had access to all sorts of information and highly placed executives from Atlantic Richfield. One particular executive that Williams befriended imparted some enlightening information when Mr. Williams asked him about the energy crisis that was occurring at the time on the east coast. The landscape of the east coast was be-speckled with scenes of people waiting in long lines for fuel. The executive told Williams that the oil companies, "were ordered by the Federal government in 1973 to close down certain cross country pipelines and to reduce the output of our refineries in certain strategic points of America for the purpose of creating an energy crisis."

Understandably, Mr. Williams was in shock when he heard this but he was not prepared for what the executive said next. To drive home the point to Mr. Williams, the executive took him on a tour of the wells of the Prudhoe Bay oil field and then related that the field, "could flow for over 20 years with natural artesian pressure, without even a pump being placed on it. He told me that this was one of the only fields in the world where this is true, and that oil would come out of the ground at 1,600 pounds pressure and at 135'-167 °F. He said quite clearly that this was one of the richest oil fields on the face of the earth. He also said that there was enough natural gas, as distinct from oil, to supply the entire United States of America for over 200 years, if that also could be produced." But this was not to be produced because of strict orders from on high. With no resistance from the oil company, Williams decided to invite an old friend of his, a state senator from Colorado, Hugh Chance, to corroborate his findings. Mr. Chance was given access to all information and asked the question, "If you developed the entire North Slope of Alaska as private enterprise what would happen?" He was told: "If we as oil companies were allowed to develop the entire North Slope oil field, that is the entire area north of the Brooks Range in Alaska, producing the oil that we already know is there, and if we were allowed to tap the numerous pools of oil that could be tapped (we are tapping only one right now), in five years the United States of America could be totally energy free, and totally independent from the rest of the world as far as energy is concerned." In his book *The Energy Non-Crisis* Williams tells us about another even bigger find on Gull Island that dwarfed Prudhoe Bay— but the rig was ordered removed and the well capped. If these resources were tapped, the price of oil per gallon would be less than a dollar, according to Williams. This testimony shows us that the goal to declare oil a scarce resource does not only take place in theoretical debates between abiogenic and biogenic scientists. Even with oil that fits the paradigm of the biogenic theory such as on the North Slope of Alaska there is a program to stanch and limit the supply of oil that is clearly available. Through rejection of the abiotic theory, oil is made to look like a precious resource when it really is not. Through political means, when oil is found in abundance such as the North Slope of Alaska as Williams tells us, the project is ordered shut down to keep the price artificially elevated.

So we see a little into the machinations of creating a myth of scarcity when it comes to oil. A scarcity of a valued good, even if it is a manufactured scarcity, creates one thing and one thing only— a price increase. What we see with the preceding testimony from a Baptist preacher and with the rejection of the abiogenic theory by scientists is a concerted attempt to increase the value of something that is in reality cheap and abundant. Williams states in his lectures that the artificial price of oil is an actual attempt, and a successful one, to further tax the population. It becomes more convincing when one does a roll call of those responsible for this. Inevitably, what one sees are personages that have interlocking interests from two different spheres— the oil companies and government. Those in positions of power are heavily vested in the oil industry and those in the oil industry have political power. The only thing less disputed is whether the sun will rise tomorrow. This arrangement, of a valued good and its suppression by a web of governmental/mercantilist accomplices . . . is this really different from what has been going on all along throughout history?

THE OIL OF THE MEDICIS

In the 15th century the political rulers of the city of Florence, Italy, were exclusively from one family— the Medicis. This powerful banking family supposedly made loans even to the Vatican. One interesting episode concerning this family should interest us concerning our topic. There are many others but this one will serve us as a sort of template or exemplar that shows us a mechanism as to how the world works when it comes to valued resources such as oil. And perhaps we shall gain some insight from this . . .

Alum was one of the most important resources in the Middle Ages because of the monolithic textile industry. Dyes could not adhere to any cloth or textile without alum being used as a sort of adhesive for the dye. There were only two other mines in western Christendom that supplied alum— the major suppliers were the Turks in the East who had a virtual monopoly over west. Because of this they exacted a high price for their product until the Tolfa mines were discovered right in the backyard of the Papal dominion. The Medici family was put in charge of all distribution and exchange with this rich mine.

What they did next is symbolic of what happens when the elite rulers run into a valuable resource. They systematically eliminated all competition in order to command an artificial price. They suppressed production at another mine in Volterra. Of course the citizens revolted, seeing their incomes disappear but Lorenzo Medici solved the problem by laying siege to the city. The Ischia mines in the kingdom of Naples were then forced to give part of their income to the Medici cartel as a fee for doing business. Graciously, the Medicis let them stay in business only if the owners would abide by all regulations set down by the Medici contract. The biggest goal was to suppress the Turkish alum which threatened the Medici/Papal cartel. This was accomplished by earmarking income from the Tolfa mines for the next crusade against the Turks and Hussite heretics which undoubtedly had as one of its goals destruction of the Turkish enterprise. The whole goal of this was to create an artificial shortage so that an artificial price could be charged.

Of course the Medicis probably were not as sophisticated as the biogenic theorists are today. They didn't propagate theories as to why there was a shortage of alum. Perhaps they could have but then again they didn't have the luck to call upon such a vaunted authority as Science to justify their rapacity . . . .

POLITICS/ECONOMICS PILLAR: THAT WHICH IS UNSEEN

3

The crowd parted, bemused, as the sheriff led his charge onto the sidewalk just in front of the bake shop. There was a mixture of laughter with some expressions of disbelief as the sheriff waited for the bakeshop owner to come outside. The growing crowd excitedly began to press a little too close to the prisoner and captor. The sheriff raised his hand and the gathering slowly became silent. A cackling voice from somewhere in the back broke the silence, "Got your man, huh Fitzy?" The sheriff, half expecting this, smiled as the crowd broke into raucous laughter. The captive began to squirm and fidget. "All right, enough of that now," said the sheriff as he tried to fortify his hold on his prisoner but to no great success. He wished he could use the handcuffs but the prisoner's wrists were much too skinny– the prisoner could not have been more than 10 years old.

Charlie, the owner of the bakeshop around which the crowd had gathered, came outside and pointed excitedly at the prisoner, "Fitzy, that's him! You got 'im!" He then kicked at the shattered glass on the sidewalk that had once been his store window. The child moved behind the sheriff as Charlie stared menacingly, shaking his fist. "Your gonna pay for this you little hoodlum! You know how much that's gonna cost? At least a thousand bucks!! Wait'll your parents find out about this!"

Don, the tailor, nodded with sadness, "Just when we took those measurements too. Ain't that a shame Charlie!"

"Just hold on a second, Don," replied Charlie. "I still want you to make the suit. I'm not out a thousand bucks. This kid's parents are gonna pay for this so don't you worry—make that suit."

Just when he said this the sheriff interrupted with some hesitancy in his voice. "Um, yeah...ah, Charlie?"

"What is it Sheriff?"

"Yeah, there's just one small matter. You see, um... he doesn't seem to have anyone...well, he has no parents. He belongs to someone I'm sure; but no one at the carnival is talkin' just now."

"What? You mean to say I'm gonna end up payin' for this out of my own pocket?!!"

A hush fell over everyone as they realized the unfortunate predicament of the baker. The townspeople began to openly commiserate with Charlie, as he was a favorite with everyone.

Amy, the florist, made her way to the front of the crowd and, being a florist, tried to spin this sad occasion into something more positive. "Charlie, I'm so sorry about what happened." Everyone nodded and gave their assent. "But...all is not lost you know. At least someone will gain from this and in the end that means that our community gains; even from something like this terrible thing happening."

The townspeople were amazed at this revelation and waited with baited breath to see what good could possibly come of this. "Well, how do ya mean?"

"This situation, as bad as it is, will create work.... Someone has to repair this don't they? That means Bill, the glazier, will have a job and he lives in this community and eventually will spend that money in this community. So out of something bad we have something good."

The crowd began discussing Amy's idea and the general consensus began to be that yes indeed, this incident, as unfortunate as it was, would actually stimulate the small towns glazing business. That a loss could actually turn out to be a gain was welcomed by all.

Just when everyone became comfortable with the idea, Old John, Charlie's friend and the owner of the general store came to the front of the crowd and addressed them. He looked at the sheriff and said, "Well sheriff, since everyone agrees I think you should let the boy go."

"No one has said anything about releasing the boy," responded the sheriff.

"Oh, but I believe we have. What I mean to say, sheriff, is this: If Miss Amy here is right as everyone here seems to agree then let the boy go. And when you do make sure you give him specific instructions. 'Blast out as many windows in the town as you can so we can stimulate the economy in this old town and 'create work', as she says. Yep, in fact, tell him the first place to go is Miss Amy's shop down the road."

Amy shrieked in protest as the crowd became agitated. Old John looked at the boy as he pointed to the florist, "You see that lad? She's shoutin' for joy 'cause she's excited that you'll be creatin' more jobs when you get through blastin' out her windows!"

The florist's objections were swallowed in the din as the crowd was now in a general uproar. "You can't say that !", came the general cry from the mob.

"Yeah, John your disturbin' the peace," said the sheriff.

"I'll tell ya what disturbs the peace sheriff!" The crowd became silent again as Old John glared at the flock and pointed at everyone. "It's idiot ideas like this that disturb the peace. Destruction does not mean growth–c'mon people! No offence to you Miss Amy but ideas like the one you brought up cause all kinds of trouble because you don't see what they come to; they ain't thought through!" With that, the crowd now was completely silent as if waiting for a rebuttal but none came from any source. Old John's logic seemed to have left everyone speechless; even Amy the florist.

THINGS UNSEEN

Our economic thinking, if flawed, will bring about policies and laws that are flawed and dangerous— as we see in the above example if the florist's idea were to become *policy*. However, the end result and impact of the florist's idea was not readily apparent to the crowd because as Old John said, things just 'ain't thought through'. Nowhere is this more apparent than in the field of economics. Amy the florist's thinking was flawed because she narrowed her thinking down to one group and did not consider the whole group or the whole picture. The glaziers in the town would definitely benefit from this 'destruction' but the town as a whole would not have. The overall wealth of the town would have suffered. How much public policy is buttressed by this thinking of 'destruction equals growth'? Initially, you may be repulsed by the phrase but historically and contemporaneously it has been packaged by economists in palatable ways. You may think it obviously illogical except for the fact that there are people walking around the earth who believe that World War 2 ended the Great Depression. In other words, a war (destruction), brought about economic growth. Are we seeing the whole picture or just one part?

All faulty thinking in economics falls under one unifying principle. The principle was elaborated by the French theorist and legislative assemblyman, Frederic Bastiat (1801-1850). Of his many pamphlets and books we will focus on one pamphlet where he states the overarching principle of all his work. The pamphlet's name is simply, *'What is Seen and What is Not Seen'*. He begins with the principle stated: "In the economic sphere an act, a habit, an institution, a law produces not only one effect, but a series of effects. Of these effects the first alone is immediate; it appears simultaneously with its cause; *it is seen*. The other effects emerge only subsequently; *they are not seen*; we are fortunate if we foresee them." Old John would agree. This is the downfall of economics. So how do we make ourselves resistant to error in economics? "There is only one difference between a bad economist and a good one: the bad economist confines himself to the visible effect; the good economist takes into account both the effect that can be seen and those effects that must be foreseen."

This foresight is lacking in most economic policy because of this narrowed focus which we saw above with Amy, the florist. She focused on *one group and her thinking had immediacy for that same person or group e.g*, the glaziers in this case. The rational person or 'good' economist will see things in their totality. Not only are the attitudes completely different from each other but so are their outcomes. Each approach has a distinct consequence when put into effect. Old John had to draw this out for the townsfolk; the ideas which Amy the florist espoused had real life after effects that were far worse than a glazier having a temporary boon. Bastiat understood the two approaches and their eventual fruit, "Yet this difference is tremendous; for it almost always happens that when the immediate consequence is favorable, the later consequences are disastrous, and vice versa. Whence it follows that the bad economist pursues a small present good that will be followed by a great evil to come, while the good economist pursues a great good to come, at the risk of a small present evil." That seems to be the calling card of the bad economists approach. The immediate results are favorable but then something happens. The effect of the policy does widespread damage throughout the economy and now, because the effect is seemingly unrelated to the cause, it almost seems absurd to pin it on the original law when in fact that is the reason for the damage. This damage, which will ultimately come, is unseen or rather unforeseen. The damage that is done, however, has the quality of *'unrelatedness'* to the original law so that it is tempting to go along with the bad economists. This dissimilarity between cause and effect is only apparent. Sometimes, one can carry the thinking all the way through much like Old John did. Other times a little more thinking is required.

'Destruction is opportunity' may not be a slogan that a government would like to overtly bandy about but around the time of World War 2 it was almost an axiom that the war brought about prosperity. Henry Hazlitt in his excellent book, *Economics in One Lesson* talks about how certain industry leaders would make proclamations about "how much better off economically we all are in war than in peace."

Working as a reporter and an editor, Hazlitt saw the broken window fallacy revived by times of war, especially WW2. As Hazlitt puts it, "In Europe after WW2 , they joyously counted the houses, the whole cities that had been leveled to the ground and that 'had to be replaced'. In America they counted the houses that could not be built during the war, the nylon stockings that could not be supplied, the worn out autos and tires, the obsolescent radios and refrigerators. They brought together formidable totals." In their glee this accounting of massive 'demand' justified their theory. Now picture Amy the florist; she would be positively overjoyed at this accounting of loss that they actually consider to be demand. However, demand is more than need. It is need plus purchasing power. When we need something the supply is created only because we have something with which to trade. This is purchasing power. We can sit around and 'need' all day but this will not create the supply— until you create something with which to trade. The creation of Charlie's suit, by Don the tailor, was based on his production of bagels. Demand is the same thing as supply. They are two sides to the same coin. No bagels produced by Charlie means no suit produced by Don. As Hazlitt puts it, "Supply creates demand because at bottom it is demand. The supply of the thing people make is all that people have, in fact, to offer in exchange for the things they want. In this sense the farmers' supply of wheat constitutes their demand for automobiles and other goods. All this is inherent in the modern division of labor in an exchange economy." So we can see, in Charlie the bakers case, the only reason there are suits to buy is because he supplies baked goods. The supply of the suit was created by his supply of bagels. But because of destruction, the suit will not get made— there will be no supply because there simply is no demand as Charlie must take the wealth he planned for the suit and divert it into reconstruction of the window . . . something he already had but now must replace. There is only one party that gains and that is the glazier but there was a loss to both Charlie and to the tailor— there was an overall loss in the community. What is interesting in all this is how war or destruction diverts an economy in a certain direction as we saw with the baker having to divert his wealth to the glazier rather than the tailor where he originally wanted it to go. In other words he is forced to *divert* his wealth in another direction. Instead of buying the suit he now must replace a window. Yes the glazier has work because of this but the overall wealth in the community has gone down. The money Charlie will use to replace the window that created that job is just a lateral transfer of wealth; nothing has been gained.

    The same principle holds on a larger scale when we speak of war. Henry Hazlitt writes about this diversion of wealth and lowered purchasing power in the aftermath of WW2: "The people of Europe built more new houses than otherwise because they had to. But when they built more houses they had just that much less manpower and productive capacity for everything else." Think of that young delinquent running amok in that town and destroying more windows than just Charlies. All of a sudden the glazier has more than his hands full of work. Now, resources get redirected for the glazier hires more help. Others begin to get the idea that that sort of business might be profitable and start to funnel time and energy in that direction. Keep in mind that this diversion of energy is *away from something else*; such as goods that the community desired. Hazlitt says, "Wherever business was increased in one direction, it was correspondingly reduced in another." The conclusion is that WW2 or any war for that matter, "changed the postwar *direction* of effort; it changed the balance of industries; it changed the structure of industry."

The last clause is rather ominous. Could we imagine a scenario where the glazier, having a depraved mind, pays the young hoodlum to break windows all around town? For a small price he hires a band of these misfits who wreak destruction which actually results in profits that redound to the glazier. What the glazier is doing is actually, as Hazlitt intimated above, *restructuring* the economy to suit his ends. This type of socio-economic engineering has occurred on a small scale historically. Is it possible that it has happened on a larger scale such as when we speak of nations and war? This is enough to make one shudder but rationally we can't forbid it. There is evidence for this occurring but we will broach this again in a further issue of *Seven Pillars*.

'FIXING PURCHASING POWER'

What occurred in America and Europe was *diversion* of demand. Europe had to divert it's wealth into rebuilding much as Charlie did. The re-builders gained much as the glazier did in Charlies case— but overall there was a loss. In America the diversion of demand was to products that could not be purchased during the war such as autos, radios, refrigerators etc. So there was a boom of demand after the war because purchases of those products were pent up, so to speak, *during* the war. Hazlitt says, "To most people this seemed like an increase in total demand." Did Americans have the purchasing power to acquire these products? Simply put, no. How then did it happen? Printing of paper money. Hazlitt makes the point that this fallacy, 'destruction breeds opportunity' gives birth to another even more pernicious fallacy and that is that *purchasing power is thought of in terms of paper money.* " Now money can be run off by the printing press...But the more money is turned out in this way, the more the value of any given unit of money falls. This falling value can be measured in rising prices of commodities."

If Charlie the baker goes down into his basement and prints out $1000.00 every week to buy a new suit from Don the tailor, well, Don the tailor will be happy about this overabundance and will begin to charge more because of this overabundance. But this new money will filter into the general community and have the same effect. Prices will begin to creep upwards on everything. This 'newfound' purchasing power by Charlie the baker actually causes an upward spiral in the cost of products. This is inflation. As Hazlitt says, "Most people are so firmly in the habit of thinking of their wealth and income in terms of money, they consider themselves better off as these monetary totals rise, in spite of the fact that in terms of things they may have less and buy less." Inflation (printing of money), is what caused the end of the depression; it wasn't the war. Hazlitt says, "Most of the 'good' economic results which people at the time attributed to WW2 were really owing to wartime inflation. *They could have been, and were, produced just as well by peacetime inflation."*(my emphasis)

We can see that this fallacy is dangerous, for it implants in the mind a historical sequence that is deleterious to our thinking. The depression of the thirties was a difficult time. Then the war came and scarcity was even greater but because of 'patriotic spirit' people willingly sacrificed. The war ends and all of a sudden there is 'prosperity'. People have been heard to say when economic times get tough, 'We need a war'. This is deadly thinking. In times of economic downturns people may support a 'war effort' thinking that that is the only way to revive a dead economy. You have more money but really it is an illusion. Prices have outpaced or kept even with the increased money in your pocket. The other thing it does is it restructures an economy falsely as we saw with the glazier and his band of hoodlums. This is not what people really want i.e. replacement windows— but because of necessity they demand it. They have no choice. The same goes for nations. Restructuring and diversion occurs because the environment (war, natural disasters, terror) forces it upon people. In this we can see that wrong economic thinking leads to destructive and hurtful policy and law. This is because we don't pay attention to what is 'unseen'; that is we must become good economists as Bastiat says and work an idea all the way through. 'Destruction brings opportunity' is an adage concocted by the devil.

PARIS IS FED

The unseen in economics has a positive aspect also. This polar facet of economics goes unnoticed in human affairs and has been a marvel to those who scrutinize it. It is unrealized and unappreciated because it lies right under our noses hiding in plain sight— nobody really concentrates on the air we breathe until it is taken away from us of course. This positive aspect of economics is just like that but even more so. It has prompted many to name it and then to try to harness it but to no avail. It is simply a miracle . . .

Bastiat was one of those that beheld this force and he was awed by it. He realized it in a serendipitous moment. There was a peculiarity that philosophers had been trying to make sense of for many years. They would even give this oddity names and such but it really remained unclassifiable because it didn't fall under any traditional philosophy like ethics or metaphysics. This peculiar force dealt with interactions between humans but it had nothing to do with ethics; it was amoral, so to speak. A conundrum wrapped within an enigma. But yet it was there; as sure as the air that we breathe, this thing was there, even if it did go unnoticed by the greater part of mankind.

Bastiat commented on this enigmatic but powerful force in his book *Economic Sophisms* in which he made the following observation: "On coming to Paris for a visit, I said to myself: Here are a million human beings who would all die in a few days if supplies did not flow into this metropolis. It staggers the imagination to try to comprehend the vast multiplicity of objects that must pass through its gates tomorrow, if it's to be preserved from the horrors of famine, insurrection and pillage. And yet all are sleeping peacefully at this moment, without being disturbed for a single instant by the idea of so frightful a prospect. On the other hand, eighty departments have worked today, *without cooperative planning or mutual arrangements*, to keep Paris supplied. How does each succeeding day manage to bring this gigantic market just what is necessary—neither too much nor too little?" (italics mine)

This is what befuddled philosophers for so long. This arrangement between humans that was not directed by a central command or agreements. Yet there was organization to the highest degree. How could this cooperation happen without some type of supervision? Each individual was just 'doing his own thing' without worrying about the end in mind which was to supply Paris; as Bastiat says, without planning or mutual arrangements. Adam Smith noted this in his book *The Wealth of Nations* book four chapter 2, when speaking of an individual engaging in an economic transaction, "he intends only his own gain, and he is in this as in many other cases, led by an 'invisible hand' to promote an end which was no part of of his intention." You can see the befuddlement at this process which magically aranges things without a planning board or governing influence. Chaos should be the rule here but it isn't. As Adam Smith mused there seemed to be an invisible force that just got things done.

THE FORCE AND THE PENCIL

So we say with some confidence, that this force *creates*. It tends to order instead of disorder. It takes disparate elements and arranges them into a good desired by all. For example, as stated above, each person looking after his own interests, with no intentions of great altruism, such as serving humanity, does, in the end, serve humanity; for *Paris is fed*. This can be applied to every situation or place. But let us take a more humble and simpler example to demonstrate the amazing sophistication of this force. We will choose a product that everyone uses and is familiar with: the pencil.

The following is a short essay by Leonard E. Read, founder of the Foundation of Economic Education. The import of what he says is grasped best when it is read in its totality. The main idea of his article can't really be summarized effectively because it has a cumulative thrust. Certain details may have changed such as places and production processes because the article was written over 50 years ago but the essence of the article remains the same.

I, Pencil, simple though I appear to be, merit your wonder and awe, a claim I shall attempt to prove. In fact, if you can understand me – no, that's too much to ask of anyone – if you can become aware of the miraculousness which I symbolize, you can help save the freedom mankind is so unhappily losing. I have a profound lesson to teach. And I can teach this lesson better than can an automobile or an airplane or a mechanical dishwasher because – well, because I am seemingly so simple.

Simple? Yet, not a single person on the face of this earth knows how to make me. This sounds fantastic, doesn't it? Especially when it is realized that there are about one and one-half billion of my kind produced in the U.S.A. each year.

Pick me up and look me over. What do you see? Not much meets the eye – there's some wood, lacquer, the printed labeling, graphite lead, a bit of metal, and an eraser.

Innumerable Antecedents

Just as you cannot trace your family tree back very far, so is it impossible for me to name and explain all my antecedents. But I would like to suggest enough of them to impress upon you the richness and complexity of my background. My family tree begins with what in fact is a tree, a cedar of straight grain that grows in Northern California and Oregon. Now contemplate all the saws and trucks and rope and the countless other gear used in harvesting and carting the cedar logs to the railroad siding. Think of all the persons and the numberless skills that went into their fabrication: the mining of ore, the making of steel and its refinement into saws, axes, motors: the growing of hemp and bringing it through all the stages to heavy and strong rope; the logging camps with their beds and mess halls, the cookery and the raising of all the foods. Why, untold thousands of persons had a hand in every cup of coffee the loggers drink!

The logs are shipped to a mill in San Leandro, California. Can you imagine the individuals who make flat cars and rails and railroad engines and who construct and install the communication systems incidental thereto? These legions are among my antecedents.

Consider the millwork in San Leandro. The cedar logs are cut into small, pencil-length slats less than one-fourth of an inch in thickness. These are kiln dried and then tinted for the same reason women put rouge on their faces. People prefer that I look pretty, not a pallid white. The slats are waxed and kiln dried again. How many skills went into the making of the tint and the kilns, into supplying the heat, the light and power, the belts, motors, and all the other things a mill requires? Sweepers in the mill among my ancestors? Yes, and included are the men who poured the concrete for the dam of a Pacific Gas & Electric Company hydroplant which supplies the mill's power!

Don't overlook the ancestors present and distant who have a hand in transporting sixty carloads of slats across the nation.

Once in the pencil factory, each slat is given eight grooves by a complex machine, after which another machine lays leads in every other slat, applies glue, and places another slat atop – a lead sandwich, so to speak. Seven brothers and I are mechanically carved from this "wood-clinched" sandwich. My "lead" itself – it contains no lead at all – is complex. The graphite is mined in Ceylon. Consider these miners and those who make their many tools and the makers of the paper sacks in which the graphite is shipped and those who make the string that ties the sacks and those who put them aboard ships and those who make the ships. Even the lighthouse keepers along the way assisted in my birth – and the harbor pilots.

The graphite is mixed with clay from Mississippi in which ammonium hydroxide is used in the refining process. Then wetting agents are added such as sulfonated tallow – animal fats chemically reacted with sulfuric acid. After passing through numerous machines, the mixture finally appears as endless extrusions – as from a sausage grinder – cut to size, dried, and baked for several hours at 1,850 degrees Fahrenheit. To increase their strength and smoothness the leads are then treated with a hot mixture which includes candelilla wax from Mexico, paraffin wax, and hydrogenated natural fats.

My cedar receives six coats of lacquer. Do you know all the ingredients of lacquer? Who would think that the growers of castor beans and the refiners of castor oil are a part of it? They are. Why, even the processes by which the lacquer is made a beautiful yellow involves the skills of more persons than one can enumerate!

Observe the labeling. That's a film formed by applying heat to carbon black mixed with resins. How do you make resins and what, pray, is carbon black?

My bit of metal – the ferrule – is brass. Think of all the persons who mine zinc and copper and those who have the skills to make shiny sheet brass from these products of nature. Those black rings on my ferrule are black nickel. What is black nickel and how is it applied? The complete story of why the center of my ferrule has no black nickel on it would take pages to explain

Then there's my crowning glory, inelegantly referred to in the trade as "the plug," the part man uses to erase the errors he makes with me. An ingredient called "factice" is what does the erasing. It is a rubber-like product made by reacting rape-seed oil from the Dutch East indies with sulfur chloride. Rubber, contrary to the common notion, is only for binding purposes. Then, too, there are numerous vulcanizing and accelerating agents. The pumice comes from Italy; and the pigment which gives "the plug" its color is cadmium sulfide.

No One Knows

Does anyone wish to challenge my earlier assertion that no single person on the face of this earth knows how to make me? Actually, millions of human beings have had a hand in my creation, no one of whom even knows more than a very few of the others. Now, you may say that I go too far in relating the picker of a coffee berry in far off Brazil and food growers elsewhere to my creation; that this is an extreme position. I shall stand by my claim. There isn't a single person in all these millions, including the president of the pencil company, who contributes more than a tiny, infinitesimal bit of know-how. From the standpoint of know-how the only difference between the miner of graphite in

Ceylon and the logger in Oregon is in the type of know-how. Neither the miner nor the logger can be dispensed with, any more than can the chemist at the factory or the worker in the oil field – paraffin being a by-product of petroleum.

Here is an astounding fact: Neither the worker in the oil field nor the chemist nor the digger of graphite or clay nor any who mans or makes the ships or trains or trucks nor the one who runs the machine that does the knurling on my bit of metal nor the president of the company performs his singular task because he wants me. Each one wants me less, perhaps, than does a child in the first grade. Indeed, there are some among this vast multitude who never saw a pencil nor would they know how to use one. Their motivation is other than me. Perhaps it is something like this: Each of these millions sees that he can thus exchange his tiny know-how for the goods and services he needs or wants. I may or may not be among these items.

No Master Mind

There is a fact still more astounding: The absence of a master mind, of anyone dictating or forcibly directing these countless actions which bring me into being. No trace of such a person can be found. Instead, we find the Invisible Hand at work. This is the mystery to which I earlier referred. It has been said that "only God can make a tree." Why do we agree with this? Isn't it because we realize that we ourselves could not make one? Indeed, can we even describe a tree? We cannot, except in superficial terms. We can say, for instance, that a certain molecular configuration manifests itself as a tree. But what mind is there among men that could even record, let alone direct, the constant changes in molecules that transpire in the life span of a tree?

Such a feat is utterly unthinkable!

I, Pencil, am a complex combination of miracles: a tree, zinc, copper, graphite, and so on. But to these miracles which manifest themselves in Nature an even more extraordinary miracle has been added: the configuration of creative human energies – millions of tiny know-hows configurating naturally and spontaneously in response to human necessity and desire and in the absence of any human masterminding! Since only God can make a tree, I insist that only God could make me. Man can no more direct these millions of know-hows to bring me into being than he can put molecules together to create a tree.

The above is what I meant when writing, "if you can become aware of the miraculousness which I symbolize, you can help save the freedom mankind is so unhappily losing" For, if one is aware that these know-hows will naturally, yea, automatically, arrange themselves into creative and productive patterns in response to human necessity and demand- that is, in the absence of governmental or any other coercive master-minding – then one will possess an absolutely essential ingredient for freedom: a faith in free people. Freedom is impossible without this faith.

Once government has had a monopoly of a creative activity such, for instance, as the delivery of the mails, most individuals will believe that the mails could not be efficiently delivered by men acting freely. And here is the reason: Each one acknowledges that he himself doesn't know how to do all the things incident to mail delivery. He also recognizes that no other individual could do it. These assumptions are correct. No individual possesses enough know-how to perform a nation's mail delivery any more than any individual *possesses enough know-how to make a pencil. Now, in the absence of faith in free people – in the unawareness that millions of tiny know-hows would naturally and miraculously form and cooperate to satisfy this necessity – the individual cannot help but reach the erroneous conclusion that mail can be delivered only by governmental "master-minding."*

Testimony Galore

If I, Pencil, were the only item that could offer testimony on what men and women can accomplish when free to try, then those with little faith would have a fair case. However, there is testimony galore: it's all about us and on every hand. Mail delivery is exceedingly simple when compared, for instance, to the making of an automobile or a calculating machine or a grain combine or a milling machine or to tens of thousands of other things. Delivery? Why, in this area where men have been left free to try, they deliver the human voice around the world in less than one second; they deliver an event visually and in motion to any person's home when it is happening; they deliver 150 passengers from Seattle to Baltimore in less than four hours; they deliver gas from Texas to one's range or furnace in New York at unbelievably low rates and without subsidy; they deliver each four pounds of oil from the Persian Gulf to our Eastern Seaboard – halfway around the world – for less money than the government charges for delivering a one-ounce letter across the street! The lesson I have to teach is this: Leave all creative energies uninhibited. Merely organize society to act in harmony with this lesson. Let society's legal apparatus remove all obstacles the best it can. Permit these creative know-hows freely to flow. Have faith that free men and women will respond to the Invisible Hand. This faith will be con-

firmed. *I, Pencil, seemingly simple though I am, offer the miracle of my creation as testimony that this is a practical faith, as practical as the sun, the rain, a cedar tree, the good earth.*

Two things must be highlighted from this article by Read.

1. There is *no coercion* involved in the process of bringing about this pencil. No one is forced to make this object, it comes into being freely.

2. None of the participants in this process performed their respective tasks because they wanted a pencil. Everyone 'did their own thing'. In other words there was only *self interest*.

ATOMIC PENCILS

The pencil is a simple item. Think of the more intricate items that surround us. Not only are the items composed of physical matter known as atoms but they are also composed of many individual know- hows. A myriad number of men and women with their own expertise and labor go into that product and so help bring it about. These atoms of individual pieces of knowledge are brought together by this mysterious force which has this characteristic of *auto-organization*. The more you contemplate it the more unfathomable it becomes. This is one of the reasons that philosophers have such trouble with this superb organizing force; it brings about design but who is doing the designing? How do the many intelligences involved who do not know the end product (neither do they care about it) bring this product about? It is a question that the best minds in the world have been miffed at for ages. At the same time it is because of this inconceivableness that we are hesitant to apply it to things that we normally would think must be taken care of by some other organizing force. But if we look at the pencil, there is no government that is established in order to undertake it's manufacture. This auto-organizational force has never been unleashed full scale to see it's possibilities in fields of endeavor that are now done by government, such as the mail system. One thing is certain, it would be far more efficient. These potentials of this force we may never know because this force is suppressed. But what is actually being suppressed here?

The pencil originates as an idea. Yes, it is a physical object but it originated in thought. Thoughts belong in minds; this is self evident. Minds belong to humans. This pencil, ultimately is a product of the human mind. The force that brings it about is still a mystery but even if we can't grasp the nature of this force we do know one thing; the whole process originates with an idea in the human mind. Then this force or law makes concrete this idea as we saw above in the creation of the pencil. If this force is interrupted or diverted in some way, logically, what is being affected, is the human mind. The more this force is suppressed the more the human mind is suppressed. The mind and this accompanying force have an inextricable connection that can actually be shown not only logically but historically. You can call it what you want. Some resort to -isms and call it capitalism. We must get away from these emotionally laden constructs and understand fundamental concepts and principles. But the important point to remember is that this force is inextricable from the human mind— they can't be separated. In fact, to the extent that this force is encouraged and aroused, is the exact extent to which the human mind will be encouraged and aroused and grow— they are commensurate with each other. One approach to history is from the viewpoint of this force. The more this force has been restrained by edict or some type of government influence the more the human mind has been restrained. Consequently, where this force is encouraged, you will see the fruit and wealth of the human mind. Where this force is suppressed you will see squalor and destitution— and the human spirit crushed.

Historically, this auto-organizational force has never been completely encouraged. It has always been stifled to some degree in every country and in every time period. In some places and times more than others. One example of this stifling is a circumstance during seventeenth century France. The French economist Turgot references this story in the *Mercure de France* gazette around 1759. The chief adviser to Louis the 14th, Jean Baptiste Colbert, desperately tried to improve commerce within France. His protectionist and indirect taxation methods had largely failed to bring in needed revenues. He regulated the trades by imposing strict standards that required a ponderous bureaucracy to supervise infringements of standards. According to Hernando Desoto, 16,000 small entrepeneurs were put to death by this regime (pg. 11 *The Mystery of Capital*). Their crime according to DeSoto was "manufacturing and importing cotton cloth in violation of France's industrial codes. " French workers began emigrating because of his oppressive policies. In desperation he called a meeting of manufacturers. He asked them what the government could do to 'help' improve manufacturing. A manufacturer named Le Gendre cried out, "Laissez nous faire!" Translated as "Leave us alone!"

BIG BUSINESS FEARS CAPITALISM

There are only two ways to acquire goods. Either through

A) Theft or

B) Directed Production. To put it simply; trade or robbery. This has been the dynamic tension in history between those who produce and those who take the fruit of that production. Whether you see it on a small scale in the local newspapers or whether we see it on the worldstage when we speak historically of nations and empires throughout the ages; it is the same. In the words of St. Augustine, "Remove justice, and what are kingdoms but gangs of criminals on a large scale? What are criminal gangs but petty kingdoms?" As he saw it the only difference between Rome and a local gang was that Rome won "so many recruits" and was thus able to 'atttain impunity'.

The fundamental thing that Colbert and the Roman empire represent is 'interference' with human transactions. The fundamental remedy is to 'leave alone' or let things be; that is do not interfere. Interference in any form is THEFT.

Historically and logically, interference with this force, results in protection of a few, while the many are plundered. This interference comes in two forms. These two forms, however , are really the same thing in the end; just different names. These two forms of interference, with the auto-organizational force, are very much deeply ingrained primal beliefs of our culture.The two forms of interference are:

1. Charters

2. Regulations

Both are forms of 'protection' for a favored group and oppression and thievery against the majority. In essence, they are the same thing. To sum it up in an easy way we will look at this interference phenomenon in a small setting, a town.

Picture a small town. Now picture that, among the populace, you are the only carpenter in the town, in fact you are the only carpenter for miles around. Business is good because you are the only game in town and pretty much you can charge whatever you want until....the new carpenter arrives in town. He starts charging lower prices in order to get some business. Now you become a little upset because your income starts to drop off because this new carpenter is charging lower prices and you think 'what am I going to do?' There are two things you can do:

1. use force— by either directly threatening the new carpenter to leave town or indirectly by utilizing the political system to pass a law which would, in effect, outlaw the new carpenter

2. use peace— improve your efficiency and skills (directed production) to make an even better product than the new carpenter or cater to a very specific need. This direction benefits everyone in the town.

So here we see again the two methods of acquisition; thievery and force or creativity and directed production. Destruction versus creation. It sort of boils down to either using peaceful means or aggression. If you decide to use aggression you can suppress your competition by charter or by regulations. Charters have been used since time immemorial by sovereigns; of course the sovereign has a vested interest. The charter is backed by the crown, that is by force of arms. If you were granted one, no one could infringe on whatever it is that the king has granted you. You have 'exclusive rights' to a particular resource, land or trade. The sovereign commits to 'protecting your rights' under this contract; this is implied or sometimetimes explicit. No one else is allowed into the domain marked out for you. Now let's say that the sovereign of your town has granted you a charter and you are once again the lone carpenter in town because your competition was unable to attain one. All competition is driven out and you can begin to relax your standards and charge any price you see fit. If there is any 'blackmarket' competition and they are found out they are prosecuted by the governing body which granted you exclusive rights. The sovereign has 'interfered' in the transactions between men and created a situation favorable to only a few— you, the lone carpenter. This is the essence of interference; exclusive favoritism to a few.

There are, however, some problems with granting exclusivity rights to someone in the form of a charter. The main thing being the marketing issue. There is a public relations problem that this form of protection has. Openly favoring one group may cause some problems amongst the general populace, especially if you are in a democracy. So to avoid this, another tactic is pursued which generally solves the image problem. This is the technique of *licensing* or instituting *regulations*. The marketing of this technique is packaged with a mantra that is usually always entwined with it; and that is, 'regulations and licensing are for the safety and benefit of the public'. They are, actually, the furthest thing removed from benefitting the public. They are in fact harmful and devastating to the public, as we shall see. In the end, by 'regulating' or licensing you have instituted the charter mechanism. They are the same thing with different spellings.

With the technique of licensing and regulations our lone carpenter, in our small town, takes a different tact now. To assure his monopoly, he dissuades further competition by actively lobbying for rules that govern anyone seeking entry into his field. The laws are passed and this makes it more difficult for someone to enter that field. This is done in the name of public safety. This allows the price of that particular item or product to be at the whim of the monopoly holder; in this case the carpenter. In the case of both the charter holder or the beneficiary of regulatory mania, there is a monopoly created. One is done by fiat (charter), the other by legislation in the publics interest.

There is hardly a trade or field of endeavor that is not protected by regulations or licensing, the modern charters. For instance, many states have a Tonsorial Board which licenses and regulates hair cutters and barbers. Each person cutting hair must not only be licensed but also must pass inspection by the local Board of Health. Even if you are retired from being a hair stylist all your life and wished to make some part time income at home this would be impossible unless one was willing to risk a jail sentence or fines. Any individual undertaking this enterprise is providing a service for people but with an attached risk of punishment if he or she is found out. Is the public being protected? The main reason for this threat is protection of a group, in whatever profession, and this can be seen historically; one hysterical example is from the 1930's during the Roosevelt administration. Due to national legislation certain industries were allowed to set fixed prices on their products. These prices then became binding upon anyone engaged in that particular industry. Jacob Maged, a successful owner of a small business pressing clothes for 22 years, did not get the memo. He was sent to jail and fined $100 for *lowering* his price for pressing a suit to 35 cents. The industrial code set by agreement was 40 cents. Big business can't make a profit if these Jacob Mageds keep running around charging lower prices taking money from big business and saving it for the rest. The fixed prices were really a means used by these industries that couldn't otherwise protect themselves through extensive regulation and licensing. They couldn't extend the rhetoric of public safety in shirt pressing for instance. Wherever there is a interference by any of these techniques there is a corresponding diminution of quality and return for the consumer.

Regulations have only one effect: monopolistic protection of a chosen group. They are not there for the benefit of consumers. This force that we have been talking about is not only organizational but it is also *self-regulatory*— it exhibits this characteristic only when it is 'left alone'. We are not able to see this, however, because it has rarely been given a chance. However, there are examples of the self-regulatory ability of this force. Since 1885 women across the country gave creedence to a magazine rather than a governmental body when it to came to food and nutrition. We must keep in mind that food was unregulated at that time— no one knew what was going into what product as preserving chemicals yet Good Housekeeping was there years before the Pure Food Act was introduced in 1906 by the federal government. In 1910 it opened it's Domestic Science Laboratory and Testing Kitchen. In 1912 Dr. Harvey Wiley, the former commissioner of the Bureau of Chemistry, worked at the magazine apprising America's housewives about the condition and nutritive value of the food they were putting on their tables before any government agency was doing this.

But for those who still believe in this primal belief that industry and the trades should be regulated and licensed, let us look at a few historical and more contemporary examples.

THE CHARTER

This event in American history is actually, in a way, magical— for that which is good was called bad and that which is bad was called good. One can only appeal to magic in order to accomplish a feat like this mass hypnotism. It forever changed the view of supposedly educated Americans. What it did was change words around in the English language so that the connotation of a word was changed and made to be associated with something that is not that thing. Down to this day, because of this event in history, capitalism is called an evil when in fact there has never been such a thing as capitalism only a dim minor representation of it. But, instead, what there has been is protection of the few to the great harm of the many.

In America, during the great expansion out west, the Pacific railroad bill was passed in 1862. Two corporations undertook this venture to lay track from Missouri to the California coast; the Union Pacific and the Central Pacific. The funding of this project was initially about $50 million dollars from government bonds.

But the Union Pacific needed a company to actually carry out the construction and they hired a company called Credit Mobilier. But there was a slight problem— this was a sham company. It was a front company which had the same owners as the Union Pacific. It was a ruse to make a quick profit for the biggest stockholders. The Credit Mobilier was to be paid by the Union Pacific to carry out construction. So, because the biggest stockholders owned both companies, they were indeed paying themselves. Of course the Credit Mobilier could charge whatever it liked...and it did. The money was coming from the American public. When you are given a domain outright and there is no competition from any source you can pretty much do whatever you like. The domain given to the Union Pacific was vast. On each side of the line, per every mile of track laid down, they were given about five square miles on either side of the track. All resources and mineral rights included. Each mile of track laid down was grossly over budget simply because the investment capital was not theirs, it was subsidized by the taxpayer. There was no reason to be efficient. The more inefficient, the more profit for the biggest stockholders. Now this is nothing but theft. It is interference with the great natural law that makes the pencil.

The objection might be that public works on this scale can't be accomplished on a private investment basis— only government is capable of carrying out massive public works like this. The Great Northern Railway lays that to rest however. This rail line extended from Minnesota to Seattle and it was all done with private money. In the Great Panic of 1893 when all other railroad companies went bankrupt, the Great Northern ended up making a profit. James Jerome

Hill was the mastermind and president of this undertaking, building the line slowly, with no taxpayer money, making sure that each extension of line was able to turn a profit before further building would commence. He did this by giving incentives to farmers; moving them to the area for free, and giving them discounts on shipping charges. This in turn inspired more interest in the project and more and more people were drawn. What was called 'Hill's Folly' became one of the great successes in American history; and not one cent of taxpayer money.

These two entities, James J. Hill and the other transcontinental railroad corporations, can't be lumped together. They are distinct creatures. One is based on theft and the other is directed production with a goal in mind.

The Central Pacific started out from the coast of California and at some point was to meet the Union Pacific rail which started in Missouri. By act of legislation the California government gave the Central Pacific complete monopoly control of the entire coastline. Basically, No Competition Allowed, said the sign; and that, for almost 30 years. As happens with state granted monopolies (read charters) they charged rates that oppressed the farmers, who had no other rail to turn to. Funny thing, this monopoly was repeatedly challenged but always ended up being protected by legislative act. The suffering wrought by this corporation was made possible courtesy of judicial and legislative assistance. The natural force was disturbed with and yet this disturbance created by government intervention was not blamed; instead what was blamed was 'capitalism'.

Because of this intervention with this natural force, widespread affliction ensued. Matthew Josephson, in his anticapitalistic book, *The Robber Barons* (pg. 165) describes the fallout from the Union Pacific and Credit mobilier scandal: "the tale of appalling waste, of crime and turpitude shook the whole country like a mighty quake and set many a weak structure to rocking . . . thousands lost their savings in Union Pacific's fall, while distress spread quickly to the grain growing regions. From the rostrums the tribunes of the people . . . began to speak out, in tones soon to become familiar whenever such provocation arose, against the giant corporations which overran the country." Some one had to be blamed, I guess. But Josephson failed to make a distinction between capitalism and theft that was going on. How was this capitalism when all the money came from public funds?

When Josephson's book was released in the middle of the Great Depression, it only solidified the deception that capitalism was this great evil at the root of the financial problems of the day. Interestingly, Josephson's book gives the evidence in support of capitalism as he details how these corporations were granted charters and funded by taxpayers. Curiously, he could not see this distinction along with the rest of the populace. The ism that was being practiced was not capitalism but statism or corporatism. What the corporation fears is a revoking of the charter which grants them rapacious abilities. The Central Pacific repressed farmers in California not because of capitalism but because of legislative aid from their cohorts in the California legislature. The Union Pacific pillaged the American taxpayer because of a monopoly charter with an open ended purse.

REGULATIONS AND LICENSING

Hernando deSoto is a true scientist. Though he is an

economist from Peru and a well known one, he is no stranger to testing his theories by taking it to the streets—literally. In his book, *The Mystery of Capital,* Hernando documents how he and his research team uncovered some amazing facts about economic life in third world countries. They did this by actually working, setting up shop. In Lima, Peru they opened up a garment shop on the outskirts of that city. It was a totally legitimate enterprise. They found out some interesting things about trying to make a living in third world countries:

"The team then began filling out the forms, standing in the queues and making the bus trips into central Lima to get all the certifications required to operate, according to the letter of the law, a small business in Peru. They spent six hours a day at it and finally registered the business—289 days later. Although the garment shop was geared to operate with only one worker, the cost of legal registration was $1,231.00—thirty-one times the monthly minimum wage. To obtain legal authorization to build a house on state owned land took six years and eleven months—requiring 207 administrative steps in 52 different government offices. To obtain a legal title for that land took 728 steps. We also found that a private bus, jitney or taxi driver who wanted to obtain official recognition of his route faced 26 months of red tape."(pgs. 17-24)

Peru was not the only place that deSoto and his researchers investigated. They encountered the same repression of working people everywhere they went; whether it was the Philipines, Egypt, Haiti or Brazil. The people could not find work 'in the system' because of the web of protective legislation protecting the elite mercantilists. DeSoto goes on to say that he found most of the people have no choice but to opt out of the repressive system and go 'underground'. We are talking about third world countries, not America or Europe. But in a sense the same thing is happening in these places also as anyone who starts a small business understands.

EPISTEME AND TECHNE

But certainly, doctors and plumbers and lawyers and drivers must be licensed? For example, in the field of medicine, you would not dare go to a doctor who was known to be unlicensed and unaccredited in his field, right? But what I will boldly proclaim here and now is that the reason you go to a doctor is not because he is licensed but rather it is because of a pragmatic nature that you go— it is because you want to be healed. In other words, do you go to someone to be healed because they lay claim to knowledge or do you go to someone to be healed? If the practical nature of your sickness is not taken care of then how does the knowledge of that healer help you? To understand this better we must understand the philosophical distinction between *episteme* and *techne*.

Aristotle is the first thinker in which the ideas of knowledge, or *episteme*, and craft, or *techne*, coalesce. Craft (techne) is knowledge (episteme) that works or has utility. Such as when a mechanic fixes your car, he is putting his episteme (knowledge) into physical actions which work well (techne)— he has used knowledge in an application which is physically fixing your car. But if there is a disjunction between episteme and techne (in other words the knowledge has no utility or is not working) then what human nature will always do is align itself with techne or craft—

that which *works*. This is easily illustrated by asking yourself this question. Would I rather have my car fixed by someone who is extremely efficient at doing so everytime or would you rather have someone who is licensed and had all the great schooling yet fails to fix your car? The latter person has a claim to knowledge (episteme) but there are complaints about his work and his ability to trouble-shoot your vehicle— his knowledge has not translated to techne— that which works. Everyone would flock to the person with techne (craft) because what he does 'works'— regardless of his educational backround. This is an inveterate characteristic of human nature that we all tend to do. Episteme is a claim to knowledge, *much like licensing*, but does this claim to knowledge convert into techne? When I pass a drivers license test all this ensures is that I have episteme, that is, I *know* how to drive a car. Does this ensure that I am a *good* driver— that I have craft or techne? Not at all. When a doctor passes a test he lays claim to a body of knowledge(episteme). Does this ensure he is a good doctor— that is, does it ensure that he will effect cure? Not at all. All that it ensures is that he has knowledge (episteme). If his patients are not being cured or helped with their problems then you can be sure that they will go to someone who has techne; in other words someone who offers something that *works*. We have actually seen this occur enmasse in the last 20 or 30 years, in medicine, where people are thronging to alternative cures not because of the fact that these cures are licensed but because the cures have utility— that is, *they work*. Human nature always is attracted to *what works*. Up until the mid-twentieth century, in the outer districts of China, there have been stories about village doctors who were paid in a most curious fashion which will illustrate this distinction between episteme and techne. The village doctors were only paid when the townsfolk were *healthy*. Whenever the village suffered from sickness or ill-health, the doctor was not paid. He was not doing his job of preventing illness. His craft was not 'working' so to speak and a doctor who wasn't paid meant a bad doctor.

So as I boldly claimed at the beginning, what human nature seeks is craft or techne— that which works. Another way to illustrate the distinction between episteme and techne and to put this into perspective is to poll the various professions and ask them what they would rather prefer: A licensing system or a rating system?

I venture to guess that everyone in those professions would favor licensing. But I bet every consumer of those professions would prefer a rating system. Licensing is rather a clever way to become inept. In other words licensing does not give you further incentive to craft or techne. 'I am a licensed mechanic' does not mean that you are a *good* mechanic. A rating system tells you how good you are doing— if whether what you claim to know has utility, whether it works. A licensing system tells you there is no need for further improvement— you have arrived, so to speak.

In a free society these rating systems would be the norm rather than the licensing systems. The apparatus of the rating system would be applied to each and every field. A *Consumer Reports* for doctors, lawyers, plumbers, contractors, baby-sitters etc. etc. That we abide by the rating system and not the licensing system is demonstrable anecdotally. Inevitably we all succumb to the rating system whenever we hear from a neighbor or friend by word of mouth about some plumber or carpenter or healer that 'worked' for them. After hearing high praise about the service in question and if you hear this repeatedly from others, would you really ask, "Yeah, but is he licensed?" I don't think so. How many times have you been pleased with something or some service that was 'word of mouth' (rating system) compared to that which you were co-erced to choose (licensing system)? For, in fact, this is a form of veiled co-ercion when you can only choose between those who are licensed rather than from those who have techne or craft.

HOW TO MAKE WHERE YOU LIVE INTO A THIRD WORLD COUNTRY

Everyone would agree that beating down and regulating the human mind is evil. But when you interfere with peaceful human action you are actually doing the same thing. It is unseen, this interference, but it will ultimately rear it's ugly head in physical reality. Poor living conditions and squalor are only suppression of the human mind; interference with a natural force that creates miracles like the pencil and far greater amenities of civilization. It seems incredible to believe but the slightest well meaning official proposing a regulation or licensing law is doing violence to the human *mind*. Anyone would feel appalled at having a 'truth council' or 'truth board' that 'regulated' ideas which told you what to think. Why is it any different when peaceful actions between humans are sanctioned? Where is the outrage? After all the idea precedes the act . . .

Thought is *potential* to act in this world, i.e., it is prior to act and therefore superior to act because it generates act. If act is suppressed you are affecting that which generates act— thought or mind. Suppressing actions equals suppressing the mind. Supressing the mind has an undeniable effect in the world outside. The potential in the world will be suppressed.

Ideas create the world around us. They create the pencil, the plane, the television, the coffee pot. If we stunt the mind then we have a truncated world. A world held short of its potential. It is just an exercise to extrapolate from what is to what could be but if we gaze into the subtleties of such things as the creation of a pencil I think we can imagine a world where abundance is the norm and scarcity is obsolete. As Buckminster Fuller said in the 1970's 'There should be 4 billion billionaires.' Though it is unseen, I believe that world is there and that it will come about when we recognize that act *is* thought and that we are only fooling ourselves when we think we can restrain actions, by modern day charters, without negating the human mind.

Until then we'll have faith in the unseen . . .

FORTEAN PILLAR: UFOS ARE SUPPRESSED TECHNOLOGY
PART ONE- 19th CENTURY BEGINNINGS

4

In the Socratic dialogue Timaeus, the philosopher Plato takes a sledgehammer to one of our cozy, modern beliefs. Though he states it demurely and unpretentiously, what he revealed was completely heretical to the Greek mind but also, if true, extremely destabilizing to our modern mind.

He illustrates, through an exchange between two characters, what the origins of myth and mythology are; what we would call today by the name of *fiction*.

Plato states through the mouth of an Egyptian priest that mythology is not what it seems, a fanciful story about fanciful characters, places and events. The Egyptian priest uses the myth of Phaethon and the chariot of his father Helios as an example to show his listener Solon, the Athenian statesman, that the myth was not just a story for entertainment's sake; instead he says the story, "has the form of myth, but really signifies a declination of the bodies moving in the heavens around the earth, and a great conflagration of things upon the earth which recurs after long intervals." In other words, the myth was actually a *chronicle of an actual astro-historical event.*

What the priest revealed was astounding. Deep beneath the layers of this myth of Helios and other myths is a fundamental historical event that is illustrated in the clothing of *story*. Socrates was executed for not giving obeisance to the gods of the Athenian state and here is a priest, almost a century before Socrates's death, telling the head of the Athenian state that the gods and their mythology are nonsense; that in fact they are a cover story. Keep in mind these myths were not only embodied in stories but also in religious ritual and visual mediums such as sculpture and later, paintings.

This dualistic nature of myth has been explored by the likes of Giorgio de Santillana, professor from MIT, and Immanuel Velikovsky and other competent researchers in the last one hundred years; what they have uncovered verifies the story that was told by that Egyptian priest to Plato. It seems that the myths are a code for the initiated, those in the know. Why they are in code would be the logical question to ask. Albertus Magnus, who we shall meet later on, seemed to think that it was for ease of remembrance. Instead of memorizing tables and facts, if one were to learn a story that could entertain, one would have entrance into vast stores of knowledge. This may have some truth to it for when we look at some of the medievalists and their enchantment with memory systems, we begin to see outlines of a sophisticated classification system in the guise of symbology. Symbols are systematically used to represent a fact, whether it is an event, place or thing. The symbols are place-holders for something else. Ramon Llull in the 13th century pioneered many of these techniques which were further developed by the likes of Giordano Bruno and Liebnitz. The sophistication of Llull's machine which he developed, has influenced modern computer scientists to dub Llull as the founder of Information Technology. It is hard to escape the fact that the people involved in these information systems, names like Llull, Bacon and Magnus have always had the aura of secrecy and furtiveness about them. Could these fellows have been a part of a long secret tradition that goes back to the ancient Egyptians of Plato's time?

There is evidence of this, that in fact there are two worlds of communication. One that is plain to see and one that is in code. Who is using the coded communication? Paolo Rossi, in his book *Logic and the Art of Memory* introduces us to some curious correspondence between a very rich man and his son. The person is Henry Percy (1564-1632) who was not only an English aristocrat but a grandee, that is an upper level nobility not to mention one of the wealthiest peers in the court of Queen Elizabeth. In one letter he encourages his son to learn the 'Universal Grammar'. This grammar is not what you and I think of as grammar. It is described by Percy as "a necessary means to express our knowledges to others or to the delivery of them to posterity." According to Percy, it did not deal with "those rules vulgarly taught" in regard to normal language but instead it was, according to him, "the best way to signify the concepts of our minds, to others in present or future, at hand, or any remote distance possible, and in any given time that is possible." This secret language is effective because it is unchanging. It does not depend on time and space. Languages change in time and languages are different all over the world but this language by means of a sophisticated symbology is not dependent on the vagaries of language entropy. As Percy said it prevents 'all equivocations which vulgar tongues are too much pestered with'; in other words there is no room for interpretation. An interesting fact to keep in mind as we go along is that Percy was known as the Wizard because of his alchemical and proto-scientific experiments.

So interestingly, is it possible that this system of transmitting knowledge through things that are not real (e. g. symbols and myth) exists to this day? Think for a second. What if we were told that some of the art and fiction around us in its various forms, was not what it was purported to be— that it was in fact part of a Universal Grammar whose language only the initiated know? What if we were told that, in *some* cases, it actually represented real events, places and people? It would surely be disorienting if the veil were cast aside and we were told that some fiction as we know it actually is not fiction but a *chronicle of actual historical events* . . .

THE HISTORIAN OF APPARENTLY IMPOSSIBLE THINGS

The author, Jules Verne, wrote a number of novels that concern 'fantastic things'. The two novels of Verne's that we are concerned with deal with a maverick inventor type named Robur who has developed aerial flight technology that is far more advanced than the gentlemen at the Weldon Institute, which is a hot air balloonists club or fliers club.

In *Robur The Conqueror* (1885), the big problem that is vexing everyone at Weldon is how to guide the balloons while in flight. Verne humorously depicts the level of technology that the Weldon Institute is pursuing. Money has been raised and an invention has been purchased that will drive the propeller except for the fact that the members can't agree as to where to put the propeller, in the front or behind. So there is dissension between the 'behindists and the beforists' as Verne puts it. Amidst the bickering at one of the meetings a visitor is announced....it is the mysterious Robur. In Robur's speech we have the contrast of two technologies; the one being developed by the Weldon Institute and that of Robur. After some self introductory bombast that even he realizes, (Perhaps you think I am talking too much about myself? It does not matter if you do!), Robur lets them have it: "After a century of experiments that have led to nothing, and trials giving no results, there still exist ill-balanced minds who believe in guiding balloons." Robur goes on to argue the silliness of their quest to achieve 'lighter than air' flight and drops a bomb when he makes the claim, "Yes....the future is for the flying machine." In other words heavier than air flight. Eventually, Robur displays his technologically advanced ship, the Albatross, to a captive audience. In his imperious desire to prove that he is right, he kidnaps three members of Weldon Institute and takes them on a three week journey around the world. Verne wrote this almost 20 years before the Wright brothers' first flight in 1903.

In the sequel, *Master of the World* (1904), the vehicle Robur has built has the characteristics of a submarine, boat, and airplane and is easily able to go from one medium to another with ease. The propellers are done away with as he had on his former ship the Albatross. We have a whole new animal with this ship for it also travels on the roadways of America, terrorizing its citizens and even enters an International Road Race held in Wisconsin, uninvited of course. It bedazzles everyone with its speed which caused a "formidable rumbling, caused a whirlwind, which tore branches from the trees along the road and killed birds, which could not resist the suction of the tremendous air currents engendered by its passage." Some machine. It led the investigator Strock, who is the narrator of the story to speculate, "that the vehicle *ran by electricity*."(my italics) The reason Strock says this is because, "It left behind no smoke, no steam, no odor of gasoline, or any other oil." And something else which disturbed Strock and the newspapers that reported it, was a detail that was "bizarre." Whenever the strange vehicle made an appearance, "the surface of the roads was scarcely even scratched by the wheels of the apparition, which left behind it no such ruts as are usually made by heavy vehicles. At most there was a . . . mere brushing of the dust. It was only the tremendous speed which raised behind the vehicle such whirlwinds of dust." So not only is it a sub and an airplane but also a hovercraft able to traverse the American roadways at speeds up to 150 miles per hour. The other quality that Strock mentions repeatedly is the utter silence of the motor that runs the ship. Clearly, even Robur's technology has advanced.

In both novels the shape of Robur's ships are of a lengthy, dirigible-type. They are both advanced for the time in the sense of maneuverability and speed. They are witnessed by many around the world as unidentified objects in the sky.

Though it is does not deal with aerial phenomena, the same theme of advanced technology developed secretly also runs through *20,000 Leagues Under The Sea*. Captain Nemo, a man who has cast aside all affiliation with mankind, roams the deep oceans in his technologically advanced submarine, the Nautilus. The ship's power source is electricity. Is all this really fiction or is Verne revealing something important and only fictionalizing names and places? As Verne tells us in book 2, chapter 9 of *20,0000 Leagues Under the Sea*, "I'm the historian of apparently impossible things and yet incontestably real."

SUB ROSA

In the book *The Morning of the Magicians* by Louis Pauwels and Jacques Bergier, we are told about a strange event that occurred in the early 17th century. In Paris, in the year 1622, people woke to find the walls of their city covered with posters bearing the following message: "We, deputies of the College of the Rosy Cross (Rosicrucians) are amongst you in this town, visibly and invisibly, through the grace of the Most High to whom the hearts of all just men are turned, in order to save our fellowmen from the error of death." They were not talking about spiritual salvation. Pauwels and Bergier then quote a historian of the occult, Serge Hutin, from his book History of the Rosy Cross, "The Rosicrucian Brethren were credited with possession of the following secrets: the transmutation of metals, the prolongation of life, knowledge of what is happening in distant places and the application of the occult sciences to the discovery of even the most deeply hidden objects." Clearly, they were the scientists of their day. But what may be troubling to our modern minds is that the claims of technological know-how predate the actual discoveries of modern scientists by almost 300 years. Even some of the machines claimed to have been possessed by the Rosicrucians are still not in modern mans possession. Are the claims by the Rosicrucians just fantasy?

Willy Schrodter in his book, *A Rosicrucian Notebook*,

compiles a list of claims from various sources of a secret knowledge the Rosicrucians held. He says, "What the old Hermeticists taught and practised was not all superstitious nonsense. These people were ahead of their time and were therefore decried as sorcerers. Hence, the *wizardry of yesterday is often the science of tomorrow*." (his italics) Some of the knowledge the Rosicrucians laid claim to according to Schroedter:

1. Perpetual Lamps

2. Wireless Communication over long distances

3. Astral Travel at will

4. Acupuncture and Touch healing

5. Hypnotism

6. Energy Healing

7. An advanced knowledge of Optics

8. An advanced knowledge of Acoustics

Some of their instruments included:

1. Cosmolothrentas—an atomizer of physical matter. By this any building could be pulverized.

2. Astronikitas—a telescope that could see the stars unobstructed through clouds

Before we dismiss devices like the Cosmolothrentas as fiction, lets examine the interesting case of one John Keely who, with one of his 'sound machines' and eyewitnesses present, 'converted a granite block into a small heap of dust in the twinkling of an eye.' This event occurred in the latter part of the 19th century.

Keely reported geometries that could intensify sound pressures without adding additional energy (recently patented and in use by MacroSonix Corp.)...

Keely reported cold in the presence of certain orders of vibration' (now patented as an *acoustic* refrigeration and cooling system)...

Keely reported that sound could be used to heal the body (note ultrasound therapy). This subject is worth in depth coverage in the future but it is worth bringing up because Keely reported these findings along with his machines, in the 1870's and 1880's...over 120 years ago. IS it possible that the scientific society of the Rosicrucian brotherhood had this knowledge even earlier, say around 1622?

CURIOUS CLAIMS AND CURIOUS EVENTS

There are two things we must keep in mind throughout this treatise. There have been 1.) *Claims,* by individuals or groups, of certain fantastic abilities either through the instrumentality of their body or through a device.

2.) There are *events* and circumstances in history that are truly *anomalous*; some would use the term miraculous. In light of these so called secret scientific societies, we are going to take a different course and declare that certain strange phenomena usually attributed to the fairy realm or the spiritual world can just as likely be explained by *invoking a technology*. It may be, as we will see later in the case of Dellschau and his club, that possession of a technology by an individual or group may account for events that their contemporaries would deem 'impossible' or miraculous. Many Roburs going about and flaunting their technological know-how, so to speak. The usual explanation in textbooks or standard historical works is to belittle the testimony of people in the Middle Ages as myth and fable when in fact these people, in a pre-technological era, may be searching for the linguistic apparatus to explain mysterious visions and anomalous events and all they can use is phenomenological language. The result is, we have reports of fairies, mystic visions, human levitation attributed to a divine power and such. They may in fact be trying to explain something that is beyond their level of technology.

Take the case of the scientist turned 'mystic', Emmanuel Swedenborg. His abilities were seen as clairvoyant and otherworldly; they definitely were not seen as scientific, though he was a brilliant scientist earlier in his life before his mystic turn. In one instance in his strange career, he began reporting, at a dinner party, about a major fire that was occurring in Stockholm three hundred miles away as if he were there; he did this for two hours in front of witnesses. When a courier from Stockholm came about three days later, he verified all that Swedenborg had said; this brought Swedenborg into prominence and made him a figure of reverence. Swedenborg, by the way, was named a Brother Rosicrucian in the Mystic Triangle, a Rosicrucian publication of the 1920s.

How about the strange case of Goodwin Wharton in the late 17th century? He was a Whig politician in the British parliament that was given permission to recover goods from one of the sunken ships of the Spanish Armada off the coast of the Isle of Mull. Everything seems fine until we hear about how he received the knowledge of where the ship was. His lover, Mary Parish, communicated with fairies and they told her where the treasure was. She then relayed this to Wharton who eventually was able to commune with this group and receive special intelligence on where ships were sunk, what certain individuals were feeling about him and based on this what moves he should make next. This is not even the strange part. The fairies promised Wharton, through Mary, a technologically advanced underwater breathing apparatus. A self contained underwater breathing apparatus more commonly known today as SCUBA. The fairies promised Mary a special 'breathing cloth' that would keep out water while allowing something from the water that was breathable, in. To be able to filter it with a magic cloth assumes that there is something in the water to be filtered, like oxygen. By all accounts oxygen was 'discovered' 100 years later. Not only this but the fairies were constructing a special mask to be worn while underwater. Are the fairies just a cover story for something else going on?

Then there is the case of the Dominican Friar and Bishop, Albertus Magnus in the 13th century. Magnus was conversant with all the fields of knowledge of the day. But his reputation was also in the esoteric fields of alchemy and astrology, for many magical writings were attributed to him. In one reported instance he threw a dinner party in which his guests were treated to a sumptuous feast and lavish entertainments. The only problem was that there was no food or entertainment and the guests were hypnotized to such an extent that they regaled everyone with wonderful stories of this grand feast. The scale of the event was such that it makes one wonder if something else was involved. That 'something else' makes one think of Anton Mesmer (from whom we get the word mesmerism) in the 18th century, who was purported to heal people by magnetizing water with strange rods in barrels and was able to induce a catatonic state in his subjects and thereby heal them with a *device he held in his hand*. No one seems to know what this device was except that it had 'magnetic properties' and made people swoon. Was Magnus privy to this technology?

A persistent rumour with Magnus is that he was purported to have made a 'talking head'. This along with reports that he constructed robots and that somehow he was able to make them talk and do menial tasks take on many variations but they all report a common thing. There is another dinner party story of how the guests of Albert were served by his automatons. Upon encountering one of these creatures, his pupil, Thomas Aquinas, went into a paroxysm and destroyed it, believing it to be the work of the devil.

Magnus was not the only one involved in technologies that were out of the ordinary in those days. Roger Bacon, philosopher and lecturer at Oxford and the university of Paris, was persecuted and repeatedly imprisoned; once by his own order, the Franciscans. The reason was clear to Roger why the superiors and brothers kept him, "under close guard and would not permit anyone to come to me, fearing that my writings would be divulged to others [rather] than to the chief pontiff and themselves." Roger clearly had some information that was threatening to the establishment. In his *Opus Majus* he talks about such things as telescopes, microscopes, hydraulics, steamships and flying machines; this work was written in the middle of the 13th century. The interesting thing is that he was accused of many magical acts by his contemporaries and those in later generations. An example from the latter is the play written by Robert Greene in the late 16th century, *Friar Bacon and Friar Bungay,* in which Roger Bacon is depicted as possessing marvelous skills such as remote surveillance, aerial flight and last but not least the artificially created talking head.

Leonardo Davinci also seemed to have the robot constructing bug. Many are familiar with Davinci's drawings of advanced apparatus such as helicopters and airplanes but do not realize that automatons and their construction consumed a good part of his time. The sketchbooks of this wonder were discovered in the 1950s. Just recently the robot was built, according to Davinci's specifications from his notebooks, by Mario Taddei and the Leonardo3 company; amazingly, the robot was able to do exactly what Leonardo intended with all it's complex gearing and levers; it was able to sit up, move it's arms and neck and even move it's jaws as if it were conversing.

This is only a smattering of the wonders that were reported in the pre-modern era. This whole phenomenon will be delved into deeper in further issues but for the sake of our argument it is enough to see that there is something out of the ordinary going on; there is a pattern that we can follow. Various individuals (or a group like the Rosicrucians) throughout history, make a claim to a knowledge that is extraordinary. There is a clatter or noise; a sort of resonance that follows in the wake of these claims. Testimonies and accusations from ecclesiastical authorities or even the vulgar- the common folk, abound; represented in plays and books and novels. Concerning the Rosicrucians, the claim has been made that they possess a knowledge that can save mankind. We can dismiss this as puerile or we can take the claim seriously and investigate it. When one does investigate without prejudice, one finds events and situations that can't be explained unless you invoke a technology.

VERNE, THE ROSICRUCIAN

In the Rosicrucian literature there is a mandate for secrecy above all else. The justification for the secrecy is based on a categorization of mankind into two groups. Those that are swine and those that are not. The swine are those who do not appreciate the value of knowledge, hence the injunction in *The Chemical Wedding of Christian Rosenkreutz,* one of the foundational Rosicrucian texts: "Mysteries made public become cheap and things profaned lose their grace. Therefore, cast not pearls before swine nor make a bed of roses for an ass." But if something is portrayed as fiction then this would certainly be a way around this warning wouldn't it? Fiction is a clever device for revealing and also leaving a way for plausible deniability, for after all it's just fiction!

Rosicrucians often left their signature, R.C., on various documents or hiding in anagram form such as Verne's Robur (R) the Conqueror (C).

Robur boasts of qualities that are strangely reminiscent of Rosicrucian accomplishments such as the elixir of life: "I am forty years old, although I look only thirty. I have an iron constitution, rigorous health, remarkable muscular strength and a stomach that even the world of ostriches would regard as excellent. That sums up my physical description." So he says in *Robur the Conqueror.* It seems odd, this bit of bombast by Robur. I mean, after all, who is asking him for his physical resume? Yet he seems compelled as if he had to or was it Verne tipping his hat to the brotherhood?

But more interesting is the name Robur itself. Robur, in Latin means oak. The oak is a prominent occult symbol associated with the ancient druids and at least one secret society in the 18th and 19th centuries, the Order of the Wood Splitters who under the name of the Carbonari (coal burners) entered Italy to initiate revolutions with the specific goal of unifying the Italian states. In fact, according to Michel Lamy in his incisive book, *The Secret Message of Jules Verne*, the word *druid* etymologically, means *oak man*. Druid comes from the Cymro-Gallic root *derw,* which in turn is the origin of the word *dervish,* a branch of the mystical, secret Sufi Order. Why the oak is a symbol of importance in the occult is a topic for another time; our concern now is the frequency of association with secretive groups. So far what we have is—

—the ancient druids, who were a secretive priesthood associated with oak.

—the Sufis, who were a mystical, secretive sect derived from Islam also associated with oak.

—the name Robur means oak.

One of the primary books of the Rosicrucians was known as the Proteus. Now Proteus was a god that could prophecy and yield knowledge of how to accomplish miraculous things such as arresting plagues, according to Virgil in the fourth *Georgic*. The problem with getting knowledge from Proteus was that he was a shape-shifter and not easily apprehended. Virgil writes in the Fourth Georgic how Aristeus had to seize Proteus and hold onto him no matter what he changed into. He eventually did so and Proteus yielded . .

. . *knowledge*. In fact, this Proteus was rumored to hold all the world's scientific knowledge. Robert Graves the English poet and novelist contends in his book that *Proteus was also called the man-king of the oak*. Is Robur (or the Rosicrucians) the Proteus of old who has a secret knowledge and craftily evades capture by the world? It is rather interesting that Robur (oak), especially in *Master of the World,* is one slippery fellow who is being hunted down by the world's governments, who want him to yield his secrets, all to no avail . . .

Michel Lamy points out in his book that, according to Verne family tradition, Verne was accomplished and fascinated with puns and wordplay and words with double and even tertiary meanings. He features this skill in his novels; Lamy calls Verne's language, "initiatory." He writes that his novels, "Often begin with the chance discovery of an indecipherable message perhaps found in a bottle cast into the sea . . . enlightenment will come as a result of its decryption and quite often the plot of the story is structured around it." The cryptic message in the novel is a mirror of what Verne is doing in real life. Lamy concludes, over and over again, from a lifetime of studying Jules Verne and his work that, "We are not dealing with common books, but enormous cryptograms that it is our task to decode."

If Verne were a Rosicrucian then we would have to face a mind expanding conclusion: Perhaps his fiction was not fiction . . .

ROBUR ATTACKS AMERICA

There was a mystery occurring all over America and the young man, recovering from a sickness in a hospital, was intrigued. Looking through all the clippings that were given to him in a package it seemed that the United States was being invaded by apparitions in the sky. He eventually ended up writing a book called *War of the Worlds* based on this phenomenon he was reading about in the States. The young man's name was H. G. Wells.

Time–Life Books published a series of books called *The Mysteries of the Unknown*. One of the books, *The UFO Phenomenon* presents what H.G Wells was reading about in those newspaper clippings on his hospital bed. "Between November 1896 and April 1897 the country reeled under an extraordinary series of sightings that started in the state of California and spread eastward."

The book continues, "It all began on the stormy afternoon of November 17, 1896 in Sacramento, the California capital, some fifty miles northeast of San Francisco. A trolleyman named Charles Lusk was standing outside his house and looking up at the sky when to his immense surprise he saw a bright light cruising perhaps 1000 feet above his head. A faint shape seemed to be moving along right behind it. Others at the nearby capital building glimpsed the 'wandering apparition', as one newspaper called it, and climbed up to the top of the rotunda for a better view. Another resident claimed to have seen not only the object–which was described as cigar shaped, with an underslung gondola and a pair of side wheels like an old riverboat–but also two men aboard it, peddling furiously on something like a bike frame; one of them was overheard saying to the other, 'We will get to San Francisco about half past twelve.' Later that evening, in fact, a similar apparition was seen gliding majestically over San Francisco, flashing a searchlight on the city and sending the local seals scurrying off their rocks into the protective waters of the Golden Gate."

H.G. Wells knew that there were no operational passenger carrying dirigibles in the world at that time. He also knew that searchlights were heavy and required heavy generators and batteries. Were these ships and their passengers from earth? His interpretation of other-worldliness is like the modern interpretation of flying saucers; that they are extraterrestrial. But as *The UFO Phenomenon* goes on to say, "Most people, however, seemed to accept the reality of the enigmatic vehicle and believed it to be an airship launched by an anonymous inventor." The *San Francisco Call* newspaper of November 19, 1896 reported the following in a front page article named The Incredible Airship From Table Mountain: "Finally the *Call* tracked down a lead which at least partially explained who was behind the mysterious happenings. Mr. George A. Collins, a prominent San Francisco attorney, stated that he had been engaged by a San Francisco man to secure the patents on a flying machine which he had built in the rugged seclusion of Table Mountain above Oroville. Collis said he could not divulge he name of his client."

The newspaper story from the *Call* was not the only thing that led people to believe that the ship or ships were man made. As was stated above with the sighting of Charles Lusk, many people who saw the ships saw humans on board or heard humans conversing. From the Algona, Iowa Republican dated April 7, 1897: " Good reliable citizens of Wesley, Iowa, declared upon their honor that on last Friday evening they saw in the heavens what they supposed to be an airship...It had the appearance of a cone in shape with window in the side through which shone bright lights....it would travel quite slowly at times, and again would move quite fast....Some had an idea that they could hear a noise coming from the ship. Some went so far as to say it was human voices..."

Keep in mind that Count Ferdinand von Zeppelin's LZ1, the first 'successful' airship, barely flew for 20 minutes and covered all of three and a half miles before it crashed. The LZ1 flew in 1900 and was the most up to date technology at the time. Contrast the LZ1 with the ship reported by the *Call*. That ship, and all the other strange ships witnessed at the time, had properties that the conventional balloonists and known inventors of the time did not possess. For instance, the speed and variability of speed of the ships is a characteristic of many of the sightings. The control and maneuverability such as landing and turning with ease are also a feature that did not exist in the development of airships that we know of such as with the Zeppelin company. In other words these ships, from all the evidence, seem to be in a distinct class of their own. Brad Steiger reports in his book, *The Rainbow Conspiracy*, of an actual landing of one of the airships near Springfield Illinois in April of 1897. Two farmhands witnessed "two normal human men and a woman" who explained to the farmhands that they had to do some maintenance to their electrical equipment and searchlight. Steiger continues, " They went on to inform the astonished Winkle and Hulle that their airship had flown from Quincy to Springfield, a distance of approximately 90 miles, in thirty minutes." This speed of 180 miles per hour is twice the speed of dirigibles that were developed after this time. Some more verifications of astounding speed were reported in the Harrisburg, Arkansas, *Modern News* newspaper. The article details an encounter that one Mr. Harris had with the occupants of the ship. An airship carrying two young men, an older man and a young woman landed just a short distance from the home of Mr. Harris around one o'clock in the morning. They were resupplying their store of water from a nearby well when Harris came upon them. A conversation ensued between Harris and the older gentleman in which he revealed that he was the inventor and that the ship was carrying a Hotchkiss machine gun that could fire 63,000 rounds a minute, a far greater capacity than guns at the time. But, according to Steiger, "the man added that his crew could take breakfast in Arkansas, do some shopping in Paris, and be back in Harrisburg for dinner without convenience." Another hint at the ability of these ships is a sighting by John Barclay of Rockland, Texas, wherein an airship landed in a pasture near his house. One of the outstanding features that Barclay noticed was the lighting. In his report he stated, " There were brilliant lights, which appeared *much brighter than electric lights* (italics mine)." Again we have a hint of development that is greater than the technology of the time. Barclay was asked by an occupant of the ship, a Mr. Smith, to procure some lubricating oil, a couple of cold chisels and some blue-stone. As they were about to leave, Barclay asked them where they were from and where they were going in which they replied, "We are from anywhere, but we will be in Greece the day after tomorrow." Steiger goes on to quote Barclay noting the speedy departure of the ship, "It was gone...like a shot out of a gun!"

Jacques Vallee in his book, *Anatomy of a Phenomenon*, reports of a sighting that took place in April of 1897. The encounter was probably reported in the first place because there was a crime committed by the airship occupants! But even more interesting, at least from the documentary aspect, is that a legal affidavit was drawn up and authenticated by many witnesses as to the reliability of the victim and his encounter. In his detailed report, the victim/observer, Alexander Hamilton, describes what happened that night when he saw the airship (ch. 1 pg16-17): " Last Monday night, about 10:30, we were awakened by a noise among the cattle....saw to my utter astonishment an airship slowly descending upon my cow lot....It consisted of a great cigar-shaped portion...with a carriage underneath...it was brilliantly lighted within and everything was plainly visible... When about 300 feet above us it seemed to pause and hover directly over a two year old heifer which was bawling and jumping... Going to her we found some red material, fastened in a slip-knot around her neck...We tried to get it off but could not, so we cut the wire loose and stood in amazement to see the ship, heifer and all, rise slowly, disappearing in the northwest. We went home but I was so frightened I could not sleep."

The next day, according to the affidavit, Hamilton positively identified the remains of the calf which had been dropped into a neighbors yard. The affidavit was attested to by and signed by community members of official standing recognizing Hamilton as, "long been a resident of Kansas...He was a member of the House of Representatives.....we have known him from one to thirty years...and that for the truth and veracity we have never heard his word questioned, and that we verily believe his statement to be true and correct." The signers of this document ranged from officials such as the sheriff and deputy sheriff, an attorney, a postmaster and also professionals in their respective fields such as the pharmacist, the banker and a state oil inspector.

These events and many more are all verifiable through documents and also newspaper reports of testimonials from various people in different paths in life. The concentration of reports seems to be in the 1890s but through a careful search of the records it seems that this airship phenomenon had been going on for at least 50 years before 1890 or even earlier.

Vallee brings our attention to reports in the 1880s; these are special because they are reported in scientific journals. The French astronomical journal *L'Astronomie* reported the following in 1885: "M. Mavrogordato, of Constantinople, calls our attention to the following strange observations which have been communicated to him. On November 1, at 9:30 P.M., there was seen, west of Adrianople, an elongated object giving off a strange luminosity. It seemed to float in the air and its apparent disk was four or five times larger than the full moon. It traveled slowly and cast light on the whole camp behind the station with a brightness about ten times greater than an electric bulb."

L'Astronomie reported at least five of these strange occurrences in 1885 alone. Vallee also informs us of the journal *Zoologis* reporting in January of 1868 on a sighting in which an "aerial construction emitting light and giving off engine noise was interpreted locally as a giant bird with shining eyes..." The *Astronomical Register*, in 1874, reported a Professor Schafarick seeing, in Prague, "an object of such a strange nature that I do not know what to say about it. It was of a blinding white and crossed slowly the face of the moon. It remained visible afterwards..." Another journal, *L'Annee Scientifique* reports that on March 23, 1877 " fiery spheres extremely luminous, came out of a cloud of a peculiar shape and went slowly toward the north for one hour." The peculiar shape according to the journal of a "cloud cigar". Also Jerome Clark through his research has stated that there was a big airship flap in France and Germany during the 1850's.

What we notice, from these instances sighted above, are a few things:

1) The form of the object in the sky, in the reports from individuals, is overwhelmingly of a 'dirigible shape'.

2) The sightings are worldwide

3) Human occupants were either sighted or heard from on these airships

4) The technology is more advanced than the conventional technology known to most of the world

5) From the compilation made by Vallee and others we can see that there was an explosion of these sightings after 1850 or the second half of the 19th century that grew in frequency with each decade;

and last but not least,

5) the details of the airships correspond to two books that Jules Verne wrote, *Robur the Conqueror* and *Master of the World*.

CRACKING THE CODE

In the year 2007, at the Slotin folk art auction in Georgia, a 'mixed media piece' was sold for $8,050. The piece was by Charles Dellschau (1830-1923) a man who emigrated from Germany possibly, by some accounts, in the early 1850's as a young adult. The piece sold was called mixed media because along with his paintings he would attach newspaper clippings from around the turn of the century, to his works. Some of his works are running in the range of $15,000 dollars. The interesting thing about his supposed art works are that they are not on a canvas but in an oversized notebook type arrangement of 15" x19"; almost as if he were documenting something. According to some researchers, he *was* documenting something; something that was supposed to be hidden and never allowed to see the light of day. Something that, if revealed, carried the greatest penalty known to man....death. A secret that was bound in oaths of blood from a secret society whose origins are still unknown and whose ghostly fingerprints may lie upon many unexplained events.

Leave it to a junkdealer to expose a secret society. Something about the tattered notebooks must have caught Fred Washington's eye that day. In a trip to a local dump, the 'antiques dealer'– as he liked to call himself– was rummaging through debris when some oversized scrapbooks caught his eye. Another scavenger happened upon them before Fred but with a little haggling that was motivated by a gut feeling, he was able to procure the "coloring books" for a hundred dollars. He cleared a space for them in his workshop while trying to find out something about the artist whose name seemed to be on every drawing. But his name, C. A. A. Dellschau, didn't spark anyone's interest and for that matter it seemed the artist was unknown to everyone he talked to.

So it seemed like an investment that wasn't likely to bloom into anything, until three college students from St. Thomas University came into his shop around early spring

1969. They were doing a project for school and they thought that Mr. Washington might be able to help them. As they told him the subject of their project for school, Washington began thinking the Dellschau scrapbooks he had picked up awhile back might just help these students. Their project was called **The History of Flight**, and here in Dellschau's paintings were some of the strangest flying vehicles that they had ever seen depicted, in fact all of his paintings were flying vehicles of assorted shapes and designs. There were single passenger and multi passenger flying vehicles to massive airships with decks and levels and all sorts of abstruse assemblages attached; all with an eerie technical detail that seemed out of place in an 'artistic piece'. Washington agreed to loan two of the scrapbooks for the exhibition. His thinking was that perhaps if the scrapbooks were exposed to the public someone would take a monetary interest in them. He was ultimately correct in his assumption as some of the scrapbooks were bought by an Art History director at Rice University. But what he didn't understand at the time is that those strange paintings would be the key to unlocking one of the strangest episodes in American history and perhaps a key to how our world works.

The person who turned the key was a man by the name of Pete Navarro. Pete owned a graphic arts company and happened to be attending an exhibition at St. Thomas university put on by a few college students, **The History of Flight**. The same gut feeling came to him when he happened upon Dellschau's paintings. Pete's graphic arts background helped him in discerning the subtle technical details that were in Dellschau's work. These were not just art, thought Pete to himself. There seemed to be something more here that was eluding everyone else. He sought out the person that loaned the works to the university, Fred Washington, and thereupon began the trip down the rabbit hole. He eventually bought some of the books from Washington and had access to the others sold to Mrs. DeMenil, the Art History Director of Rice University.

Navarro felt that something was of great importance here but there was a problem in trying to piece everything together. On each page of the scrapbook there was a smattering of runic type script. Each page had notes in English, German and this curious symbolic script. It was this script that Navarro felt was the key to Dellschau's secret; the enigma of Dellschau would depend on cracking the code that he left. Navarro had an interest in cryptography and recognized general principles of the craft. After fifteen months of indefatigable persistence, Navarro cracked the code. Then, thirty years of additional research and decoding led him to piece together a most remarkable story that is truly stranger than fiction. With the help of writer/researcher Dennis Crenshaw, Navarro put together part of his life's work on Dellschau into a book called *The Secrets of Dellschau*. Dellschau's story lies before us in all it's strangeness . . .

SECRETS OF THE SONORA AEROCLUB

This just may be stranger than fiction or in this case science fiction. Navarro's decipherment shows us that Dellschau in his scrapbooks was actually documenting the accomplishments of a group of men who were secretly developing heavier than air flying vehicles that used a *gravity negating gas* which also propelled the ships. This all at a time at least 50 years before the Wright brothers were even heard of. The group built and tested their craft in Sonora, California and in the nearby town of Columbia. They were funded by a shadowy group that called the shots and were referred to as NYMZA; whether a name or an anagram for something, nobody is really quite sure. Dellschau was the 'historian and draftsman' of the group. Unfortunately for us, it was to be a history that was not to be propagated but kept secret. Yet, something could not keep Dellschau from recording it even if it was in code and enigmatic sayings. He had to let it be known but in a careful, encrypted manner, for as we shall see he was dealing with powerful forces that did not want to reveal this hidden technology. Even when the code was deciphered and translated from German into English, Dellschau still spoke mystically and enigmatically. The writer/researcher Jerome Clark noted this strange way of Dellschau in an article for FATE magazine: " Dellschau was of two minds about what he was doing. On the one hand he wanted his 'secrets' known; on the other he seemed afraid to speak directly. So he compromised and wrote in a fashion aimed to discourage all but the most determined investigator. He was writing for an audience. If not for one in his own day, for one in some future period." This may be why there are certain portions where Dellschau refers to a 'Wonder Weaver' who "*will unriddle these writings. They are my stock of open knowledge.*"—from plate number 2048.

Almost every page in the scrapbooks of Dellschau has a distinct style of airship with a particular name that is in English. Along with these drawings on each page there is writing, whether in symbolic script or English or German, Dellschau gives us vignettes or stories involving the history of this peculiar, secretive Aeroclub. As Crenshaw says in *The Secrets of Dellschau*, in chapter 32, "As Pete studied the Dellschau books he began to recognize the various individuals and characters pictured in the airship drawings as members of the Aero Club. Before long he grew to recognize the physical and personal characteristics of each of Dellschau's friends and they became quite familiar to him, not unlike Pete's friends and acquaintances." In certain places Dellschau even draws the faces of the individuals.

Each page, or plate as Dellschau called them, was numbered by Dellschau himself. For instance in plate 1878 we have a vehicle of the name Goosey, built by a Peter Mennis, one of the main members of the club. He was the inventor of the mysterious NB Gas that powered the ships. His *Goosey* was the prototype of all subsequent Aeros as Dellschau hints in plate 2009, "...Peter Mennis' Goose, the mother of all!" In the 1878 plate of Mennis' *Goosey* Dellschau writes, *Nothing new on earth, says Brother Caro*, referring to another member, Louis Caro. Another line from plate 1879 divulges perhaps the motivation for Dellschau's work, *Old friends and their deeds not forgotten*. Again he says of Peter Mennis, *Peter flew for years, in lull or blow, in his Goosey, like air a good old buggy trap*. Crenshaw and Navarro take this to mean that in good or bad weather, Mennis flew in the Goosey like it was a buggy. In plates 1850 and 1851 we have the Aero Trump designed by a Monsieur Jordan designed as a warcraft. In plate 1851 the title line reads *Droppings—- Aero Trump* and a quoted line that reads *The people below needs protection for all this nuisance, I say!* The plate shows the Aero Trump with a bomb bay or either a waste disposal opening.

There were evidently some failures of design with some of the ships. In plate 1875 and 1876 Dellschau compares the design of the Goosey with the Aero Des Hehtnich which in German means literally, " the airship that won't go." And in plate 1856 referring to this ship, *..but who of our members, did not say, say No Sir—won't go!* Another Aero that was not sky worthy is found in plate 2101, where the caption reads *A joke...Aero...Wont Goe...George Newell proposer.*

It seems the group had various demands put upon them from heads of state to military leaders; again, from plate 1856, *Now Kaiser Wilhelm wants sleeping rooms attached to his ballons. Say Jourdan, can't you supply his majesty?* Jourdan was Monsieur Jourdan, a Frenchman who belonged to the club and also designed the Aero Trump according to Dellschau. One of the countries that may have approached the group for military aeros is Prussia. The sense is that there may have been others but what is clear is the annoyance that the Aeroclub members had with these military men (from plate 1743): *And who are you to question our board? Now what takes practical military airship 10 or 100 miles an hour?? Hell! Those acting officers act just like racetrack gamblers. No such questions asked as bulletproof...good gas reservoir...fallease...antiballast! ....And what say I to that long legged Prussian officer?* Dellschau does not hide the fact that there were Aeros for military purposes as we see in plate 1788 he paints the *War Aero* and as we saw above the Aero Trump which may have had war uses.

In plate 1930 Dellschau painted the Aero Newell which was designed by George Newell the second most important member of the club. Here we have a photo of the plate of the Newell airship:

The following account from the St. Louis Star, April 20, 1897, conforms well with the Aero Newell. Under the headline of :
THAT SHIP
Postmaster at Greenfield Ill. Gets a Look at It.

"The most interesting report of the aerial wonder comes from Illinois and seems to be well authenticated.. . . M.G. Sisson, postmaster at this place, was the most favored spectator. He was out walking in the woods that line the banks of Taylor Creek about three miles east of here. He had just started to return to the city when his dog which had accompanied him, ran to him and crouched down at his feet in abject terror. . . Presently he heard a noise which seemed to come from above, and looking upward and to the northwest he beheld the airship approaching him. It was about 150 feet from the ground, but was not traveling very rapidly . . . it passed about 100 feet above him and by its close proximity he was enabled to get a very good view of it. It was about 100 feet in length and about fifteen in diameter at its largest point. Its depth was probably twenty-five feet. It looked as if it was made of metal and around its sides was a walk or deck which was protected by some sort of railing or net work." This walk or deck is precisely what we see in the photo above. Also, the size in relation to the people pictured in the photo accords well with the estimation of length by the postmaster.

One member, Jacob Mischer, designed the Aero Gander which *cost him a pile of money*, relates Dellschau. He goes on to say that Mischer, probably since he financed it himself, wanted to make money with the ship by fixing it up as a *gambling hall*. This was a no-no to the NYMZA overseers, for Mischer ended up dead. As Dellschau put it, *But a box of matches sent Jachob and the Gander up to heaven as flame and smoke...goodbye Jacob*. Crenshaw speculates that, "It was probably the fact that they wanted the airships to remain a secret for the time being and any profitable use would surely expose them to outsiders." This may account for the reason that Dellschau seemed to be of two minds as Jerome Clark theorized.

As mentioned above, Dellschau also would paint mini portraits of the members interspersed amongst the paintings. There are pictures of Peter Mennis, a Michael Gore and August Shoetler just to name a few. By Navarro's accounting there were at least 60 members of this club. August Schoetler seems to have been the actual builder of the vehicles. In plate 1644 Dellschau relates the occasion in which a demand for a ship was made upon Schoetler: *Schoetler, the machine must look aweful dangerous! Must look so I say! Or there is no money to be made with it. The dear good people up here are anxious as anything...*

PRESS BLUMEN

The oddest but yet most revealing thing about the scrapbooks is the press clippings Dellschau attached to the paintings throughout. Dellschau referred to them as press blumen or press blooms. Many of them have to do with scientific findings and aerial news of the day, such as the following: On plates 1939 and 1940 there are pictures and articles about the Wright Brothers and their accomplishments with their Aeroplane; Dellschau writes, *Goosey beats them all.* This, of course, is referring to the Aero Goosey of Peter Mennis.

The comments, which are usually in English, may help us shed some light on some things. How about this one? In plate 4607 we have just one clipping which is rare for there usually are more than one. The title of the clipping is **New York –'Frisco Air Mail Soon Will Be A Reality.** The strange thing is the comments that Dellschau paints on the plate. At the bottom he writes CRIMINAL DOOING (the spelling is his). Then in the upper right of the plate he writes NONSENSE which is a common sentiment in a few other plates. What is Dellschau trying to tell us? Who is/are the criminal(s)? What have they done and what relation does it have to the fact that soon air mail will be transcontinental? Here is that plate on the next page:

The words 'nonsense' and 'humbug' are a common refrain in Dellschau's plates that have clippings. What is he trying to say? In plate 4563 there are several clippings which range from safety of parachutes to an airmen being killed in a crash to a picture from some paper of a searchlight with the subheading of World's Most Powerful Light. What does Dellschau have to say about all this? In the lower right hand corner of the plate he spells out: GRAND NONSENSE. On the next page is plate 4563:

What is 'grand nonsense'? The worlds most powerful light? The parachute safety or the fact that an airman died? It seems that he is categorically renouncing and ridiculing the claims of all of these articles. What in them is he repudiating however?

In plate 4513 Dellschau features an article from Scientific American from 1919 in which we read the title **Aboard A Giant Passenger Carrying Airplane.** Dellschau writes in his own peculiar spelling, WHAT MAY HAPPN...WONT PAY. Then in another plate, whose number was blurred out, there is a press clipping with the title **World's Largest Hydro-Plane Will Carry 100 Across the Atlantic**.

The comments Dellschau writes below the article are, WILL 100 RISK THIR LIVES (again, his spelling).

Gianni Caproni made the first Italian aircraft around 1911. In plate 4605, Dellschau paints a likeness of Caproni under the title of Men Who Did. Then at the bottom he comments enigmatically, MONEY COST PLENTY...AND DONT PAY.

What can we glean from this sampling of Dellschau' comments? He seems to belittle modern progress and invention from the repeated comments of HUMBUG and NONSENSE. But why would someone do that? If Dellschau did indeed belong to a club that was developing technology that was slightly ahead of the times then his comments begin to make sense. For instance if Dellschau was aware that there was a group that was hiding technology then we can see why he calls the NewYork to Frisco airmail as criminal. It is criminal because this should have been happening much earlier in mankinds history but it was being intentionally suppressed by a group that obviously did not have the best of intentions. It is criminal because the inventions of Dellschaus group didn't put people at risk as evidenced by his comments on the passenger plane crossing the Atlantic. It is almost as if Dellschau is feeling great remorse and anger at this shadowy group that funded the airclub while at the same time expressing his distaste at the ignorance of the press in reporting 'modern progress'. NYMZA would be powerless if the knowledge was leaked out to people and perhaps they are involved in metering out just enough so that 'progress' can be controlled by them. So what seems like an invention by someone is really only something that has been given the green light by this group.

In plate 4773 Dellschau has various clippings that are divided into two columns by a painted pillar. In the space to the left of the pillar we have clippings under the title HAZBIN. To the right of the pillar we have clippings under the title of WILLBE. Spelling was not Dellschau's strong point, whether due to the fact that English was undoubtedly a second or third language to him or if he meant to mispell for the purpose of obscuring the message, one can only guess. But considering the context, HAZBIN is surely HAS BEEN. Under the title HAZBIN (HAS BEEN) we have clippings of modern inventions such as **Fire Proofing For Airplane Given Test** and another, **New Invention Prevents Fire On Airplanes**. Then another under the same column, **Vera Cruz–Yucatan Air Service to Start**. Is Dellschau telling us that this was a possibility or already happened when the Aero club was in operation? Then under the WILLBE (WILL BE) column he has the clipping **Airplane Tumbles, Flyers Are Lucky and Escape Injury**. Above that in the same column, **Houston Man's Invention Praised By Newspaper**. Is he saying that accidents *will be* inevitable as a result of the inferior airplane that was being accepted by the public? Remember when he said *The Goosey Beats Them All*. Were the Aero Club's designs superior to the point where accidents were not an issue to be worried about? And were inventions to pop up from time to time by 'inventors' when they were actually common knowledge many years ago to a select few? Is this what Dellschau was intimating? There must have been something special Dellschau knew that made him so dismissive of the 'modern discoveries', something that made him so confident in saying 'nonsense' to groundbreaking (for the times) technology.

THE SOUP OF PETER MENNIS

From the many paintings of Dellschau, researchers have been able to ascertain features of the vehicles that were advanced for the time; things like the lighting system with its spotlights, retractable wings and landing gear and compressed air which one of the members, August Schoetler, invented and used on a vehicle of his called the Crippel Wagon. The system of compressed air was called the air squeezers in which air was compressed and delivered through a tube to be ejected as work.

But nothing compares to the biggest secret the Aeroclub held in their possession—the mysterious NB Gas. This gas or liquid is what kept the airships afloat and propelled them. And the death of its discoverer may have been the reason for the disbandment of the AeroClub.

Lighter than air vehicles had been flying around for along time, since at least 1790. Balloons are kept afloat by either heating of the air or using a gas that has a lower molecular weight than the ambient air surrounding it such as helium. So the balloon rises and becomes buoyant because of the disparity of the gasses .....the balloon's gasses are lighter than the gasses of the atmosphere, hence lift. This is why they are called lighter than air aircraft as opposed to the airplane which is heavier than air. BUT according to Dellschau NB gas was not a lighter gas but instead an antigravity gas....it nullified the effects of gravity. It was discovered by one of the associates in the group, Peter Mennis. This was THE SECRET. It was the motherlode of their operation, the reason for their existence as a club.

In several plates Dellschau illustrates the technical details of what the motive power for the ships really was. According to plate 4308 water was an important component of the system it seemed for there are two tanks shown; one of supe (colored green) and one of wather, most likely water (it was colored blue). NB gas was produced from mixing water with 'supe'. The NB gas in turn negated the weight of the object and also acted as propellant.

The reliance on water as part of the power system seems to corroborate one aspect of the airship sightings in the 1890's. In many of the sightings crewmembers of the airships are found by people restocking the ship with water. In Conroe, Texas April 22, 1897 from The Galveston Daily News " A social game of dominoes at the Conroe Hotel was interrupted by two men who said they were from the airship and needed water....The four men were somewhat skeptical until they actually saw the 'wonderful aerial traveling machine'...rise majestically from the earth, illuminated by brilliant electric lights, and plow its way through space." A sheriff H. W. Baylor heard some strange voices in back of his residence on April 20th in Uvalde,Texas. According to the report there were three men from an airship that were looking for water and procured some from Baylor's hydrant in his backyard. Then in Harrisburg, Arkansas the aeronauts ran into an ex- Senator named Harris....they were taking on a fresh supply of water when Harris encountered them.

A green powder or liquid mixing with water and creating a fuel of some sort seems to have a very strange history. From Rex Research online: "In 1916, Louis Enricht announced that he had invented "a substitute for gasoline that can be manufactured for a penny a gallon". As a demonstration, Enricht allowed reporters to inspect the empty gas tank of an automobile. The reporters also tasted the water that Enricht then poured into the tank. He added a green pill, started the car, and gave the reporters a ride around Farmingdale, Long Island. William Haskell, publisher of the Chicago Herald, investigated Enricht's claims. He wrote:

"I examined the entire engine and tank. I even tasted the water before the mysterious green pill was dropped into the tank. Then I opened the petcock and examined the liquid, which now tasted like bitter almonds. I also tasted the liquid at the carburetor which was the same. I was amazed when the auto started. We drove it around the city without any trouble"."

Again from Rex Research: "In 1917, John Andrews approached the US Navy with his claim that he could convert fresh or salt water into a fuel with the same power as gasoline. The chemical costs were about 2 cents/gallon.

Andrews was allowed to demonstrate his invention at the Brooklyn Navy Yard, where a motor boat was fitted with a dynamometer for the test. Commander Earl P. Jessup, who was Captain of the yard, said:

"We gave Andrews a bucket of water drawn from the Navy Yard [fresh water] hydrant by one of the yard attaches. He got into his car with a gallon can which we inspected and found to be empty and a little satchel he carried with him. In about a minute he handed out the filled can which I personally carried to the open fuel tank. While pouring the liquid into the tank, Andrews held a lighted cigarette close to the liquid, which did not ignite. That showed it was not gaseous or inflammable at that part of the demonstration, which to me was most important. The engine caught just as quickly as it would have done with gasoline, and after a moment's adjustment of the carburator, it settled down to its work, developing 75% of its rated horsepower, a remarkable showing with any fuel with so slight a readjustment of the carburator.'"" It was reported that a 'green powder' was in the satchel.

A more recent claim occurred in 1973 when a former coal miner revealed that a German rocket scientist had shown him how to turn water into 105-octane fuel by means of a mysterious 'green powder' which he called Mota.

From Rex Research: "The fuel is produced with one pound of the reagent in 50 gallons of water. It burns clean and leaves no residue. In one demonstration with a lawnmower, it ran for about 15 minutes on a small amount of Mota-treated water. An equal amount of gasoline lasted only 3 minutes. Mota fuel is very sensitive to sunlight, which will turn it back to water with a white powder residue.

Gary Bolz, a consultant on carburetion and fuel engineering, was able to test Mota with the help of chemists at Michigan State University and Havoline Chemical Laboratories. Bolz stated:

"The granules are dark olive green. As they enter water, they dissolve in a string of green, which begins to spread fiber-like throughout the water. As the water begins to react, there is a swirling effect. Reaction is complete in a few minutes. If the crystals are mixed in 1:1 ratio with water, the resulting fluid is highly explosive and can be detonated by a small shock. But it isn't shock-sensitive when mixed at a normal ratio of one ounce of powder per half gallon of water. The finished fuel is lighter than water.""

It is interesting to note this long pattern from the 1850's to at least the 1970's with a 'green substance' reacting with water. Now, it seems that what Peter Mennis had was of an entirely different order because it provided lift as Dellschau said. But it still is rather intriguing that there is this commonality. A *German* scientist reveals it to Franch....Dellschau and other members of the AeroClub were from *Germany*....the NYMZA overlords speculated to be from *Germany...maybe there is something here.* But the 'green soupe' of Mennis was not meant for the masses. Mennis was so secretive of the formula that according to Navarro and a fellow researcher of his, Jimmy Ward, Dellschau was 'always moaning about not having the soupe and not being able to accomplish his aims.' In plate 2576 Dellschau says, *If I could solve the soup riddle–and someone will find it out yet.* Alas this has not happened yet or maybe it has? Whether Mennis discovered the formula for NB gas or whether he was put in charge of it, is not really clear. It's just as likely that he may have been the steward entrusted with it by NYMZA. Either way the formula was highly guarded by Mennis as Dellschau tells us in a plate that is unnumbered, *but P. Mennis would sell no soupe——and they could not make it themselves. They had to stay on earth.*

The NB gas was superior to what was being used by AeroClub's contemporaries: *When material is used other than Peter's fuel even the Army using fire to ascend, cannot stay up long, because nothing travels like the Goosey.* Crenshaw believes that this is referring to the Armies use of hot air balloons for observation purposes during the War Between the States which used fire to produce the hot air which in turn provides lift. According to Crenshaw, in a plate dated in the year of 1908 Dellschau asked, *Is Peter Mennis' Lift Power Forgotten?* The science of that time still had not caught up to the uniqueness of the AeroClub's main motive force . . .

PETER I HAVEN FORGOT YOU

In plate 2002 is the following notation:

Goosey

Sonora, 1857 California

Have you never heard of Peter Mennis?

Goose and his offspring?

Peter I haven forgot you!

The bare outline seems like this. At some time during' the 1850's, a group of men came together in California to construct aircraft powered by a secret formula discovered by or entrusted to a single individual named Peter Mennis. They designed and built and tested these different vehicles. Some of them were sighted by people on the ground and thereupon reported to various authorities and media. The prototype seems to have been The Goosey design which Dellschau hints at when he says *Goose and his offspring?* It was the basis for all the other airship designs. The group was funded and overseen by an organization named NYMZA. Navarro found this NYMZA in code in many of Dellschau's plates. What they really were/are is anybody's guess but there does seem to be another interesting parallel in fiction.

WOW

"They had no country but the world, and no law save those which governed their Brotherhood." This line is from the novel, *Angel of the Revolution*, written in 1893 by George Griffith. The jist of the story is that of a Secret Brotherhood which strives, through the invention of one of its members, to control the world and institute world peace. This world peace would have to come at a price though, as the worlds governments will only submit to an overwhelming force but this is just what the Brotherhood has. What may this weapon be but an aerial ship, first of its kind, with great speed (120 MPH) and a secret motive force— two liquids which, when combined give the ship its great power. The Brotherhood consists of members from all over the world and controls events through other groups and those groups in turn control other groups known as the Outer Circle. The hierarchy is demonstrated in this quote from one of the members, "[we are an]international secret society underlying and directing the operations of the various...organisations which have for their object the reform or destruction, by peaceful or violent means, of Society as it is at present constituted." But this would be achieved with finality only by means of an advanced technology embodied in the Ariel, their first airship of war.

In the movie *Things to Come* written by H. G. Wells we run into the (same?)Brotherhood who call themselves Wings Over The World (WOW) who have an advanced technology that they use to consolidate the world into one government. In the words of one of their members, "We are the Brotherhood of Efficiency, The FreeMasonry of Science..." This technology is typified in their advanced aircraft. This mastery of flight will enable this band of 'engineers and mechanics' to rule the world incorporating it into a one world government. C. S. Lewis gives us more of the same in his book *Out of the Silent Planet*. This secret society is a bit on a smaller scale with just a mad professor and his acolyte but nevertheless we have here the same secrecy and belief that technology is best left in the hands of an elite. The physicist gone bad is Professor Weston and he has developed an interplanetary spacecraft which he hopes will be the first of many so that mankind will expand to the stars..for it is their right as he says in a speech to the Martians, "Our right to supersede you is the right of the higher over the lower..." Lewis wrote this in 1938.

WE WILL FALL

Criminal Dooing, wrote Dellschau in one of his plates, in his strange spelling. Thanks to Dellschau, we can gain some insight into the way the world works or at least a fragment of the picture of how things really function. In the 1800s and early 1900s there were two programs of technology: One that the public was familiar with, and one that was secretly being developed alongside it, that was significantly more advanced. But Dellschau seemed to think that there was a criminal aspect to this group and its technology. Was it his conscience declaring that hiding this technology from mankind was wrong, or was it something else? Was he aware of a plan being hatched involving this technology being used against mankind?

Possibly, the following plates might help us to piece together a world view that may serve us in understanding this group and its intentions. Crenshaw writes that in, "plate 2039...is a drawing of the devil, who is looking down at the scene below through a rip in the fabric of the sky, as though he was looking down through an opening into this from another dimension." This same plate has a drawing of Peter Mennis with his black cocker spaniel. Does the devil represent the shadowy NYMZA spying on Peter, making sure his job is getting done? Or, does it mean the source of this technology is otherworldly? Or worse, is there a diabolical aspect to this group and their aims?

In one of the plates that Crenshaw deciphered, plate 1644, Dellschau says, " . . . the time is here when awful things are simply possible to do and have been so a long time ago."

In plate 4417, there is an inscription that is in Latin, *Do Mino Est*. Translated into English, it means "God Exists." This affirmation seems out of place in his paintings; it is the sole religious observation that Dellschau makes. It doesn't make sense unless we take a holistic view of his work; we must see these odd statements in their totality to see if they can make some sense. Perhaps throughout his work, during the process of painting, he was having one long, continual subconscious conversation with himself and from time to time the strands of thought would rise to the surface of his conscious mind resulting in what seems to us as disconnected banalities when, in fact, they are actually connected and intertwined into a meaningful web of interpretation. With this awareness we can perhaps connect these strange emissions such as in plate 2594, where there is a notation with skull and crossbones that reads, "We . . .will . . .fall." Another notation alongside it reads, "Forbidden forever."

I suggest that, though these statements are on separate plates, there is a thread that ties them together. These comments of Dellschau suggest that this group holding this knowledge, is on the verge of betraying mankind in a mighty way while at the same time aligning itself with dark forces that even they do not understand. Like a child playing with a handgun Dellschau tells us that they will meet their end because they have infringed upon a higher law; an area that is forbidden to mankind as told to us in the Promethean myth of old. Strangely, in their very pursuit of ultimate power, the chronicler Dellschau may have shed some light on an Achilles heel of theirs— that they might have run into a wall which made them realize their limitations and finiteness compared to Divine Sovereignty. What it was that they ran into, one can only imagine, but it led the painter to write: God Exists . . .

GENERAL PHILOSOPHY PILLAR: THE POISON FOUNTAIN OF EDUCATION

5

Schools have a secret curriculum that is not known to most. This secret curriculum is taught to the student unbeknownst to the student. The subtlety of the secret curriculum is striking in that it, rather than the overt curriculum, is what is absorbed and integrated into the student. It has a demonstrable lasting impact that say, algebra or grammar does not have. The overt curriculum is what everyone is familiar with; it is out in the open, it is subject to inspection and analysis. It is what we send our children to school for— to learn grammar, history et cetera. But alongside this instruction in reading, writing, history and science, there is another instruction that is imparted to the student. Because this hidden curriculum is not always revealed, and the fact that most don't know it exists, makes it all the more binding upon everyone to know what it is that is actually being taught.

It is actually astounding that at its inception, the architects of our modern schooling system made it clear that there was to be a two-fold curriculum. They did not hide the fact that there was a second curriculum but wrote and spoke about it openly and embraced it. The problem lies in this however . . . the hidden curriculum is the principal, predominant doctrine that the architects of mass schooling want to have embedded in a persons nature. The ABCs and Reading and History are not the goals of schooling, according to these engineers of the 'school system'— it is something completely different. If this is the case why do the common lot worry about their children being 'educated' when that is not the goal of so called 'education'? You surely could buy a car for the purpose of storing clothes in it but I can guarantee no one purchases a car for this purpose; the car designer has designed the car for something else, mainly transportation. Yet this is exactly what we do when we send our children off to school in hopes of them 'getting an education.' The mass schooling system was not designed for this by it's engineers— yet the common folk flock to it in hopes that their child will have an 'education'.

Hidden in the mists of time, however, is documentation that shows there was a rebellion against this secret curriculum. The rebellion was widespread but soon lost its legs when further generations succumbed to the schooling process. The question of mass education is not even challenged today— it is a primary assumption, like an axiom of logic. But at one time this was not the case . . .

THE HIDDEN CURRICULUM IS SPOTTED

In the year 1917, rioting broke out in New York City at a public school, PS 171 to be exact. The usual things that accompany such gatherings were involved: broken windows, people being beat up, threats being made and police tires slashed. The rioting spread to other areas such as in East Harlem and in the boroughs of Brooklyn and the Bronx. Schools were stoned and demonstrators blocked entrances to schools suspending school operations. At one point close to five thousand demonstrators marched. In light of all this the press tried to downplay the debacle as minor immigrant unrest. True it was mostly immigrants that were responsible but what was truly strange is that the participants in this protest were both parents and children. In Yorkville, mostly a German immigrant section, over a thousand mothers were reported to have gathered to protest. Parents along with student volunteers picketed schools with signs and shouting their protests. The newspapers belittled the cause of these people by calling them "street corner agitators" without really clarifying what these people were so inflamed about. The revolt went on for ten days until concessions were made and a mayor having to be tossed out of office. What mobilized this alliance of anger?

It is illuminating to listen to some of the complaints from parents as to why they undertook this action. John Taylor Gatto compiles for us many of the reactions in his splendid book *Underground History of American Education* (pgs.223-225). For instance, the mothers in Yorkville complained that their children had been put on "half-rations" of education. Here are some other comments: "too much play and time wasting".... "the cult of the easy".... "a step backwards in human development".... "they change class every forty minutes".... "they focus on the group instead of the individual." These are just some of the comments preserved for us. There was something in this new learning method that had parents upset. Some principals and teachers also recognized this high strangeness as one principal is on record saying that the new philosophy in schooling would cause mental retardation... and he wasn't kidding. These people recognized that something was wrong, that they were being shortchanged in getting an education, that in fact, they were being given "half-rations."

When Horace Mann proposed his radical changes for public schools in Massachusetts, the Boston school teachers were not having any of his shenanigans. They published a 150 page rebuttal in which they cited Mann's proposed changes as "hot bed theories in which projectors have disregarded experience and observation." Mann wanted to institute the Prussian philosophy of schooling but the schoolmasters believed it would be psychologically damaging and that they would lose the ability for "forming the habit of independent and individual effort." Three years earlier in 1840, Mann's Board of Education was excoriated by the Massachusetts Legislature for undertaking to build a teacher's college with $10,000 put up by the industrialist Edmund Dwight. The existence of the Board itself was even questioned: "If then the Board has any actual power, it is a dangerous power, touching directly upon the rights and duties of the Legislature; if it has no power, why continue it's existence at an annual expense to the commonwealth?"(Underground History pg 174) And further, that Mann's Prussian system would put "a monopoly of power in a few hands, contrary in every respect to our democratical institutions." However, the House voted to overturn the recommendation of its own committee and Horace Mann had his way. What is going on here?

So we see that something didn't sit well even with those in the education field. Bruce Curtis, in his book *Building the Educational State 1836-1871* recounts the antipathy of parents in Canada when state schooling threatened. According to school records, in Ontario, Canada, a teacher was locked in a school house by the students while parents stood by encouraging them. They "threw mud and mire into his face and over his clothes." Curtis cites many examples of this kind of resistance to the changes or reforms and this is surprising because as he says, " . . . many educational historians . . . argue that state schooling was desired by the population as whole." But Curtis chronicles a time period, in Canada specifically, that has all the marks of a resistance movement from parents and the general populace. It was not a resistance to learning but it was a resistance to something else that was not as tangible. The parents, in their perspicuity, realized that something more subtle was being learned in the classrooms. In his summary of the matter Curtis believes that schooling was for one purpose: "The creation in the population of new habits, attitudes, or orientations, desires; the channeling of popular energy, into particular regulatory forms.... - these were the objectives of education. Over time, these objectives have been absorbed into the texture of state schooling." (Curtis, 1988, p.366) And we all thought that reading and writing was the primary purpose. Yet, even Curtis is vague in his assertions about the aim of schooling. It is our goal to clarify this, dear reader, in this article.

The version of education history that is often told has been demolished by those in the education establishment itself. The myth is repeated time and again that there was a popular demand from the working class for state run education. In the book *The Irony of Early School Reform* (2001) by Michael B. Katz, the author conclusively demonstrates that this was clearly not so. Through primary documents, Katz reveals an interesting episode from education history which takes place in Beverly, Massachusetts, where the townsmen actually rejected a proposed high school that was for the benefit of their children.

A TALE OF TWO COMMUNITIES: THE HIDDEN CURRICULUM PART 2

IN his book *The Poison Fountain* (1878), the lawyer, writer and activist Zachariah Montgomery, asks his readers to take a journey of imagination. Before he does this he asks the reader to consider a basic assumption. Does education make a person better, that is morally wise? Just consider your impressions. We all associate crime, especially hideous doings, more readily to an illiterate highschool dropout than to a physician or engineer for example. This was the common assumption held at that time also and to some extent now, that education does make you better, that *ignorance is the mother of vice*. Around that time, this doctrine was well summed up in *The Commentaries on American Law* by the legal scholar James Kent when he says in his second volume of Commentaries what a lack of education would lead to: "...children of all conditions would probably become idle and vicious when they grow up."

We don't have to agree with the assumption but in order to take up that trip of imagination offered by Montgomery, we must at least understand it. To illustrate the assumption let us imagine two distinct communities living side by side. What is the distinction? Well, one community is educated and the other is illiterate and uneducated. Then Montgomery asks us to imagine a *what if.*

What if we found out that the *educated* community had six criminals to the one criminal of the illiterate, uneducated?

What if the *educated* community had two paupers to the one pauper in the uneducated community?

What if the *educated* community had four suicides to the one suicide in the uneducated community?

What if these statistics were consistent for a little over 200 years?

Obviously it is disturbing to see this in an *educated* community, so Montgomery asks, "What conclusion would you arrive at with reference to *that kind* of education?"(italics his)

From the years 1647 to 1860, Montgomery compared two distinct school systems. For this time period they happened to be distinct geographically also. But when he distinguished them he called them separate names based on their philosophy. The New England style of schooling or *antiparental* as he called it was predominant in the New England states. The *parental* style of schooling was the main system of schooling in the states of Georgia, North Carolina Maryland, Delaware, South Carolina and Virginia. It wasn't until the second half of the 1800s that these states accepted the New England style of schooling and became compulsory.

Parental style of schooling was simply up to the parents who took it upon themselves to educate their children without any State interference. This was the main system of schooling since the beginning of time. In America, antiparental or non-parental began in Massachusetts in 1647 when the colonists of Massachusetts decided by statute that "...each town consisting of 50 householders was directed to maintain a school to teach their children to read and write; and every town of 100 families was to maintain a grammar school to fit youth for the college. The common schools have been kept up to this day by direct tax..." Again from the *Poison Fountain*, Montgomery quoting Kent's Commentaries, "In New England...it was the right and duty of the government to provide, by means of fair and just taxation for the instruction of all the youth in the elements of learning."

Virginia, on the other hand, according to Montgomery, as late as 1856 had no free school system. Parents did what they thought was right in regards to their childrens's education. Cornelius Heatwole's *History of Education in Virginia* delves into the non-compulsory aspect of Virginia education. In 1810 the Literary Fund was set up to support education for the poor and indigent. The source of the fund was miscellaneous fines and fees levied on the general public for minor transgressions. No system of primary schools was set up. The schooling was a combination of this fund and also tuition from parents if they so wished to enroll their child. Again, schooling was not compulsory.

These two States represent the two *systems* of education according to Montgomery. The educated State, which was *nonparental*, being Massachusetts and the relatively non-educated State, which was *parental*, being Virginia. The imaginative scenario that he asked us to envision was not imaginary or fictional, however. The striking facts are that the statistics he cited were exactly what corresponded to a real life situation. The New England States that utilized the new philosophy of school or as Montgomery calls it, the anti-parental system, which soon spread to the rest of the country after the civil war, had a direct correlation with high criminality and suicide and insanity and pauperism. For 200 years, side by side, these systems yielded a social result that was appalling to those who studied it. It was Montgomery's contention that these ills of society were and are a direct byproduct of this style of education. A system that was supposedly put in place to curtail such things actually increased it. In distinction to the anti-parental system we have the parental system that the South utilized, in which there were low crime rates and social ills. In his book Montgomery establishes an amazing correspondence between expenditures on public education and civil breakdown in society. Simply put, the more each of the New England states, where schooling was compulsory, spent on each child, the more criminality and social deviance occurred.

From our brief survey we have seen that parents reacted to this system but what is hardly publicized is that media outlets actually noticed and criticized this system of schooling also. A leading newspaper of the time, the Alta California, in its editorial of January 31, 1872, condemned the system as "our anaconda" and declared that to "judge this system by its apparent fruits, we shall have to pronounce it not only a melancholy, but a most disastrous failure, and that it will be idle to look for the cause of the general rowdyism, idleness and viciousness of the rising generation anywhere but in the training which it is receiving?" The new system was encroaching upon California and the San Francisco *Morning Call* warned " that a large number of public school men have come to the conclusion that the public school system of that city is a failure." The city being referred to is Boston and the year of publication is 1877 August 5th for this particular article.

CONFESSIONS

In the mid 1950's Rudolf Flesch wrote *Why Johnny Can't Read*. The book was an outgrowth of a personal experience he had with his twelve year old grandson who couldn't make out new words that were presented to him. Flesch, in a letter to his daughter said, "What I found is absolutely fantastic. The teaching of reading – all over the United States, in all the schools, in all the textbooks – is totally wrong and flies in the face of all logic and common sense. Johnny couldn't read until half a year ago for the simple reason that *nobody ever showed him how.*"(italics mine) It may be, however, that, shocking as it sounds, reading may not be the goal of modern schooling; for that matter, learning itself may not be the intention of modern education.

But let us hear what the architects of modern education have to say on the matter. Did these originators and founders of modern schooling know what they were doing? That is, did they intentionally subvert traditional learning and institute a *hidden curriculum?* And, if so, for what purpose?

This is from John Dewey, one of the theoreticians of modern schooling: (In all quotes that follow, all italics are mine)

"There is, however, a false educational god whose idolaters are legion, and whose cult influences the entire educational system. This is *language study* – the study not of foreign language, but *of English*; not in higher, but in primary education. It is almost an unquestioned assumption, of educational theory and practice both, that the first three years of a child's school-life shall be mainly taken up with learning to read and write his own language."

From Edmund Burke Huey who wrote *The Psychology and Pedagogy of Reading* which justified 'scientifically' the *look-say* method of reading and squashed the traditional reading methods and in fact, negated the importance of reading:

"As child nature is being systematically studied, the feeling grows that these golden years of childhood, like the Golden Age of our race, belong naturally to quite other subjects and performances than reading, and to quite other objects than books; and that reading is a "Fetich of Primary Education" which only holds its place by the power of tradition and the stifling of questions asked concerning it."

Granville Stanley Hall, the apostle and main expounder of the new education philosophy in America:

"Very many men have lived and died and been great, even the leaders of their age, without any acquaintance with letters. The knowledge which illiterates acquire is probably a much larger proportion of it practical. Moreover, they escape much eyestrain and mental excitement, and, other things being equal, are probably more active and less sedentary. It is possible, despite the stigma our bepedagogued age puts upon this disability, for those who are under it not only to lead a useful, happy, virtuous life, but to be really well educated in many other ways. Illiterates escape certain temptations, such as vacuous and vicious reading. Perhaps we are prone to put too high a value both upon the ability required to attain this art and the discipline involved in doing so, as well as the culture value that comes to the citizen with his average of only six grades of schooling by the acquisition of this art."

Edward L. Thorndike, who injected the new educational philosophy into America from his post at Columbia Teachers College, with his books such as *Educational Psychology*(1903), *The Principles of Teaching Based on Psychology*(1906) and *Elementary Principles of Education*(1929), inculcated the new philosophy to armies of minds...the future teachers of America. Let's hear some of this philosophy:

"Studies ...indicate the advisability of placing little emphasis before the age of six upon either the acquisition of those intellectual resources known as the formal tools–reading, spelling, arithmetic, writing, etc.–or upon abstract intellectual analysis."(*Elementary Principles of Education* pg. 308)

"...the program of the average elementary school is too narrow and academic in character. Traditionally the elementary school primarily devoted to teaching the fundamental subjects, the three R's, and closely related disciplines...Artificial exercises, like drills on phonetics, multiplication tables, and formal writing movements, are used to a wasteful degree. Subjects such as arithmetic, language and history include content that is intrinsically of little value." (*Elementary Principles of Education* pg. 311-312)

DON'T ROCK THE BOAT

Most parents enrolling their children would be surprised to learn that the three R's are wasteful as Thorndike says. These men were the primary movers and designers of modern education. We can already see that the curriculum which is obvious, like reading, writing and math is not an emphasis or main goal of education. Keep in mind that this is only a brief survey and that pages with these types of quotes could be filled. So then, if not for reading, writing and arithmetic what is school for? What is the aim of education according to these architects?

From Edward Lee Thorndike, the apostle of the new education philosophy:

"Education is interested primarily in the general interrelation of man and his environment, in all the changes which make possible a better adjustment of human nature to its surroundings."(*The Principles of Teaching Based on Psychology* pg. 3)

Almost all educators speak and write obliquely, their prose is dense and formidable at times. Richard Mitchell, in his book *The Graves of Academe* gives some hilarious examples of the way educators cloud their meaning with either prolixity or just outright nonsense. Mitchell read widely in education theory and came to the conclusion that what educators were writing was actually anti-knowledge: "The clouded language of educational theory is an evolved, protective adaptation that hinders thought and understanding . . . those who give themselves to the promulgation of educational theory are usually both deceivers and deceived. The murky language where their minds habitually dwell, at once unminds them and gives them the power to unmind others." This inclination of educators is highly amusing but I only bring it up to make you the reader aware that this is going on as in the quote above from Thorndike. Obviously, as Mitchell concluded, they are either ashamed or fearful of being found out. So we must interpret through the veil.

Thorndike, above, is saying that education and learning

have one goal. Become one with the direction of society. Don't rock the boat. This is the theme that you will see time and time again. That the aim is not learning but being what is known as *socialized*. That is, conditioning of an individual must make him a co-operating member of society. In order to accomplish this he must be 'educated' . . . some would say mind controlled. A person, after the education process, is a *planned individual*. The planned individual is paramount in the machinations of these architects as we shall see for a very specific reason. In other words there is a specific role that the planned individual plays in a wider context, i.e., society.

From John Dewey's, My Pedagogic Creed - Article 2:

"I believe that the school is primarily a social institution. Education being a social process, the school is simply that form of community life in which all those agencies are concentrated that will be most effective in bringing the child to share in the inherited resources of the race, and to use his own powers for social ends."

Not a word here about learning in the sense of what most people understand, like reading and writing to prepare for life ahead. In fact, according to Dewey, education is not about preparation at all: "I believe that education, therefore, is a process of living and not a preparation for future living."(also from Article 2) In other words, we need you to act a certain way— to have predictable behavior.

We can see from this sampling, the fanaticism with words like, *environment* and *surroundings* and *relationship*. These are the buzzwords that have a sort of foggy double meaning. They seem like such nice words . . . so you really couldn't mean anything bad by them. The obliqueness of the words are designed, however, to hide a very specific meaning which we will soon understand.

Ellwood P. Cubberley, the 'evangelist' of American education, who wrote *Public Education in the United States*, the book through which all subsequent historical thinking about education was filtered, had this to say: "Through all the complicated machinery of the school, some way must be found to awaken a social consciousness...Reading, writing, arithmetic, geography, and history, the staples of the elementary curriculum are really of little value...Our teachers must become more effective social workers." (from *Changing Conceptions of Education*-1909, pgs. 66-68)

We can gather from the above that there is something more that is intended in public education than the traditional three R's. Over the years there have been many books and articles on the subject admitting that public schools have *'failed.'* But this is from a completely wrong conceptual viewpoint. The fact is, they have not failed at all. They have been the most successful institution on the face of the earth. To say they have failed is to argue from a completely different framework of reference. The designers never meant for learning, in the sense that we like to think of learning, to occur. If we grant that something else was their goal then we can judge the whole differently. For now we can safely say, however, that they intended to create a specific kind of individual— the *socialized individual*. The rhetoric is indeed murky from these Architects but based on these and many of their other comments it seems that the goal of education is to *subsume the individuality of a person into the whole*. It is to create a homogeneity of opinion, morality, character and standards— in short, a consensus opinion of reality. It is a constructed society, a planned society that has a self-regulating preservative function for itself. And it is this: Because there is consensus, anyone stepping outside of this consensus is surely mad or on the fringe— the message from early on to every individual is Don't Rock the Boat. However, the consensus is a construct and anyone inside it is actually parroting the engineers of the construct. We must investigate who is responsile for this construct and their motives. In this volume we shall cover those who sponsor and fund this operation. In the next volume we shall discover the intellectual underpinnings and the actual mechanics of this philosphy in the classroom.

But it is enough to see, for now, that overall there was a defiance to this educational process by concerned parents and individuals— simply because education was not and is not the thing intended. They had the insight that escapes us today. The canvas of educational history is not like what is usually painted; an eager and willing populace that is zealous for education for their children. The picture is far different and these parents understood that the planned individual of these Architects was really only the precursor and necessary ingredient for the *planned society*.

THE TIES WHICH BIND THE HUMAN MIND

Charles DeGarmo hints, in his book, *Herbart and the Herbartians*, that the typical subjects like the Three Rs are only a cover for the real teaching. He says in chapter 7 of his book that, "Instruction in knowledge . . . performs an important function in the development of *moral character*." In chapter 5 he says that education, "can alone bring the youthful will into the desired activity and direction." What then is the goal of education? Frederic H. Hayward in his book

The Secret of Herbart (1903) gives us a piece to the puzzle. Now, Hayward was not one of the theoreticians but more of an apologist for the Method and Aim of Modern Schooling. The aim of modern schooling says Hayward, as we can probably guess, is not to learn subject matter but instead its purpose is to form the character of man. He laments, "If education had ever had one tenth of the chance that religion has had over the centuries...moral wonders would long ago have been effected." The *nature* of man can be changed for the good if Education is just given the chance, for as he says, "the best men have not thrown themselves into it; public sympathy has never yet been fully on its side; it has never yet discovered a standpoint or a standing for itself." And what has kept this from happening? Why has the public been so averse to accepting Education as the shaper of men's souls? The problem is Religion has dominated this venue of character shaping. Religion has had its chance and judging from human history it has failed miserably. As Hayward puts it, we need a "scientific gospel." Human behavior must be treated "as a scientific problem is treated."

Edward Alsworth Ross, whose book, *Social Control* (1901), influenced social theory in the 20th century, crystallizes this outlook. Although it was not a new distinction, Ross maintains that there are two forms of living on this earth. One of them he calls *community* living, the other is life in a *society*.

Community life implies 'concord' as he calls it, that is, agreement. It is implicit agreement of individuals and between individuals on the duties and privileges within a group...the individual gives his wholehearted assent to the structure of the community life. There is no outside imposition or laws; instead these are generated from within.

Actually, an individual in this setting would think laws were a strange thing for each person has a role to fulfill and the pressure of alignment with the group comes from within the individual, within the group. Think of a family or a clan of families having roles that are not dictated to them but are rather 'understood'— there is no coercion involved.

Society is different. Whereas community was homogeneous, society is heterogeneous. This means that there are different groups with different ideas and values, different belief systems. One group's beliefs would surely clash with anothers and sooner or later chaos and anarchy would reign. Headhunters and cannibals would probably not get on well with the Lutherans, so to speak. This distinction of community and society was expounded by the German sociologist, Ferdinand Tonnies in the 19th century as *gemeinschaft* (community) and *gesellschaft* (society). Whereas, order in gemeinschaft is natural or integral to it, in gesellschaft, order must be imposed from without. For in gesellschaft we have self serving individuals who have no natural ties to each other as we see in gemeinschaft. The art of creating ties in a heterogeneous society like gesellschaft is called *social control*. This will create the desired homogeneity or uniformity of society.

Now, according to Ross and those of his set, *community* has broken down or if it has not entirely, the last vestiges of it are due to disappear. With the dawning of *society*, new methods for stabilizing the social order are called for. But, the methods used in the past were unsuccessful says Ross. Coercion has not been fruitful for mankind, it has only multiplied the problem. The superior methods of control are inward, coming from within the individual as they did in the setting of *community*. This will be the task of the social engineer... to get a person to have the same attitude in society as he would in a community setting. This, admits Ross, is not natural but artificial so the social engineer will have to rely on artificial constructions that will engender this attitude. These artificial constructions are known to us as *institutions;* education or compulsory schooling being one of them. In fact, this is the primary means to persuade individuals rather than use coercion: "If, now, society will lure him, he will cause no trouble. The moulding of his will by social suggestion, the shaping of his ideas by education...these, if skillfully done, do not arouse the insurgent Spirit." (pg. 438, Social Control) As a consequence, education serves the purposes of maintaining order in society and will save that society a great deal of trouble if behavior is moulded at an early age: "A far sighted policy, such as the training of the young, is preferable to the summary regulation of the adult."

The social philosophers have compared their view of regulating society with the former regulation of society under a religious institution, i.e. the church, whether Catholic or Protestant. But the religious institutions have not worked and this has been a criticism of religion by contemporary social commentators. Christopher Hitchens, in his book, *God is Not Great* (God is not capitalized in his title) says that religion has historically shown that ethics or 'good works' are not grounded in a religious metaphysics. Hitchens concludes, as a result of his selective and delimited examples, that "charity and relief work . . . are the inheritors of modernism and the Enlightenment." In other words, if a society is to prosper a new paradigm must overtake the religious one, a paradigm rooted in education. For when this happens, the good things that accrue to a society like 'charity and relief work' take place, when we become 'educated'. Hitchens' belief is the fundamental belief that permeated educational thinking in the 19th and early part of the 20th century and of course today. Education must fulfill the role that was poorly filled by the Church.

We started off by asserting that there is a secret curriculum and we showed this by quoting the architects and implementers of the new philosophy. There was resistance to this hidden curriculum because people smelled a rat. The theoreticians of modern schooling confirm the rat by telling us that education serves a purpose other than 'education' as we know it, and they used cloudy words and phrases to make an even cloudier point. Words and phrases like *socialized* and *relation to the environment* are bandied about without clarification but the inference is clear: students are not there for grammar and algebra. There is an overarching purpose. This purpose is also alluded to by the theoreticians but again cloudy language is used like *formation of character* and such. What is clear, however, is that they do want to form an individual and the new system of education must be used because religion has failed to form the proper individual. A planned individual is the goal of the architects by means of their secret curriculum which is taught in the public schools. But this planned individual has specificity. He or she is constructed, by means of public education, to fill a particular role in society. This role is a well kept secret to the masses because it is clouded by opaque and dense language that really does not get to the point. The final product of education, the individual, is a certain type of individual that is meant to act in a certain type of way.

INSURANCE POLICY

Michael Katz was compiling masses of information like all good scholars do and trying to edit it but to no avail—he could not find a vantage point from which he could make sense of the data. The trees were very clear but the forest was not. The clarity finally came in the form of an anecdote about a historical incident in the town of Beverly, Massachusetts. When he followed up to verify the anecdote, he had to refashion his thinking on education. In fact, in the Introduction to his book that we have already cited above, *The Irony of Early School Reform*, he expresses his ambivalence about his work and states, "There is then, an inconsistency between *Irony* and my later work, which I am not sure how to resolve." You see, I believe that Katz was an honest scholar. What he found did not accord with his world views and when the implications of his research were drawn out by those whose world views were different from his, he tried to re-evaluate the data and maybe he thought of shaping it to suit his views, but thankfully for us he remained an honest scholar and published his work anyway.

What Katz found through his research is *representational*. It is an isolated historical incident that has broad significance in reality. He has captured under a microscope of investigation, what has happened and is happening on a wider scale in the world at large. The principles of social behavior regarding class can be gleaned from this episode and applied to reality. When we understand what he uncovered it will provide a key to interpreting the driving force behind education and the mechanics of world events. Katz has revealed the lynch-pin that holds the whole picture together.

The town of Beverly, Massachusetts was in rebellion. The year was 1850, a good deal removed from the revolutionary forefathers. Though there were no guns in this rebellion, the defiance against the powers that be was real nevertheless. This time it was not England but the state of Massachusetts that the townspeople of Beverly were fighting against. State law required a high school to be established at a certain population number and Beverly, Mass was required to build such a thing since they met this requirement. In 1858 the law was passed in Beverly to institute a highschool. But a funny thing happened, two years later the citizens voted to abolish the high school.

What Katz found was the peculiarity of who was voting for abolition of the school and who fought to keep the school. Almost unanimously the upper class, the wealthy, voted for the high school. The working class voted to abolish it. This does not sit well with contemporary recasting of history in which the poor are portrayed as demanding schooling for their progeny. But what was unsettling to Katz was the fact that the greater tax burden would be on the wealthy and in many cases, the childless wealthy; yet they vehemently opposed the closing of the school. As Katz asks, "Why did the wealthy and prestigious favor a high school? Why did the working class oppose?" Is this really heavenly beneficence and charity that the rich are bestowing onto the poor or is there some other motive?

One of the clues to the answer lies in the person of Robert Rantoul, a primary advocate and promoter of the high school. Rantoul's son was the famous Democratic senator who founded the Free Soil Party before his untimely death. Senior was a prominent, not to mention wealthy, member of Beverly. His success in his apothecary business catapulted him into other lucrative ventures such as founding an insurance company, being director of a bank and renting and selling real property in addition to having been a local magistrate. Katz also mentions the fact that the man was a money lender due to the fact of the uncollected debts he left behind when he died. He was definitely wealthy and he was definitely a *promoter* for the high school in Beverly.

Rantoul, according to speeches and some writings left behind, pined for the good old days in which there was 'unity' and 'mutual dependence'. An example he uses is the voluntary fire fighting which had provided, "a favorable influence upon the mass of the community, provoking a generous desire to aid one another by personal efforts and sacrifices." In the cholera epidemic of 1832 the citizens of Beverly banded together in a way that would not have been possible in later years lamented Rantoul. There just wasn't that sense of community spirit any longer for Rantoul.

What is Rantoul getting at? What does he think caused the change from those glory days of community and participation in comparison to the time he was speaking? Rantoul attributes the problem to, "a manufacturing population in the main." According to Katz, Rantoul told a local audience that farming was better than trade as an occupation. Rantoul believed that, with trade, there were, "too many mean artifices and tricks, too much overreaching and even gross atrocious frauds, and a reckless sacrifice of health, morals, comfort and of the vast number of lives. . ." Katz sums up Rantoul's position from various speeches and writings: "On the whole then, agriculture provided a better life than trading...And how much superior was the idyllic life on the farm to the uncertainties and questionable morality of trade." Katz then quotes Rantoul mourning over the loss of people from farms, flocking to the cities in pursuit of ignoble trade: "large and disproportionate number. . . .withdrawn from the laborious and productive classes in rural life, to engage in the unproductive pursuits of trade. . ."

Here is what should stick out like the proverbial sore thumb . . . (And this was not missed by Katz as it led him to write a whole book on the topic) . . . the man for his whole adult life was a MERCHANT— engaging in, what else? Trade! Katz puts it well: "Thus spoke Robert Rantoul, merchant, lawyer, promoter: a man who never was a farmer, who grew up in the city, who directed a bank, who sent neither son nor grandson to a farm, who subscribed faithfully to that agent of the mercantile spirit, Hunt's Merchants Magazine."(pg.26) Our key to historical truth will be actions and not words.

With this in mind we come to the interesting year of 1857 in Beverly, where Mr. Rantoul, retired from public life, decided to unretire briefly, by attending the annual spring town meeting. His main purpose in attending was to speak in favor of the proposed town high school. In his autobiography he notes the outcome of this meeting, in which he says that, "I spoke at some length but by the result of the vote with very little effect as there was a large majority against the measure." Because of this, another town meeting was called and Rantoul attended again but this time with some firepower. At his sides were his two grandsons. One was a lawyer, Robert S. Rantoul, who let the townspeople know the implications of defying state law. The other was a wealthy druggist, William Endicott, who championed the cause of bringing back the high school after its abolishment in 1860. Why is this successful entrepreneur so vehement about enforcing education on the poor? Does he feel that these wretches don't know any better or is it something else?

Another champion of the high school was a neighbor of Rantoul's, Dr. Wyatt C. Boyden, who, when he died, left even more money behind than did Rantoul. Though they were on opposite sides of the fence politically, they both served on the local school committee and were wholeheartedly in agreement regarding the high school. His basic supposition was the same as many of these promoters of education: "the prosperity of the country — and the permanence of our civil, political and religious Institutions . . . depend on the intelligence and virtue of the people." As he says in another place the State had an interest in the education of the best talent in the community. . ."

Boyden knew about prosperity. . .it wasn't only doctoring that gave him his wealth but a substantial investment in shoe manufacturing in Lynn that made him so. So, it is not hesitantly that we might take that term, that he uses so generally, in an amorphous sense, and apply it directly to Boyden himself. The "prosperity of the country" really could be restated as the 'prosperity of Wyatt Boyden'. When we amend it like so, we can begin to see through the rhetoric that these altruistic, compassionate terms might actually have a rather specific meaning that is unclouded by words like, 'country', 'state' or 'humanity'. This rhetoric and the push for public education has a source (the wealthy), that is undeniable historically. The ultimate question is why does a high school make the Wyatt Bordens 'prosperous'? We will strive to answer this but first we must see that Beverly, Massachusetts will illustrate for us a principle that is universal and worldwide—the over-concern of those with wealth in industry and commerce to educate the commoner.

In the middle 1800's it is astounding to see the energy expended by those with wealth in promoting education. The resistance was from the poor who sadly could not 'see' the benefits of an education. There was an interesting tie between those that promoted education and those that held the wealth in the State- - -*they were one and the same.* As Katz says in *Irony*, "school promoters throughout Massachusetts were people intimately connected with the economic transformation of the state."(pg.35) Katz supports this contention with the following:

Horace Mann, head of the first Board of Education in the country, "helped push through the Massachusetts legislature bills supporting and assisting railroad construction."

George Boutwell, Governor of Massachusetts, head of the Board of Education(1855-1861), state bank commissioner, appointed first commissioner of the Internal Revenue Service by Abe Lincoln was a merchant.

Henry K. Oliver, state representative and a mayor at one point, was, according to Katz, " the most vocal school promoter". Also according to Katz's research, Oliver was "agent for one of the largest cotton mills in the state."

Also an agent for the cotton industry was Joseph White who was fourth secretary of the Board of education.

William Thorndike of Beverly, was president of Hamilton Bank in Boston and also president of the National Insurance Company. In the History of Beverly (1843) by Edwin M. Stone we read how Thorndike became a " director of all the principal monied institutions in the place (Beverly)." Stone tells us this busy man had time to be "one of the school committee...in which last capacity, he devoted much time and labor to the improvement of the schools."(pg.151)

Katz's conclusion to all this: "And so it was throughout the commonwealth. The supporters of education *wrote the legislation, invested the money, and ran the enterprises* that brought about the economic and social transformation of Massachusetts."(*Irony* pg. 35)

What we have is an equation: business interests equals education promotion. Katz lauds this undertaking as being unique in American history, for this was the only time when lay (amateur) individuals reformed and were involved in education, whereas consequently until this day this has been the provenance of professionals (those who are trained and make their living in education). But there had to be an overarching reason for their involvement. There seems to be some sort of game plan that these monied interests are following.

The crystal ball becomes clearer when Katz recounts the following episode of a meeting between the prominent merchants of New England: "On the night of June 9, 1834, a group of men, "chiefly engaged in commerce," gathered to discuss the education of their sons. Among those present were Nathan Appleton, and the secretary of the meeting was the eminent William Ellery Channing. The merchants agreed that the *"present system of apprenticeship had become inefficient* and wasteful of their sons' time." (*Irony* pg. 36–italics mine) What is good for the goose *is not* good for the gander? Lets explain . . .

Apprenticeship was the gateway to riches for Rantoul

as well as Appleton who, though he had schooling, only came into his riches as a result of apprenticing himself to his brother in his business. Apprenticing was the way of mankind in every culture in every time period since the beginning of time. The only time when it has been completely supplanted has been this modern era. Apprenticeship was the way to wealth for many of the founders of America, including the wealthy Benjamin Franklin who was a lowly apprentice to his brother James in the printing business. Yet these wealthy merchants believed that a system that had brought them to great wealth and prosperity was no longer sufficient for their progeny and anyone else. Instead they sought to implement a system that

1.) Was *unproven* and more importantly

2.) Was *not accepted* by the general population. It was only implemented by force of law by men of wealth who also, at the same time, were men of public office.

There was wisdom, however, in their dismissal of this proposition by the rich for education. The working class understood well that 'education' was really an insurance policy for the rich. Insurance policies are for protection . . . protection of ones assets and against loss. Rantoul's impassioned plea for education is a plea that we will see many times— coming from the mouths of wealthy elites. 'Education' is a guaranteed protection that the masses of humanity will not develop skills or abilities that threaten the monopolistic holdings of the likes of Rantoul and company. It is a mass diversion of resources into that which is unprofitable. The parents realized that no skill would be learned in a school setting. The only jobs would be repetitive labor such as in the factories and mills that the rich were already heavily vested in. High school served the dual purpose of shunting talent from profitable ventures that the Rantouls of the world were in, thereby protecting their monopolies, and it also incapacitated a person so that he was only able to do repetitive manual labor in a factory that the Rantoul's of the world owned . . .

BEVERLY WRIT LARGE

If this isolated incident in a small town, in a small state, in one country has anything to with what is happening on earth, what is it— what does Beverly have anything to do with the rest of the planet?

The latter half of the 19th century saw an unprecedented patronage by the wealthy in behalf of education. The richest men in the world were founding and endowing universities with vast wealth. The University of Chicago was created due to the funding of John D. Rockefeller. To quote Paolo Lionni from his book *The Leipzig Connection*, "By 1910, when a glass of beer cost a penny and a loaf of bread less than a nickel, when a three-room apartment went for five dollars a month and a good pair of shoes for a dollar, Rockefeller had assets of over $800 million." In the year 2010 that amount equates to over 20 billion dollars. We see this pattern of generosity throughout that time period but as will become more clear as we go on, these endowments by the rich have specific targets that are meant to serve a specific purpose as in the case of the University of Chicago. In other words, the funding is done with extreme *precision*.

Another target of Rockefeller funds was Teachers College in New York. This was the premier institution in the land for training future teachers. Both of these universities were fundamental to the spread of the new philosophy in education. Frederick T. Gates, the man hired by Rockefeller to disperse these funds in a targeted manner had a vision that the Rockefeller fortune would be used to forward "civilization in all its elements in this land and *all lands.*"(italics mine) The world could be changed, according to Gates, as long as people understood that this was for their own good, "In our dreams, we have limitless resources and the people yield themselves with perfect docility to our molding hands. . . .we work our own good will upon a grateful and responsive rural folk." The preceding was from the *Occasional Letter No.1* , a publication of the Rockefeller funded General Education Board.

If you remember, there were two distinct schooling methods in America that could, more or less be distinguished geographically. The South was parental, whereas the North invoked the powers of the State in educating their young rather than leaving it in the hands of parents; therefore the North was nonparental, in the words of Zach Montgomery. This was not to last. One of the main goals of the General Education Board was to strong arm the South into public schooling with the generous funds from Rockefeller and company. So the reluctant and backwards South was shepherded by the magnanimous Rockefeller inspired General Education Board toward the antiparental philosophy and compulsory state schooling. What Rantoul and company did on a small level in Beverly, Rockefeller achieved on a national and world wide scale. The wealthy promoting education semed to be the spirit of the times— or is it a game plan?

THE GOSPEL OF WEALTH . . . FOR THE FEW

Education was among the many philanthropic interests

of Andrew Carnegie, also known in the late 19th century as the 'richest man in the world.' Carnegie wrote that only in "popular education can man erect the structure of an enduring civilization." According to Carnegie, in his book *Triumphant Democracy*, education, "is the basis of all stability, and underlies all progress. Without it the State architect builds in vain."(pg.131) Here is a man who fully embraces the educational system. What we should find hard to understand is his disavowal and criticism of the system of apprenticing— since he was a direct product of this system.

In fact Carnegie writes that the apprenticeship system which enabled him to become so wealthy is the exact thing which has held humanity back. He, perhaps forgetting his own situation and all those who attained wealth in this manner, endeavors to illustrate this for us: "In the manufacture of products we have the whole story. . . Formerly articles were manufactured at the domestic hearth or in small shops which formed part of the household. The master and his apprentices worked side by side, the latter living with the master, and therefore subject to the same conditions. When these apprentices rose to be masters, there was little or no change in their mode of life, and they, in turn, educated in the same routine succeeding apprentices." He forgot to mention his own life story just as Rantoul from Beverly decried manufacturing (the thing which made him wealthy) and longed for the farming life for everyone except himself.

In the North American Review of June 1889, in a piece entitled *The Gospel of Wealth*, Carnegie tells us that the "The problem of our age is the proper administration of wealth, so that the ties of brotherhood may still bind together the rich and poor in harmonious relationship." The general idea of the piece is that wealth has accumulated in the hands of the few like Carnegie. This condition of wealth that has favored the few, such as Carnegie and his ilk, should not be criticized for "Much better this great irregularity than universal squalor." As he says, "A relapse to old conditions would be disastrous . . . not the least so to him who serves – and would sweep away civilization with it."

He unabashedly states that only a monopoly by the few can bring these results to civilization when he says, "it is best for the race, because it insures the survival of the fittest in every department. We accept and welcome, therefore, as conditions to which we must accommodate ourselves, great inequality of environment, the concentration of business, industrial and commercial, in the hands of a few, and the law of competition between these, as being not only beneficial, but essential for the future progress of the race."

Since the concentration of wealth can only be held by the few, it is necessary for these kind men to see to it that the harmonious relationship between rich and poor is brought about by their wealth "administered for the common good." But instead of Carnegie dispersing the cash equally amongst his fellow citizens he says that he will decide what to do with the money— it will be "spent for public purposes, from which the masses reap the principal benefit."

Carnegie really is stating that he will be a sort of manager of mankind by dispersing his funds in a targeted manner. One of these targets, of course was education. In 1905 the Carnegie Foundation For the Advancement of Teaching was established with 15 million dollars. By doing this he was subsidizing those who would preach and institute the new educational philosophy— mass education for all in the name of progress.

Carnegie, like Rantoul and the others, gained there wealth from a system that is antithetical to the one they espouse for the rest of humanity. Carnegie did not go to school as he would have everyone else. At the age of thirteen he was working 12 hours a day in a bobbin factory and at 18, with skills learned from his telegraph/messenger boy position began his ascent in the business world by working as a secretary/telegraph operator for the Pennsylvania Railroad Company. Looking back one wonders if Carnegie would have wished he could have just gone to school to learn Latin and Greek and his Abc's instead of gaining the skills that allowed him to gain wealth just like the Rantouls and Boyden's of the world. This captain of industry instead criticized the apprenticeship system that put him in the position to become what he was. Do we start to see a pattern here with these people?

It is no wonder then that Carnegie disparaged the parental system that was dominant in the South, since this system implied and endorsed apprenticeship, the very thing Carnegie castigated but ironically was reared in. He has a few choice words for this system in the South, in his book *Triumphant Democracy*, calling it, in one instance, "cursed". He goes on to imply that the parental, apprenticing system is anti-democratic or old world aristocratic. The connotation is not pleasant because he then associates this with slavery and slave-holding. In contrast, the Northern system of State schooling is democratic and freedom loving and not associated with slavery. This contrast is rather interesting because one could easily see the comparison melt away when one considers the hundreds and then thousands of mini-plantations, called *factories*, which dotted the New England country side in the late 19th century. When some of these 'slaves' in Homestead, Pennsylvania that worked for Carnegie's Steel Company believed that Carnegie should pay them more, due to his 60 percent increase in profits, they were shot at with guns (seven were killed) by Pinkerton guards hired *by* Carnegie. Sounds like something a slave owner would do. But this is all just to say that some things bear a little closer examination and sometimes when they are, remarkable similarities come to light.

Carnegie sheds light on the motive for the elites interest in education perhaps unwittingly when he reveals in *Triumphant Democracy*, "The moral to be drawn . . . is this: Seek ye first the education of the people, and all other political blessings will be added to you." (pg 119) For who? Who is the recipient of these blessings? Don't the political blessings accrue to the Rantouls and Carnegies and their monopolistic corporations which gain their status and protection by charters from the State? Carnegie reveals the game somewhat and is convinced that everything falls into place once the emphasis is put on education when he says, "The quarrels of party, the game of politics. . . are but surface affairs of little moment. The education of the people is the real underlying work for earnest men who would best serve their country." An investment implies a return at some future time and Carnegie, shrewd businessman he was, understood that investing in education guaranteed a great return for those of his ilk by diverting talent from enterprises that would conflict with those that held the great monopolies . . . just as with Rantoul and company in

Beverly. Gold for the few . . . Education for the many.

THE GREAT DIVERSION OF HUMANITY

The same pattern that we see in Beverly, we see on a larger scale in the world, with the rich and powerful. The wealthy and powerful supporting and backing education with hardly a peep from the working class 'demanding education'. What is happening here?

The historical context serves us well. In the latter half of the 19th century, America was on the verge of having the greatest industrial output in the world. This is not debatable. What still seems to be debated is how this came about. The 'how' has many layers that are worthy of discussion but for our purposes we must narrow down an aspect of this phenomenon that is highly remarkable. The conclusion is inescapable and frightening at the same time.

Those that held the wealth shunted, as a river with many tributaries, to the side any competition they may have had from worthy hard working folk into a field that was not profitable called education. This unprofitable field was then, in turn, used as a preparation ground for needed workers in the profitable fields of the elite.

The great combinations, as Carnegie would call the monopolies, were born at this time, the great monoliths of industry that required human fodder to work in their mills and their factories day and night. The thing that Beverly and the Massachusetts Board of Education and Carnegie and Rockefeller and all the usual suspects were interested in was absolutely no competition in their monopolistic empires in their Great Work which they were on the cusp of. Behind it all were industrialists that only had in mind 'education' for the poor and wealth for them and theirs. Every law, every injunction, every book and every learned man that came along evangelizing the masses, was an agent, wittingly and unwittingly, of the industrial elite that had a vested interest in their own profits. Steak for the rich and crumbs for the poor. Isn't it interesting that compulsory schooling and the great monopolies came about at the same time? The school also was necessary to build a unique skill in the human being for preparation in order to work in the mills of the industrialists. The capacity to tolerate and endure boredom and non-sensical work was needed and schooling fit the bill. This would prepare the individual for long, grueling, boring hours at the factory.

This push for mass education by the elite should actually be called The Great Diversion of Humanity, when the masses were shunted into another course that was non-threatening to those same elite. Because of this great concentration of wealth in a few hands the Corporation as *the* mode of commerce came into being and was given the breath of life in that century. The specter of education, which would feed the Corporation, was appalling to the working class as I have shown but through force of law it became the way of life for all around the globe.

What is lost to us 'moderns' is the epic scale of this battle between rich and poor. The working class, at that time, had the ability to see through the machinations and double dealing that was going on and they resisted the change. This aspect obviously has been filtered out and lost to us by both deception and neglect. Because a true sense of what really went on would raise obvious questions. Why was there resistance from the poor and why were the rich so fanatical about seeing to the education of the working class?

THE CORPORATION HATCHED

In order to have an individual accept this mode of living (individualism vs corporatism) of working in the factory system, he had to be trained in a certain way. The essence of corporatism is *submergence* of the individual. The individual must submit his individuality into the corporate body which has an overriding goal that is the dominant direction. He or she had to be prepared. This was the undertaking of the educational Architects. In order for the corporation to be the fundamental instrument of trade for all humanity these theorists really borrowed their material from a much earlier time. The submergence of individuality into the factory system and thereby the corporate body is not new. The minimization of individuality was the frontispiece to monastic life in the Middle Ages.

The grand idea that St. Benedict of Nursia had, was a sort of synthesis of old Roman ideas of commerce mixed in with Christianity. The monastery was the body that would serve God in the world. Each person or monk, in the monastery, submerged their identities into this one common goal. St. Benedict's 'handbook' for monastic life, *The Rule of St. Benedict* was a piece of handicraft in accomplishing this. In the succeeding centuries after Benedict's own (5th century), his Rule became the standard for the monastery. With the help of Pope Gregory in the 6th century, most monasteries fell under the principles set down in the *Rule of St. Benedict*.

We must keep in mind that this type of lifestyle devoted to God's work was one that, previously to Benedict, was highly fragmented and unorganized. The proliferation of the 'desert monks' in the 3rd and 4th centuries, informs us that the monastery was yet a thing of the future though there were hints of organization coming. Athanasius was compelled to say that "the desert became a city" when masses of men and women sought to copy the lifestyle of the Desert Father himself, Anthony the Great. Every monastery had its own rule of operation and Benedict himself was well aware of this. With his Rule he crystallized the important points that eventually became an organizing force for this raw horde of manpower, creating a highly efficient machine that was able to impose its will (convert) on to Britain and Germany. Bruce Brown in his book the *History of the Corporation* says this, "The Benedictine Rule is a blueprint for incorporating the spirit of God. Hundreds of rules had been written before, but Benedict was the one who got it right. He was the first to craft a tolerable yoke for the corporation's human attendants and effectively harness their energies toward a collective goal. Before Benedict, the ideal of Christian asceticism was probably best expressed by St. Simeon Stylites, who spent 35 years living alone at the top of a narrow pillar. Benedict vanquished this ideal forever, and replaced it with the ideal of physical moderation and coordinated labor."

What was the immediate goal of this new Rule? To channel and pre-empt a persons life goal and then shaping it to conform to the higher goal of the monastery or corporate body. This could only be done by treating the individual a certain way. As Brown says in Chapter 2 of *History of the Corporation*, "Benedict's fundamental aim was to destroy the independence, and with it the individuality, of the monks, so that they could be merged into the greater corporate persona. "Let no one presume to give or receive anything without leave of the abbot, or retain anything as his own. He should have nothing at all," the Benedictine Rule reads. "For indeed it is not allowed to the monks to have bodies or wills in their own power. But for all things necessary they must look to the abbot of the monastery."" The abbot after all was God's representative in the flesh. Here is Brown again from chapter 2, "The abbot – the chief executive officer or CEO in modern corporate argot – was the cornerstone of Benedict's monastic edifice. Elected for life by the members of the monastery, his power was virtually unlimited, except that it might not directly contradict the Rule. His selection was seen as the work of the Holy Spirit, expressly and fervently prayed for in the hymn, Veni, Creator Spiritus ("Come down, Creator Spirit"). His instructions came as from God, and he was regarded as the representative of Jesus within his monastery."

This is all well and good but surely there must have been a greater cause for all this organization. The great energy expended in this organizing must have had some higher purpose than keeping monks in line. Another way of looking at this is to ask,'Was this done strictly for the benefit of the monk and his personal salvation or was there an ulterior motive for systematizing and codifying the lifestyles of great numbers of men and women?' The evidence points to higher, covert designs. . .

FOR THE SAKE OF GOD OR MAN?

In the *Encyclopaedia of Monasticism Volume 1*, by William M. Johnston we run into this quote: "In China, where patronage was a major source of income, Buddhist monasteries, partly *because of their production of wealth*, became associated with the nobility and *have always been associated with wealthy and powerful families.*"(italics mine) This is a good introductory statement because it broaches the two major themes of this section:

1) The fact that monasteries have a curious history of being supported by the wealthy.

2) The production of wealth by monasteries

These two facts are inextricable from each other. Johnston, in his encyclopedia, claims that the economic sphere that the Buddhist monasteries delved in was wide ranging and varied: " Religious festivals and market fairs were frequently held in the same place in China, and Buddhist monks were very active in trading. Some of the commercial activities Chinese Buddhist monks were engaged in include tea production, salt trade, silver smelting, pawnshops and lotteries . . . Buddhist monasteries held auctions, produced paper, ink stick and ink stones; and were actively engaged in the printing and production of books. Certain monasteries became well known as medical dispensaries . . . Other monasteries produced silk, selling it at a profit. Still others engaged in embroidery practices (convents were the primary producers in this area), and some produced lead powder, operated hostels, and made and sold food."

Not only that but Johnston goes on to explain how the monasteries undertook services that were capital intensive, that is, services that the common folk could not undertake due to the expense. Mainly such things as oil presses, which also required technical knowledge, and milling of grains which the monasteries then sold to the populace. Milling in particular was a primary source of income to the monasteries during the Sung period (960-1279) for instance. But oil production was wide ranging and had applications in many fields such as cooking, lighting and cosmetics; in ship construction; in the manufacture of weapons and lacquered goods; in rust prevention; in construction and in the manufacture of ink. The monasteries held this monopoly.

It truly is dizzying to think of every pie the monasteries in the East had their fingers in. What is not so widely known is the multifarious nature of the monasteries in the West. In the book *Sacred Trust: The Medieval Church as an Economic Firm* the authors authenticate the extent to which the monasteries were involved in various fields of economic endeavor. One such field was sheep-herding and its attendant product, wool: "Several historical accounts indicate that monastic expansion into the wool trade was substantial, and that the monasteries generated enormous demand for their wool because of its high quality. One such account is contained in the commercial list of English monasteries collected by Pegolotti, an Italian businessman. The list records that the finest wool was produced by Tintern Abbey, Dore Abbey and Stanfield Abbey. Their wool commanded a price of 28 marks per sack compared with a price of 7 marks per sack of low quality wool." In France, the Cistercians were world renowned for their wine making abilities.

The medieval historian Jacques Le Goff claims that monasteries gave out loans secured by real property until the 12th century. He says in his study of usury in the middle ages, *Your Money or Your Life*, "Certain monasteries for their part, offered types of credit, especially the mortgage, which was censured at the end of the 12th century."This is interesting because during the 12th century another group began to be involved in that very avocation, and they were known as the Knights Templar. If this is true we have a succession of the banking privilege that was undertaken by monasteries until the 12th century and then handed over to the Knights Templar and their monasteries. This function of banking was also undertaken in the East in the Buddhist monasteries. Johnston from his Encyclopedia of Monasticism: "By at least the 6th century Chinese Buddhists developed what came to be known as the 'Inexhaustible Treasuries' — storehouses of gifts, goods and items of value. Loans from these treasuries were regularly lent out to merchants at high interest rates and generated immense profits for many Chinese Buddhist monasteries." Back in the West the very same thing became a science under the Knights Templar who established international banking with their system of using paper or checks that could be drawn against an account that was held in one of their depository/fortresses. This innovation created a great deal of flexibility in transfers and hastened economic growth. As James Wasserman writes in his *Templars and Assassins*, "Funds deposited with the Order in Europe could be claimed on arrival in the Holy Land as needed."

Whatever could be marketed, it seemed the monastics took it upon themselves to develop and sell. The keen eye of the monastics in this respect can be seen even for the food item of chocolate. When Cortes conquered Mexico the monks with him sent back the cocoa beans to Europe. Chocolate making employed many a nun at many a convent. The monasteries also made chocolate, so much so that the small room over the cloisters was known as the chocolate room, where chocolate was made and tasted.

It would seem that this brief survey of monasteries in

their enterprises would be an excellent portfolio to invest in if one had the funds to do so. The contention here is that it indeed was invested in to a great degree by the nobility and monarchies of the world. But somehow this is seen as 'patronage' by modern historians, when in fact it was an investment vehicle for the wealthy. There was a return on these investments to those who bequeathed gifts and lands to these monasteries. They were nothing but workhouses and factories for the poor for raw material production and manufacturing.

There are two medieval facts that have been glossed over but which corroborate this. First, the problem of the oblates. The story of parents dedicating their child or children to the monastic Order was not a spiritual sacrifice but a reflection of the economic deprivation for many people at that time. The same thing occurred with those of an older age. Many men and women went into these Orders because of economic necessity. It was a case of 'getting a job' which was relatively secure for the times. In other words it meant bread on the table rather than risking your life in establishing your skill as a business which probably could not compete with the monopolistic powerhouse known as the monastery. This is much like today where everyone 'gets a job' rather than developing and then marketing their skill which is their love or their essence as a person. Secondly, there is the matter of the *conversi*. This will turn out to be like a wart on the nose of an otherwise beautiful woman if it is investigated in depth by historians. When most people think of monkdom we have a picture of monks praying, reading, studying and singing psalms. Yes, we also got the idea that they worked in their gardens. This, however, is not the complete picture. There was a whole other strata of people in those monasteries called conversi, that had completely different functions from these choir monks which we are more familiar with. The conversi were the workers, the production line and were recruited from the common people to work on the granges, which were the outlying areas of a monastery that were for economic production. Though they dressed like monks they did not share the same duties of the choir monks who we are more familiar with. In fact, the conversi outnumbered the choir monks in most monasteries. The authors of Sacred Trust write, "At Rievaulx in 1167, for example, there were approximately 500 lay brothers as compared with 140, whereas Pontigny had 300 lay brothers and only one third as many choir monks . . . at Himmerod in 1224 there were 200 lay brothers and only 60 choir monks. Not only did these monks have separate duties, they were also housed separately, and they were set apart from the choir monks by a screen at services." These lay brothers or conversi, as we see, were laborers for the monastery in its particular enterprise.

Remarkably the connection is never made between the patronage of the wealthy and the economic output of the monasteries by scholars. Karen Stober, the author of *Late Medieval Monasteries and Their Patrons,* is typical of the attitude by today's scholars when she says, "The spiritual benefits which the patrons of religious houses could expect in return for their patronage were normally the chief motivation behind monastic endowment." We are led to believe that these rich and super rich were exclusively motivated by spiritual reasons and not monetary. Again she says, "Prayers for the patron's soul, and the burial of his body, were certainly the nucleus of the privileges a lay patron enjoyed." (pg72 and 74 of Late Medieval Monasteries- Stober) This is the common belief but ironically these same scholars uncover evidence that is anomalous to their theory. In her book Stober chronicles the stories of five families that endowed various monasteries. One can't help but notice that once a family was given the rights to a piece of land by monarchical decree that family would in turn give a piece of that land to the building of a monastery. Then an interesting thing happens. Take the case of the Montagues. They were given their land by William the Conqueror in the 11th century way back in the mists of time; they in turn gave some of it away for the establishing of a monastery. This family was not wealthy nor high-aristocracy, but yet an astounding thing happens— in two centuries time when we meet up with them again in the 14th century, they are fabulously wealthy and now have many more monasteries under their patronage. Edward the 3rd granted them a monastery that had reverted to the crown and now he was granting this family a charter for it in which is stated the Montagues had the right to "ordain and dispose, as shall seem best for their own convenience and the usefulness of the priory, *the issues and profits thence proceeding* . . .(italics mine) Stober doesn't seem to notice this association that patronage equals profits as is clear from the preceding but she at least records the incomes of some of the monasteries under the patronage of these various families and surprise, surprise they were profitable . . . some very profitable; still, no connection is made behind the patronage, only that the patrons are overly concerned about their spiritual life. It rather should be re-termed as startup capital or costs . . .

NOTHING NEW UNDER THE SUN

In essence, the corporation is not new. The thing that distinguishes the modern corporation is it's global dominance and primary means of trade in the world.

To sum this up we must try to see this whole thing as a problem which had to be solved. The problem was this for the elite: How do we extend this successful venture we call monasticism, which is really cheap labor and suppression of competition, to a worldwide universal scale so that we can restrict and then dominate and monopolize access to all the worlds resources and industries? Though monasticism was widespread it was not as breathtakingly universal as the corporation is today. The breeding ground for the universality of the corporation had to be something in itself that was universal— public schooling. The method for doing this took time because the path had to be cleared by philosophers of the first rate such as Hegel and Kant. As we will see in the next volume of *Seven Pillars,* Hegel created the metaphysical justification for this acceptance by mankind of universal education and Kant provided the vital epistemological apparatus that was used to create the modern, planned individual. His philosophy was the basic tool used for manipulating the human mind to make it more *sociable,* as we heard from many of the apostles of education at the beginning of the chapter.

Also, we will find out that monasticism served as somewhat of a laboratory for the perfection of the techniques that would be used in a universal setting like the modern classroom. For, education was to be the instrument through which the promise of the Serpent in the Garden of Eden, and later Plato's dream, would be fulfilled. A promise of salvation for man by creating heaven on earth. At least for the few . . .

HEALTH PILLAR: FOR THOSE WHO HAVE EYES TO SEE

6

To the medical establishment, there was something very unnerving about the discovery. When the good doctor made the discovery he thought it a great boon for humanity and was puzzled by the response from his peers. Perhaps the good doctor hadn't thought out the consequences and repercussions of his discovery. Perhaps his peers had worked out these implications and were upset at the eventual outcome of this discovery of the good doctor. Perhaps we could even empathize with their plight. After all, who would want to be labeled redundant? For the fact of the matter is, if the central discovery of Dr. William Bates were perfected and refined, there could only be one conclusion: The power and influence of the current medical system would be greatly diminished . . .

PRELUDE TO THE CAUSE OF ALL SICKNESS

In 1885 an obscure physician, William Bates (born 1860) of New York, began his medical practice. It began innocuously enough, until a patient came in who happened to have a slight degree of myopia or near-sightedness. Then, as with most discoveries throughout history, serendipity struck. He was not searching for it–*it* came to him.

The prevailing theory at that time was the same as it is today. Myopia (nearsightedness) is an inherited or rather, a 'genetic' disorder. Cause unknown. The treatment as it still stands to this day was a) the diagnosis through various eye tests, and, b) the prognosis or prescription, which consists of a pair of lenses attached to a frame that you place on your nose until the day you die. In medical pathology texts it is common to run into the phrase 'aetiology unknown' which means origin or cause unknown— in other words, untreatable or no cure, unless you consider eyeglasses as a cure..

As he was testing the eyes of that particular patient, he began to notice something strange. The eyesight of the patient was changing right in front of his eyes. In fact, at one point the patients eyesight returned to normal—for a short time. This was impossible according to his training and the prevailing expert opinion of the time. In fact, he confirmed the patient was not always nearsighted; his sight was somewhat dynamic, changing according to.....according to something. But what? Was it just a fluke or could he manipulate it? When the patient was looking at a blank wall and not trying to see anything, his eyes would return to normal–for a short time. What could this be about? In all his training, he was not told about this. Eye defects were supposed to be irreversible. The same prognosis holds today.

Thinking he was on to something, he encouraged the patient to go without his glasses. A funny thing happened; the patient's sight returned to normal–this time permanently.

He was able to duplicate this in other patients with vision problems. He even helped fellow doctors improve their sight while he was with the NewYork Post Graduate Medical School and Hospital. Myopia reversed. Not only that, but hyperopia (far sightedness) and astigmatism.

The story should have ended like this: The medical profession bestowed great honors upon him and he was lauded far and wide for his discovery as this good news was instantly propagated throughout the world and utilized for the good of all mankind. Instead we have this from the Scientific American of January 12, 1918: "Bates' remarkable experiments on the eyes of animals and the startling conclusions that he has drawn from them have, as yet, attracted comparatively little attention. Reported only in a *few isolated* articles, they have not yet found their way into the general literature of the subject and have *scarcely been heard of by the lay public.*"(italics mine) From Better Eyesight magazine, April 1923: "When Dr. Bates explained and illustrated this (his findings) to his doctor friends, it disturbed them greatly. The surgeon who had charge of the laboratory came to him and said, 'Do you know that you have proven that Helmholtz is wrong and furthermore if you wish to be accepted by scientific men you will have to show how or why he blundered?'"

Yes, his findings flatly contradicted the establishment theories and he was castigated for it. These theories were not laid down by lightweights; we have some big names here. In particular, Herman Helmholtz. But really, the punishment does not seem to fit the crime; why wouldn't they at least try to verify his claims? This is from the May, 1921 Journal of the Allied Medical Associations: "The facts came to the knowledge of the head of the institution, a Dr. Roosa, one of the most prominent ophthalmologists of the day, and were regarded as highly discreditable, since Donders and the other masters of ophthalmology had declared that myopia was irreversible. Dr. Bates was accordingly expelled from the faculty, even the privilege of resignation being denied him." Why all the long faces from these scientific men? Why do we see such zeal in carrying out their persecution of Bates? It is because Bates stumbled on to something that was not immediately evident. When the implications are drawn out and made evident, it becomes clear that Bates held the ignition switch to a destructive bomb that threatened to destroy the establishment of medicine as we know it. When the establishment finally put two and two together the assault on Bates began and has really never ended. This underlying, explosive premise was the explanation for their disproportionate persecution but it also serves as evidence against them.

We can't help but seeing parallels in other, more illustrious cases. One could almost hear the voice of Galileo, through the centuries, to his persecutors– "Just look through the telescope." Or, in the case of Dr. Bates, "Just look through the ophthalmoscope." But they wouldn't look . . . in either case. Strangely, this seems to be a pattern with discoverers and their findings when presenting them to the establishment. What was the establishment so afraid of ?

ORIGINS

Every wave and every wind of doctrine that carries and exerts its influence upon the masses has a distinct point of origin. Even if that origin is mistaken in its logic it still can wend its way into a system of thought and become the

Archimedean point of that system, from which all things are judged. Hermann Helmholtz was (and still is) in the pantheon of science at the time Dr. Bates made his discovery. Helmholtz was trained as a physician, he later became professor of physics. There is barely a field of knowledge that has not been affected by his work. He defined the theorems of fluid dynamics which are still in use today. The law of the conservation of energy coalesced under his writings. Not only did he investigate properties of sound and acoustics but he also invented (independently of Charles Babbage) the ophthalmoscope. His students, just to name a few were Max Planck, Wilhelm Wundt and Heinrich Hertz; these were men of renown in their fields. This just skims the surface of his influence. If a scientist, at that time, took issue with Helmholtz, it was akin to a Rabbi arguing with Moses about the Decalogue.

In one of his forays he thought he discovered how the eyeball accommodated. When we change focus from something we see in the distance to an object that is close to us, our ability to maintain clear sight depends on a mechanism of adjustment in our eye. This is what is known as accommodation. Helmholtz believed it was the lens structure that did this. The lens would change its shape by means of the ciliary muscle surrounding it, and thereby refract light and focus it on to the retina. The following in figure 1 is the normal eyeball in normal vision:

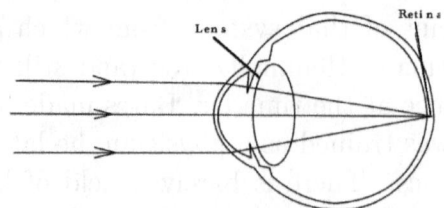

Fig 1.

As we can see, the light rays are refracted by the lens and converge directly onto the retina. The result is normal vision. Now according to Helmholtzs' theory, when we accommodate, the lens itself is what is responsible for the proper refraction of the light rays onto the retina. So with variations in our sight, the lens will alternately widen or become thinner depending on where we are looking.

Our sight is constantly accommodating to our environment. In the figure below, to the left, we have the eye focusing on something in the distance, hence, the thinness of the lens. This refracts light properly onto the retina. The eye to the right is focusing on something at the near point; hence the width of the lens allowing proper refraction onto the retina. This flexibility of the lens, according to Helmholtz, is what allows us to see clearly; it is the means of accommodation.   Fig. 2

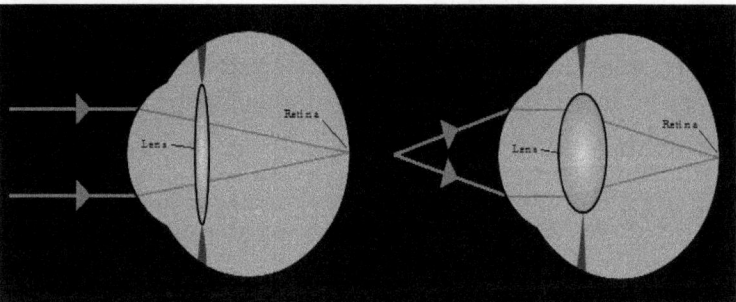

In nearsightedness (myopia) and farsightedness (hyperopia) the light rays do not hit the retina as they should. This is illustrated below in Figure 3; the eye at the top demonstrates hyperopia. Notice the point of refraction is beyond the retina. This will cause blur for objects close by. The middle eyeball demonstrates proper refraction; as you can see, the light lands perfectly onto the retina. The eyeball at the bottom is myopic. The light falls short of the retina causing blur while viewing distant objects.

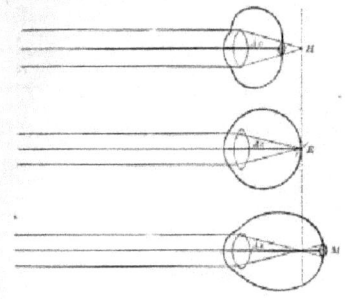

Fig. 3

To remedy the error of the refraction, a lens from outside the eye structure can bend the light so that the rays focus properly on the retina. We can see this in the image of a myopic eye on the next page in fig.4. In myopia the light comes to a convergence just short of the retina causing blur. The lens or eyeglasses in front of the eye refocuses the light on to the retina and the vision is corrected due to this lens in front of the eye.

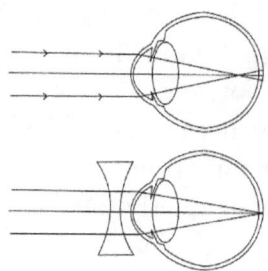

Fig. 4

Even though this was set down by the Goliath named Helmholtz and the legions have followed the theory to this very day, Dr. Bates proved him wrong. Bates also has something that the orthodoxy will not pay attention to—testimonials of people who have had their eyesight improved.

A BRAVE NEW WAY TO SEE

Though it is not the book he is well known for, Aldous Huxley wrote a book, *The Art of Seeing*, which is just as important as his other works. He wrote it to, " repay a debt of gratitude–gratitude to the pioneer of visual education, the late Dr. W. H. Bates." You see, Mr. Huxley was nearly blind due to a disease he had contracted when he was sixteen years old. In one eye he was only capable of light perception while the other eye could barely make out letters. He could only read with a powerful magnifying glass and later with spectacles provided that he kept his good eye dilated with atropine, a drug that paralyzes the ciliary muscle of the eye. In time, he said, " I found the task of reading increasingly difficult and fatiguing. There could be no doubt of it: my capacity to see was steadily and quite rapidly failing." His anxiety was great as he, "was wondering apprehensively what on earth I could do, if reading were to become impossible."

Open-minded as he was, he decided to try out an alternative method he had heard about. What did he have to lose? The contemporary treatment of his ailment had not helped nor given him hope. He happened upon a teacher who taught the principles discovered by Dr. Bates. This teacher showed him the truth about eyesight and he commenced upon a program to restore his sight. This was the result: "Within a couple of months I was reading without spectacles...the chronic tensions and spells of complete exhaustion, were things of the past...my vision is about twice as good as it used to be when I wore spectacles." And even more astounding, his bad eye which could only distinguish light from darkness, could now read print. No operation was performed on him, he just acted upon the principles that Dr. Bates had discovered.

Huxley understood well what Dr. Bates was up against; he wrote, "In spite of the long period during which it has been known, in spite of the quality and quantity of the results obtained through its employment by competent instructors, Dr. Bates' technique still remains unrecognized by the medical and optometrical professions." Even more so, as a result of his dramatic change in vision, he realized the way that establishment medicine looked at the individual was incomplete. He believed that Bates' approach brought back the ancient but correct philosophy of healing the body—*vis medicatrix naturae*. Translated, it means 'the healing power of nature' but the connotation of the phrase has more depth to it than is obvious. To illustrate with an example is better and Huxley provides us with one, that of a broken leg. When a person's leg is broken, doctors do not heal the bone. What they do is provide an *environment* that is safe and secure so that the bone will be able to heal itself. The doctors only are aids in healing, the body does the rest. In this light, we can understand why a cast for a broken leg comes off; the bone is healed. There is no doctor in the world in their right mind that would prescribe the cast permanently as a remedy for a broken bone. So Aldous Huxley asks the question, "If such things can be done for crippled legs, why should it not be possible to do something analogous for defective eyes? . . .to this the orthodox theory provides no answer." That is, why are they given permanent crutches like eyeglasses? The eyes are as much a part of the body as the bones so why do they have different methods of treatment. One method of treatment as in the broken bone results in *cure* the other results in a *palliative* treatment - - - eyeglasses, which are not a cure.

Huxley along with Bates believed that the body is a unity and that the same principle of healing should be used whether it is for the eyes or the bone or the skin or an organ. This principle is used in many healing modalities in the East and by holistic practitioners as an age-old praxis. Unfortunately, most of western medicine is palliative in it's nature; it does not cure. Instead the symptom is treated and not the cause which would result in cure. If we were to apply this philosophy to a person who had a broken leg we would give pain killers for his pain and provide him with all sorts of implements for getting about; all the while his leg is still broken and not set in a cast to allow for healing but nevertheless it is still deemed a success because his symptoms, which were pain and lack of mobility, were treated. How absurd would this be and in what type of righteous anger would a western doctor have if he encountered such a scene:

"Why, you are not treating the cause (and thereby effecting the cure), you are only treating the symptom!" Yes, this they would all exclaim not understanding that everything they do is *palliative* as in the absurd example we have given. The only area that they effect *cure* is in broken limbs. To seek palliatives is a persons prerogative but one should run from those who peddle such things. It is wise and common sense to seek cure and, in eyesight, this is just what Dr. Bates did.

THE ELEPHANT IN THE ROOM

When Dr. Bates made his discovery and began reversing myopia and hyperopia in patients, he found he had to abandon the reigning theory of the day. This meant he was opposing the establishment and the mighty Helmholtz himself. To put it simply, what he found was that *clarity of sight depends upon the shape of the entire eyeball not the shape of the lens.*

If you take the time to look at figure 3 you will notice something very interesting and also something that completely escapes the orthodox mindset. In every person that has myopia their eyeball is slightly longer than a normal eyeball. In every person that is hyperbolic or farsighted the eyeball is shorter than the normal eyeball. It is simply a principle of refraction. The defect of vision is due to the length of the eyeball. Curiously, the orthodoxy agree that this is what is causing the defective vision.

However, the orthodoxy has no explanation for the structure being either long or short, in a word it is a genetic abnormality. As Dr. Bates found, the length of the eyeball is not hereditary or genetic or some unaccounted for phenomenon. *The length of the eyeball can be changed and is due to its surrounding anatomy.* The length of the eyeball according to Dr. Bates was so flexible that it could change from instant to instant. How is this so? It is the elephant in the room; something so obvious yet disregarded.

Surrounding each eye is a set of muscles that control the movement of the eyeball in every which way possible. And here is the crucial discovery by Dr. Bates: *these same muscles also control accommodation.* In other words they are what is responsible for the length of the eyeball. It is dynamic and instantaneous and true. Through the conduit of the optic nerve, the musculature adjusts for all viewing situations. The optic nerve, of course, is connected to the brain. The muscles surround the eyeball globally. There are six:

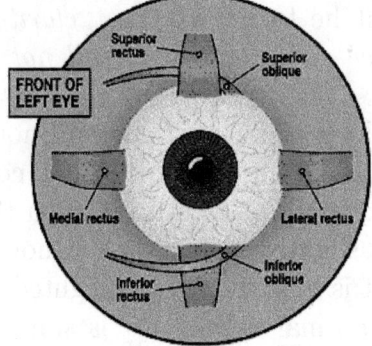

When we adjust our vision for near or far focusing the musculature configures the eyeball into a shape, either extending the length or shortening the length of it. Dr. Bates did not discover the muscles surrounding the eye, this was obviously a known fact. What he did discover was that the muscles made the eyeball short or long depending on the viewing circumstance. This lengthening and shortening by means of the surrounding muscles was how the eyeball accommodated. But since Helmholtz said that accommodation occurred only through the lens, there could then be no further inquiry into accommodation. The law had been laid down. But Dr. Bates ran into some anomalies that could not be accounted for under the prevailing theory of Helmholtz. And he did what every good scientist should do; either revamp the old theory or discard it. But perhaps establishment science is based more on faith in authority than on reason. Dr. Bates followed reason.

As the establishment theory goes, our ability to see near and far is due to the action of the lens. So the lens either gets wider or thinner depending on our focus. Keep in mind according to establishment thinking this action is still going on with those that have near or far vision. It's just that those people have an additional problem of refraction ,or bending of light rays, and that is the length of the eyeball, of which, cause is unknown. This is where Dr. Bates diverges with the establishment through his accumulated observations. The facts that prevailed against the establishment theory were there for everyone to see.

People who had their lenses removed due to cataracts were still accommodating. How could this be if the lens was solely responsible for accommodation? Bates observed these anomalies repeatedly. If the thing responsible for focus, the lens, has been removed and people are still able to focus or accommodate there must be some other mechanism of focus. This finding of Bates in itself should have destroyed the old theory.

In his extensive experiments upon the eyes of animals, he proved that accommodation was due to the extrinsic muscles of the eye. He was able to, in his words, "produce or prevent accommodation at will, to produce myopia, hyperopia and astigmatism, or to prevent these conditions." These findings were even published in medical journals. In his prelude to a study he published in the New York Medical Journal he wrote, "In most textbooks on ophthalmology it is clearly stated that errors of refraction are incurable, and that relief of the symptoms can be obtained only with the aid of glasses. My investigations during the past twenty-five years have convinced me and others that errors of refraction can be cured by treatment without glasses." (New York Medical Journal May 8, 1915 vol. 101 no.19 pp.925-933) He went on to explain the how and the why of his experiments which he performed on fish and other lab animals. By electrically stimulating the nerve connected to any muscle of the eyeball he was able to manipulate the eyeball at will. One of the surrounding muscles of the eye was paralyzed with atropine. No amount of electrical stimulation of this muscle produced accommodation. Sometimes the muscle was severed and then sewn back. When it was severed, no accommodation *whatsoever*. When sewn back, accommodation returned. He repeated this hundreds of times and got the same result. He clearly showed, through these experiments that Helmholtz was wrong and that, instead, it was the surrounding musculature that was responsible for accommodation.

Clearly, these were repeatable experiments; so why didn't anyone try to at least prove him wrong? The answer is simple - - - they would have obtained the same results as Bates did; there is no way around it. If that happened, Bates' theory would gain acceptance and his underlying thesis would be integrated into mainstream medicine. This was not what they wanted. The best thing to do was to ignore his results on the one hand and then to label him a quack on the other. But really it is not these experiments that had everyone worried; it was the underlying premise of Bates' theory that was damaging to the orthodoxy.

Since the method of accommodation had been found by Bates why was this mechanism not working in individuals with poor vision? The answer that Bates gave as to why the muscles around the eye acted the way they did had them all running for cover. They had no choice but to take up positions and label him a quack. If they didn't, the medical establishment would fall, or rather, all of science would have to be reworked . . .

A TESTIMONIAL FROM THE BACKYARD

At a young age I accepted the sentence handed down to me by the 'orthodoxy', as Huxley called them. I was diagnosed and then prognosed. The prescription was a pair of glasses and I was told that those metal frames would always come between me and blue skies and birds and God's green earth. Not only that but also a disfiguring of ones countenance, unless one could get contact lenses which were some sort of consolation in that they masked your infirmity. But people with normal vision didn't have to put on their eyes each morning like I did, now did they? There was no alternative; I had been to those who claimed to know the truth in this matter and if there was something to be known about eyesight it surely was the eye doctor. If someone came to me and said that my condition could be reversed I would give them a perfectly logical answer–How in the world did this little piece of information escape the minds of those who are in this profession? Surely they would have known of some other option . . .

But then it happened. It was an experience, in which I could not reconcile reality to my observations. I asked the experts and they had no explanation for it. If there ever was something that could be called a cold hard fact, this was it— staring me right in the face, mocking and capsizing my entrenched world view, as if saying "What are you going to do about me?" As with all things that don't seem to fit into one's world-view, a general loss of equilibrium followed, in which I felt a slight pressure in my head as if my brain were being stretched. This was far greater than realizing Santa doesn't exist when you are seven years old. I had to re-evaluate reality; strangely, I felt a loss.

I was not functional without my eyeglasses in day to day living and I definitely could not drive without them. The top letter in a Snellen eye-chart can be seen by someone with 20/20 vision from 200 feet away. I could barely see it from 10 feet away. I was doomed to wear these crutches forever until that fateful encounter with the 'cold hard fact'.

The cold hard fact happened on a rather hot day. On vacation, I was just happy to be away from work. It was the beginning of summer, so I was working on the pool getting it ready for the children who were running around playing with our two dogs in the backyard. After the work was done and everyone was content I decided to take a little break. Because of the heat of the day and the intense glare from the sun I lay my glasses on a tree stump. This is something I only did when going to bed; that's how much one comes to depend on them. I basked in the warm sun as I breathed in the smells of summer, the sound of the laughter of the children in the pool, the dogs barking; the blue sky and the birds singing and bees humming all conspired to put me into a deep state of repose. Everything was right in the world. My breath was steady and deep. I was completely relaxed as I sat there with my eyes closed. If I had known what was to happen next I might have kept my eyes closed, that's how disorienting it was. When I opened them, as they say, I could hardly believe my eyes. My sight was, to say the least,— PERFECT. Everything was sharp and in even greater detail than when I wore my glasses. I simply could not believe it, I could not remember how sight actually felt. This miracle lasted for almost a minute but the questions it raised lasted far longer. Now, I thought, here is a quirky thing. How can a person who has had corrective lenses for 15 years revert instantaneously to perfect vision?

BODY EQUALS MIND

The answer was given by Dr. Bates over a hundred years ago, and this is what had his enemies running for cover. The following quote is from chapter nine of his book *Perfect Sight Without Glasses*, "It has been demonstrated in thousands of cases that all abnormal action of the external muscles of the eyeball is accompanied by a *strain of effort to see*, and that with the *relief of this strain* the action of the muscles becomes normal and all errors of refraction disappear...this fact furnishes us with the means by which all these conditions, so long held to be irreversible, may be reversed."(italics mine)

Here is the CRUX: How do we relieve this strain that Bates is talking about? If we follow the anatomical structure of the eye we can see that all six muscles connect to the optic nerve. The optic nerve *connects to the brain*. The brain is where we *think*. Here is Dr. Bates again, "The cause of any error of refraction, of a squint, or of any other functional disturbance of the eye, is *simply a thought- a wrong thought-* and the reversal is as quick as the thought that relaxes."(italics mine) Now, that is the reason that the incident of complete clarity occurred to me in the backyard. My thoughts were changed; I was relaxed. As Dr. Bates says in chapter ten of the same book "In a fraction of a second the highest degrees of refractive error may be corrected." And also, "the strain to see, results in the production of errors of refraction; but its foundation lies in wrong habits of thought."(italics mine)

This was an astounding thing to say, especially at that time. The body and the mind were looked at, and still are today, as completely separate entities. They have no contact with each other and certainly the mind has little to do with physiology. The establishment has a completely antithetical approach to psycho-physiology and herein lies the potentially damaging threat to the physical scientist. If mind or thought is *primary* in matters of physiology where has our focus been for the last few hundred years? We may think ourselves advanced but are we really? It is just possible that mankind may look at this time period as barbaric and childish in its approach to human pathologies of the body. It may be that research has been intentionally diverted from this area, for there is a frightening aspect to it; at least to those who stand to lose, namely the medical profession.

A massive shift would occur if the focus of modern science were to change in this direction. If we use the business of eyesight as an example we can see that there is a whole industry built up around it. To put it simply, if harnessing our thoughts changes the body then there is a diminished need for those who treat the body. We must magnify this to see the logical outcome. The field of medicine is large and varied. The eye and its treatment is only a small piece of this large field. What if this is applied to all problems of the body? Certainly, there are other ailments. Imagine going to visit your eye doctor and instead of the usual battery of tests he says 'How are your thoughts?' Instead of fitting you with glasses, your mind is the focus of relaxation treatments; you are taught to use your mind in a positive way. Now project this into other areas of medicine. Instead of being diagnosed with cancer and going in for chemical oblivion, what if instead, you learned about thought integration. Sound strange? The funny thing is, this kind of thing has already happened and, in fact, always has.

Norman Cousins was an editor of the Saturday Review for thirty years, and came to write some rather thought provoking books that deal with this very subject of the mind and human disease. Cousins had a special vantage point in the topic, since he was diagnosed with a degenerative disease (ankylosing spondylitis) of which he was told there was no hope of recovery. His battle with this irreversible disease is detailed in his book, The Anatomy of an Illness. He did recover, though, but not through conventional medicine— he attributed it to massive doses of the Marx brother's movies. "I made the joyous discovery that ten minutes of genuine belly laughter had an anesthetic effect..." (*Anatomy of an Illness* Pg.43) Change the mind, change the body. This does not bode well for conventional medicine which treats the body as if it were alien, an enemy , a thing only to be measured, prodded and poked. A thing to be cajoled into changing when really the change must come from somewhere else.

There are countless cases of this happening but then again they are considered *anecdotal*. Conventional medicine is still somewhat rigid in its distinction between body and mind even though some doctors have made some headway in considering the mind as a source of physical pathologies, such as Dr. Herbert Benson, who wrote the book, *The Relaxation Response*, which was based on studies at Beth Israel Hospital and Harvard Medical School. But still when all is said and done it is only looked at as a part of the puzzle when it may be actually primary. This distinction has done a disservice to mankind and its cost in human well being can never be counted. You have cases where under hypnosis people have changed a physical condition. The evidence is so compelling that it can't be relegated anymore to the quackery bin.

LIAR LIAR

Thoughts, according to Bates, are what caused strain which in turn caused lowered vision. What kind of thoughts? "A patient 25 years old had no error of refraction (perfect vision) ...but if he said he was 26, or someone else said he was 26, he became myopic. The same thing happened when he said or tried to imagine he was 24. When he stated or remembered the truth his vision was normal, but when he stated or imagined an error he had an error of refraction (worse vision than normal)." This same phenomena occurred in the case of a little girl who told a lie. When she lied, in response to a question, she became myopic. When she gave truthful answers "the retina-scope indicated no error of refraction." Again, from *Perfect Sight Without Glasses*, "A child whose vision was ordinarily so acute that she could see the moons of Jupiter with the naked eye became myopic when asked to do a sum in mental arithmetic, mathematics being a subject which was extremely distasteful to her..."(pg. 58) Lies that we tell to ourselves; things we believe about ourselves that we shouldn't believe and things that make us upset; if we don't deal with these things they affect the body.

A thought can not be weighed. A thought can not be measured. In the scientific, mechanistic world view this ethereal object has no place. It surely has no bearing on the physical world such as the body. These are the same thoughts that men of the microscope and telescope assure themselves of as they go on whistling past the graveyard of past scientific dogmas. In fact each person that rose up and recognized the truth of the matter, such as William Bates, was systematically persecuted with a religious zealotry. The fact that their physics may be incomplete and lacking is too disconcerting for them. The fact that other cultures, which are 'primitive' in their estimation, may actually be much further advanced in their conceptual framework is incredible to them. Tibetans historically have said that thoughts are 'things'. The Huna philosophy of the Polynesians recognizes thoughts as real objects which can bring good or evil into the physical world.

Dr. Bates would have wholeheartedly agreed with this conclusion, for he saw through a multitude of observations that these thoughts cause strain; manifesting themselves in the physical world by means of tension in the muscles which surround the eye, squeezing the entire eyeball out of shape. This distortion of the eyeball causes light to fall where it shouldn't. The tenacity with which we hold onto these thoughts is the variable that can cause a 'permanent' distortion. This in turn gets diagnosed as myopia, or hyperopia or astigmatism. And you are told that it is irreversible. By surveying the case histories we can see that he discovered the eye could change in an instant according to the thought the person was holding. By inference we can see that if the wrong thought is held onto with tenacity for a long period of time, the physical distortion will also be for a greater period of time. The longer you hold this thought or complex of thoughts, the more it becomes second nature and you begin to not even realize it. The eyeball then takes on its new 'shape' as the habit has actually given birth to a new physical structure that is not in harmony with nature.

This 'new' structure now affects your life and you don't even realize its origin. This is the great mystery with pathologies of the body. They seem to come from 'nowhere' or 'aetiology unknown' in doctor parlance. Because we have been indoctrinated that the mind and body are separate, we treat the body, leaving the mind behind. That which has the answers we neglect; to the detriment of our bodies. We accept crutches when we really could be free. How do we get back to ourselves? How do we 'fix' the mind? Is it as easy as deciding to change our thoughts? Fortunately for us, Dr. Bates also found out that because the mind and body have this intimate connection they have a reciprocal effect on each other. Just as the mind can affect the body and effect a change in it so can the body affect the mind and effect change in it. It's a two way street. This is why the Bates method for restoring sight is associated with 'exercises', which they are not. In actuality, they are what the relaxed mind habitually does. By studying the habits of the relaxed mind and implementing these same habits in the daily lives of people with lowered vision, he was able to restore vision in countless subjects. Something like reverse-engineering. Behind these habits were three general principles of correct vision and possibly of life in general because in the end they are habits of a healthy mind . . .

Each principle has an attendant habit that is associated with it. These three habits, in turn, are all aspects of the *act of relaxation*, because strangely, we shall uncover that relaxation is an 'act' and that tension and strain are actually a 'freezing' of the organism. Tension is non-motion; in other words, death.

The three principle with their attendant habits are:

1. Relaxation; with its attendant habit–the breath or breathing. Then, in no particular order..

2. Movement; with its attendant habit of blinking and body movement

3. Centralization; with its attendant habit of sketching or tracing

CENTRALIZATION

In the book *Relearning to See* by Thomas Quackenbush, he relates something that Bates wrote in the May 18, 1915, issue of the New York Medical Journal: "The sole cause of all uncomplicated or functional errors of refraction is a conscious or an unconscious effort or strain to see. The only solution to this strain is relaxation. *Relaxation or rest of the eyes is accomplished only by centralization.*" Focus, but a very particular focus.

An illustration is best here and Thomas Quackenbush provides us with one from *Relearning to See*: "Close your eyes and pretend you are in a large auditorium. Imagine there are a hundred people encircling you about fifty feet away. Now, imagine there are fifty conversations going on simultaneously (two people per conversation). Try to comprehend all of the conversations at the same time. Do this for about thirty seconds...if you can!"

Mr. Quackenbush actually uses this with his vision students when he introduces centralization. After this little visualization exercise, he then surveys the students by asking them about their reactions to it. Here are some of the feelings and responses he has recorded: confusion, tension, irregular breath, breath stopping, chaos, body freezing, strain and blurred vision.

Centralization is a laser. It is paying attention to one conversation. In vision, it is paying attention to a particular aspect of the visual field. A person with normal vision does not see the 'whole' visual landscape in front of her anymore then she can hear every conversation in that auditorium. The eye with normal vision focuses on one small area at a time. How can a person with normal vision have a clear field of vision if they can only see one aspect or point of the visual landscape at a time ? The movements of the eye are rapid. This rapidity of movement is natural and not perceptible to the person with normal vision, thereby giving the illusion that the whole field is clear when really the eye is transitioning from point to point with amazing speed.

Diffusion, the opposite of centralization, is trying to listen to all conversations at once. In vision, it is trying to take in the whole field of vision all at once. This habit is actually a reflection of the state of mind of an individual. A diffused and muddled mind equals diffused vision. Trying to do too many tasks at once or thinking of many different things at once reflects itself in our vision. From *Relearning to See*, "Now, pretend you are listening to only one of the conversations. Let it be a pleasant conversation. Do this now for thirty seconds, and for the rest of your life ."

How do we implement this principle back into our life? We practice what is known as sketching. It is as if you are outlining an object with your eyes instead of a pencil — never staying on one point for more than a couple seconds. Sketching teaches us the habit of a normal eye. From Dr. Bates' Better Eyesight magazine, September 1927, "Shift your glance from one point to another. That is, when you look at a chair or any other object do not try to see the whole object at once. Look at a specific point then look at another...This is centralizing. Your head and eyes are moving all day long." Although it may seem odd to do at first; with time, they become second nature and are unnoticed. This particular exercise was my introduction to the Bates method. I began tracing or outlining letters from a book I was holding in front of me. Within a few minutes my vision began to clear.

The bigger picture is this: Centralizing means focusing on one thing at a time, whether in vision or in life. It is actually how we are made. But this is the exact opposite of what our culture teaches us. Anyone heard of multitasking? Do we know that we are actually creating tension when we engage in the wrong philosophy and that that tension eventually materializes? In other words, the tension becomes a physical manifestation. We are designed to do one thing at a time.

MOVEMENT

From Better Eyesight magazine, January 1924: "The normal eye is only at rest when it is moving..." Usually, when we think of something at rest we think of non-movement. But, strangely, this is not the case in nature. Nobody would say that a non-moving heart muscle is relaxing. This only illustrates that our ideas of relaxation may have to be re-examined. From Relearning to See, "While teaching students to improve their vision, Bates emphasized head movement. People who have blurred vision have a tight neck, head and shoulders. These tensions are caused by rigid staring and shallow or even stopped breath." The whole organism freezes. You can create blur in a person with normal vision, by having them stare at an object without blinking. Blinking releases the frozen eyeball from its stare.

As we saw with the example of the heart, it may be that everything has a cycle or frequency that is integral to its nature. It may be that relaxation itself is movement. Interestingly, the psychologist T. Ribot in his book, *The Psychology of Attention,* makes the point that a thing like attention, is not what it seems. When you think of paying attention you think of something that is unbroken, seamless; otherwise it wouldn't be attention right? "Let us here note a fact of considerable importance in the mechanism of attention. This real intermission in an apparent continuity alone renders possible any long attention."(pg. 10) In other words to keep attention we must break away every so often. He goes on to adduce examples and interestingly brings up the eyes. "If we keep our eyes fixed upon any single point, after awhile our vision becomes confused; a cloud is formed between the object and ourselves, and finally we see nothing at all. If we lay our hand flat upon a table motionless, and without pressure (for pressure itself is a movement), by slow degrees the sensation wears off, and finally disappears. The reason is, there is no perception without movement, be it ever so weak."(pg.17) Non-movement equals non-perception; and as we saw in the case of the heart, death. Non-movement is death. As Ribot put it, "Movement is the condition of change, which is a condition of consciousness."(pg.17)

Blinking is associated with movement. When we stare we want to freeze the world and tend not to blink; we want to lock in the world. Blinking breaks the stare or the freeze thereby encouraging movement. While studying people as they looked at normal pictures Bates noted, "In all cases where the sight was normal, blinking occurred almost every second." Better Eyesight magazine, September 1923: "Blinking is only another name for dodging. Dodging what? Dodging the harmful tendency to look steadily at things all the time." From the December, 1925 issue: "Blinking is necessary to maintain normal vision in the normal eye. When blinking is prevented the eyes become tired, and the vision very soon becomes worse . . . blinking is very important. It is not the brief periods of rest from closing the eyes which helps the sight so much, as the shifting or movements of the eyes. It should be repeatedly demonstrated that the eyes are only at rest when they are shifting (moving)."

Centralizing and blinking are all modes of movement. This movement is the natural state of the eyeball. The eye is only at rest when it is moving. And this movement, as we have seen, is relaxation. All the principles are really just an explication of what relaxation is, when speaking of the eye.

They are just reminders that this is the way things work in a normal eye. So, we relearn, in a sense, what we have forgotten. Through tension we learn new habits that escape our notice. Meanwhile, we dispense with healthy habits. This is a somatic reaction to stress of some kind. The body reacts to a stimulus and before too long we incorporate this reaction into our being which lead to inadequacies in our health. An indicator of this is the way we breathe.

RELAXATION

When we are relaxed our breath is different from our breath under tension. The person with lowered vision will invariably have breathing that is shallow and restricted. From Better Eyesight magazine, January 1923: "Many people with imperfect sight are benefited by breathing....at one time I experimented with a number of students. They became able to demonstrate that holding their breath was a strain and caused imperfect sight and fatigue, while the deep breathing at once gave them relief." Good breathing attends relaxation. When we are relaxed the breath is rhythmical and smooth. Bates also related a story of a man who through repetition of deep breathing had an improvement of vision that became more permanent. So, breath is really like our vision, it is an outcome of a relaxed mind. But by focusing on our breath we can induce a relaxed state of mind. Sort of 'reverse engineering' a relaxed state by manipulating the breath consciously. As Joy Manne says in her book, *Conscious Breathing*, "How we breathe affects what we feel, how we relate, how we live, how we think."

The wide variety of mental states each have a corresponding breathing pattern. As she says, the breath is actually a language with a distinct vocabulary. From Conscious

Breathing, "Breath language is a psychological language. All spoken languages are rich in expressions that relate our breath to our inner state of being. In English, we wait with bated breath. We catch our breath when we are exhausted. We hold our breath during moments of fear, anticipation, tension strain, anxiety, danger and excitement. And when we are at ease again we breathe freely." Emotional states affect our breathing. Our emotional states affect our vision. This was Bates' genius. But if we change the breath we can change the state of mind, thereby changing our vision.

This language of the breath is barely noticeable to us. It is because it is not something that we have to do consciously. It is done autonomically by our body. Because of this we take it for granted; it just happens. But we would do well to recognize this language which has substantial impact not just on our vision but on our health. From *Conscious Breathing*, "As our breath awareness develops, we realize that our breath is a language. It is a language that tells us how we are, moment by moment. When we do breathwork we learn its vocabulary. We learn the different features of breathing such as where it takes place in the body, its length, its degree of ease or tension; its lightness or heaviness; its quickness or slowness, shallowness or depth, its rhythm. We observe whether it is strong or weak, confident or fearful, flowing or restricted, tight or relaxed, comfortable or uncomfortable. Our breath brings up emotions, augments or diminishes sensations, evokes memories and in every way puts us into contact with ourselves...breath language speaks only the truth." That would be a good language to analyze.

THE BREATH IS EVERYWHERE

Now, Ms. Manne specializes in the field of breath-work

so we can appreciate her observations. What is interesting, however, is how the study of the breath turns up in unrelated fields of research. In the book *Yoga: Immortality and Freedom*, the philosopher and historian Mircea Eliade states, "The respiration of ordinary man is generally arrhythmic; it varies in accordance with external circumstances or with mental tension. This irregularity produces a dangerous psychic fluidity, with consequent instability and *diffusion of attention.*"(my italics) Sound familiar? Seems like Eliade was talking to William Bates. He continues, "respiration must be made rhythmical; if not in such a way that it can be forgotten entirely, at least in such a way that it no longer troubles us by its discontinuity. Hence, through *pranayama* one attempts to do away with the effort of respiration; rhythmic breathing must become so automatic that the yogin can forget it." As far as I know, Eliade had no knowledge of Dr. Bates and his method. It is interesting to see the same ideas presented though.

It doesn't end there, however. The literature on the subject of breath is wide and deep. Eliade was a historian and professor. Here we shall turn to a neuroscientist/pharmacologist, Candace Pert. In her book *Molecules of Emotion* she states, "Conscious breathing, the technique employed by both the yogi and the woman in labor, is extremely powerful. There is a wealth of data showing that changes in the rate and depth of breathing produce changes in the quantity and kind of peptides that are released from the brain stem. By bringing this process into consciousness and doing something to alter it- either holding your breath or breathing extra fast- you cause the peptides to diffuse rapidly throughout the cerebral spinal fluid in an attempt to restore homeostasis (the bodies feedback mechanism for restoring and maintaining balance). And since many of these peptides are endorphins, the body's natural opiates, as well as other kinds of pain relieving substances,you soon achieve a diminution of your pain. So it's no wonder that so many modalities, both ancient and New Age, have discovered the power of controlled breathing. The peptide-respiratory link is well documented. Virtually any peptide found anywhere else can be found in the respiratory center. This peptide substrate may provide the scientific rationale for the powerful healing effects of consciously controlled breath patterns."

So there is a conscious connection between our breath and endorphins which make us *feel* a certain way. Our mental states change according to the breath or vice versa. Joy Manne says, "Our breathing massages our organs. It keeps their energy flowing and thus it keeps them functioning effectively." What follows from all this? We can change our state of mind by consciously changing our breathing. Stress moves our breathing from our belly, where it should be, to our chest or worse, even higher, to what is known as 'clavicle breathing'. When we inhale, our belly should expand outwards. If the chest is expanding instead, our breathing is compromised and air is only getting into the top half of the lungs. Deep inhale ; belly out. Simple right? Not at first as the old shallow breathing from the top of the chest is hard to let go of.

SYNTHESIS

It must be stressed again that these habits, derived from the principles, arc not exercises. They are what the the person with normal vision *does.* The habits must become *un-*

conscious. The only way to do that is to incorporate them as much as possible in daily living. Here's a promise from Bates himself from Better Eyesight magazine, September 1927: "If you learn the fundamental principles of perfect sight and will consciously keep them in mind your defective vision will disappear...all errors of refraction are functional, therefore reversible...all defective vision is due to strain in some form. You can demonstrate to your own satisfaction that strain lowers vision. When you stare you strain. Look fixedly at one object for five seconds or longer without blinking or moving. What happens? The object blurs and finally disappears . . . strain is removed by relaxation. To use your eyes correctly all day long it is necessary that you:

1. Blink frequently. Staring is a strain and always lowers vision.

2. Shift your glance constantly from one point to another. Blink when transitioning to another point.

3. Your head and eyes are moving all day long.

Better Eyesight magazine December, 1927: "The normal eye does these things unconsciously and the imperfect eye must at first practice them consciously until it becomes an unconscious habit."

MOSES AND DR. BATES

All these principles however, are outcomes of a mind that is relaxed. A mind that is divided against itself seems to have a reaction upon the physical body. Remember Bates' research in this area when several of his patients were asked to lie. When they lied their physiology changed. Let us use a thought experiment here. What if, in fact, morality or ethical behaviour has a physical basis or dimension that has been, until now, overlooked? Could bad behaviour actually be bad for us, i.e. physiologically? We can imagine that it doesn't stop at lying; perhaps, covetousness, lust, cursing and adultery also have a negative effect on our bodies. The Decalogue of Moses may have greater dimensions to it in wisdom than we can possibly fathom. It may be that we are designed to act a certain way for our own physiological benefit. Why then wasn't this relationship revealed before? We can appreciate this if we understand the rhetorical axiom in which the message must fit the audience or occasion—it must be shaped according to the hearer not the deliverer. It's not like the Israelites would have understood the following: "Thou shalt not lie . . . because if you do, not only do you hurt someone else but you stimulate your endocrine system to produce ACTH from your pituitary which in turn stimulates your adrenal glands to produce excess cortisol which in turn affects the functionality of your organs,etc.—thereby hurting yourself." We shape a message according to our audience; children can't understand a message intended for adults, it must be modified.

Possibly we have been looking at ethics and morality the wrong way or in an incomplete way. It was long ago contended by Plato and Socrates that doing something immoral was more damaging to the individual performing the immoral act. When you hit someone out of anger it's obvious who is damaged right? But the Platonic argument has been that the person doing the hitting has been damaged as well, possibly even more so. This bit of insight has been generally glossed over perhaps because of the counter-intuitiveness of it or maybe the lack of evidence to bolster the argument. I believe we have that evidence today in the form of physiological responses in our body.

In most moral law we have a direction or orientation. What I mean is that we are prescribed a behaviour to follow so that we do not encroach upon another person and his property. The moral law always has a trajectory that implies another person. To illustrate, how much law or morality would there be if you were the only one on the planet? So we can see that most law has *the other* in mind. But what if morality were *bi-directional*? What if it affected us as well as the other person?

It is rather interesting at this point to bring up what the philosopher Socrates always contended— that wrongdoing affects us as much or more than it does the other to whom the wrong is done. In the dialogue of Plato known as *Gorgias*, Socrates defends one of his primary beliefs which is that to do wrong, ". . . is far more disgraceful and evil to the doer of the wrong than to me who am the sufferer."(section 509, *Gorgias*) And in the *Apology*, he actually warns his accusers that more harm would come to them than to him if they killed him. "Rest assured that if you kill me—since I am the person I say I am—you wouldn't harm me more than you harm yourselves."(*Apology* section 30) The affect on us as individuals is not as readily seen but still there— if we have the proper tools for measurement. We can talk about how it harms the soul and such but how does it do this? Possibly, through a lowering of physiological processes. In other words, wrongdoing may enervate or devitalize the human physiology which in turn affects the mind and its thought processes. In the example that Dr. Bates gave with the patients who lied, the stress of that act significantly altered the body's physiology. The fact that stress alters the body's physiology is not disputed today thanks to the work of Hans Selye and Franz Alexander in the first half of the 20th century but Dr. Bates preceded them all.

HAVE WE FOUND THE CAUSE OF ALL SICKNESS?

That the mind can influence physiology is beginning to be explored more by scientists but how deep does it go? To what extent can the mind transform/alter the body? We have seen what it does in eyesight but what about other pathologies? Well, there is no worse pathology than death itself. Walter Cannon was a prominent physiologist who taught at Harvard for over 30 years. He chronicled instances of strange yet illuminating import for mind/body interaction. He labeled a particular phenomena that kept creeping up calling it the *Voodoo death* phenomenon. These were cases that he compiled, where an alarming transformation overcame men or women in aboriginal societies, who had been "pointed at with the bone." The witch doctor in these societies would point a human thigh bone at a person for breaking some sort of taboo cursing him with some sort of punishment like death or injury of some sort.

In one case, where a Dr. Lambert was present, in a North Queensland Mission, a medicine man had to be persuaded to recant a curse that he had put on a man for fear the subject would die. Dr. Lambert performed an in depth examination and could find nothing wrong with the man yet he became steadily weaker all the while claiming he had been pointed at with the bone by the local witch doctor. Thereupon, Lambert took it upon himself to confront the witch doctor and finally had to threaten him with sanctions upon his food supply that the Mission had been assigning to that area.

When the witch doctor took back his 'curse', apologizing to the man personally, Lambert noticed an astonishing thing . . . the cursed man instantly became better and his vital signs, which had been deteriorating, became normal. Lambert reported another case to Cannon that did not end so well. This was about a Kanaka (a name Polynesians use to refer to themselves) that came to a hospital to tell a Dr. Clarke that soon, he (the Kanaka) would be dead due to a curse put on him. The same thing happens here also. The doctor does a thorough examination, including blood and stool samples, but as with the previous case, nothing was found yet the man dies within a few days. (*The Psychobiology of Mind-Body Healing* ch. 1, Ernest Rossi)

It is rather interesting that auto-suggestion and suggestion from an outside source have long been claimed to influence human behaviour but human physiology has been kept out of the picture. What is known as hypnosis is nothing but suggestion which is also used in scientific studies when a person or group of persons have been told that a certain pill will have 'thus and thus' benefit for their body. The strange thing is that a certain percentage of the group are physiologically affected by the pill even though the pill has nothing in it. The placebo effect has been well documented but it is still sometimes labeled 'anecdotal'.

Regarding the power of suggestion and the placebo effect, the classic case of Mr. Wright bears telling. Ernest Rossi, in his book has the best summary of this case in his book *The Psychobiology of Mind-Body Healing*. (pg. 3-7) First of all, Rossi makes the point that Mr. Wright's case was documented by at least two professionals in their respective fields, his physician Dr. Philip West and the psychologist Bruno Klopfer who was famously known for popularizing the Rorschach ink-blot test and writing the standard work about it. Now Mr. Wright was a cancer patient who was not responding to conventional treatments. His lymphosarcoma had advanced to the point where he had tumors the size of oranges in his neck, groin and stomach areas. According to Klopfer who chronicled the case, "The spleen and liver were enormous. The thoracic duct was obstructed, and between 1 and 2 liters of milky fluid had to be drawn from his chest every other day." At about this time the Medical Association was testing a new cancer drug, Krebiozen, and as luck would have it, one of the institutions chosen for the testing was the hospital where Mr. Wright was a patient.

Unfortunately, Mr. Wright did not qualify for the testing because his life expectancy was far too short; one of the stipulations for recipients of the drug testing was that their projected survival was at least three to six months. The claims that accompanied the drug were published in the media and this sparked hope in Mr. Wright, who then pleaded with his doctor to include him in the trial; he was a goner anyways so what could they lose? Three days after his first injection, the doctor visited Mr. Wright expecting him to be dead or at least well on his way but instead was greeted by an incredible sight. According to his treating physician, "The tumour masses had melted like snowballs in a hot stove, and in only these few days were half their original size". Talk about coming back from the dead. That was not all though— in ten days Mr. Wright, from whom they had been draining two liters of lymphoid pus from his body every two days, was discharged from the hospital with "practically all signs of his disease having vanished." While the trial was going on other patients were taking the drug . . . and there was absolutely no improvement in their conditions. For two months, Mr. Wright experienced good health but then reports in the media began to circulate on the ineffectiveness of the new cancer drug Krebiozen. Soon Mr. Wright began to decline in health. His treating physician began to suspect that maybe it was a placebo effect and tried to help by extending the so called placebo effect. The physician told him not to worry, that they were expecting a new shipment of krebiozen that was 'extra-strength' and far more powerful than the drug he had been injected with two months previously. Mr. Wright agreed; in the meantime, the doctors hatched a plan to enhance the psychological effect by telling him the shipment of the new krebiozen was delayed for some reason, thus creating anticipation and high hopes . . . faith. The plan worked as they began injecting Mr. Wright with, yes—water. Again they saw the same effect; the tumor masses melted away and Mr. Wright recovered, "the picture of health." Two months passed before a report appeared in the press; this time it was official. The AMA reported that Krebiozen was a bust; the drug was completely useless in its treatment of cancer. Within a few days of learning about this Mr. Wright was readmitted to the hospital, his condition drastically worsened. Within days of his re-admittance, he was dead.

"MAN IS NOT A REASONING BEING"

There are far worse things than poor eyesight that can affect a human being, as we have just seen with Mr. Wright. Cancer and other diseases kill and maim people, some far too early in life. In light of our brief survey we can see that there is something deeper at work when it comes to illness;

there is a connection between the ills of the body and the thoughts of the mind. If scientists in the time of Dr. Bates had given heed to the phenomena that he was uncovering, where would we be today? Would disease be nonexistent?

Because in the end, we must ask the question that has a million repercussions: What did Mr. Wright die of? In fact let us expand this to the question—What does anyone die of? Since Dr. Bates proved that poor eyesight is really a thought and we have seen the case of Mr. Wright, who proved that cancer is a thought, can we really say that people die from thoughts? I think the evidence must be followed down this strange road. What is interesting is how medicine is not pursuing this with an excitement and zeal as, for instance, when antibiotics were first developed. The extreme power of this phenomenon has been shown in many other cases than the one of Mr. Wright. How many cancer drugs or even natural remedies could effect a breathtaking change, that quickly, like the one Mr. Wright experienced?

There is a sickness that is far greater than the one Mr. Wright succumbed to, and that is the human mind that refuses to look at the truth. This sickness is pervasive; medicine is not the only place that this dogmatic ignorance shows up. Every field of human knowledge is infected with this malady of the mind. This malady is marked by the distinct refusal to investigate an anomaly in whatever field it may be. This ingrained ignorance actually results in stagnation in science; the result is that people end up suffering, when instead they could be reaping the fruit of sincere truth-seeking done by scientists and doctors. Bates puts it best in the very last paragraph of *Perfect Sight Without Glasses*: "The fact is that, except in rare cases, man is not a reasoning being. He is dominated by authority, and when the facts are not in accord with the view imposed by authority, so much the worse for the facts. They may and indeed must, win in the long run; but in the meantime the world gropes needlessly in darkness and endures much suffering that might have been avoided."

The end?

THEOLOGY/METAPHYSICS PILLAR: A NEW ARGUMENT FOR MURDER

7

If evolution is true the evolutionists should be evolving toward better arguments for their theory.

The biologist/author, Richard Dawkins, has achieved somewhat of a celebrity status by refashioning old arguments in the evolutionary/atheistic worldview and presenting them to audiences that do not seem to understand . . . they are still old arguments. Nevertheless Dawkins claims to have found the key to understanding *natural selection*, the mechanism behind evolution. We will investigate that new argument of Dawkins and find that it actually compounds the main problem of natural selection and hence, evolution. Then we will investigate the pillar that evolution along with atheism, is built on— it is an incomplete conception of causality. In fact, we will see that the evolutionist/atheist really has an illogical and rather dangerous view of reality— *all because of their incomplete notion of causality*. The danger I speak of is not only an intellectual blunder but a danger in the sense of causing pain in this world.

However, before Dawkins presents his arguments in his book, *The God Delusion*, he invokes a curious principle of interpretation that he calls upon his readers to embrace *before* looking at the evidence . . . .

THE *ALTER* CALL

In his book, Dawkins tells us that we must look at evolution in a new light, to reconsider it with a fresh approach. This approach entails us *raising our consciousness*, as he states more than once. He draws an analogy between this and normal everyday things in our life such as maps of the earth being configured with the northern hemisphere on the top as a 'northern hemispheric chauvinism'. He says maps could be displayed showing the southern hemisphere on top and that these would be 'consciousness raisers' in our Northern hemisphere classrooms. The same with the issue of feminism. When we substitute her-story for history this makes us aware of our bias and our consciousness is raised. He then pleads that the same must occur with our view toward the mechanism behind what drives evolution— natural selection. The only reason these 'consciousness raisers' enlighten us to some reality is that they can be empirically or logically deduced. In other words, if the evidence leads us there, then one is justified in seeing things in a 'new light'. However, you can not alter your view on something that is demonstrably wrong. Or rather, you *can*— but only while bypassing the critical factor known as the reasoning mind. I believe Dawkins is well aware of the shortcomings of evolutionary theory and this awareness leads him to call for a 'jump before you look' attitude in his readers.

So, what exactly does it mean to have ones consciousness raised regarding evolution? It really is a call to *faith*.

What he battles most in his opponents is their faith based religion where faith is given a priority to evidence. Yet in his book, before any evidence is presented, we have a call from the altar to alter our beliefs *before* looking at the evidence. Seems strange coming from supposedly a scientific, rational man. The reason for this is obvious; the modification proposed by Dawkins, for rehabilitating natural selection and thus evolution, is even more problematical than the original theory.

THE DANCE OF DAWKINS

Natural selection is a process of nature that selects beneficial developments in an organism over those that are non-beneficial. These beneficial developments will allow the organism to survive in the environment. The dynamic between the organism and the environment are what is primary. It is somewhat of a feedback loop. The environment has certain conditions that must be met by an organism in order to survive. The organism that displays 'adaptability' survives and is able to transmit this to its progeny. This transmittal ensures survival of the organism.

But the problem begins upon closer inspection of this process. In this process there is a continuum in which the organism develops from A to B. Let us say that B is the full development of that organ and A is the organ's premature stage where it is supposedly just beginning to adapt to environmental conditions. Before the organ reaches its fully adaptable state, B, it is in an incomplete state. This continuum between the two points is exactly where the problem lies, however. For instance, how is half an eye a benefit to an organism— how does an incomplete state favor selection? Presumably, as the evolutionists say, the process is a slow one with millions of years involved and development taking as long. But before getting to a fully functioning eye there had to be something that wasn't what we would call . . . an eye. This partial eye would serve as no benefit to the organism, so the environment would surely smother a development of this sort. This goes for any organ or body part. What benefit would these inoperable, non-functioning half-formed appendages or organs serve? If we follow the rationale of natural selection it compels us to say . . . NONE. The theory folds in upon itself with a breathtaking collapse. The vaunted mechanism of evolution cannot explain itself. But have no fear, Richard Dawkins now comes along and says we must believe in it by 'raising our consciousness'; or rather, is he saying 'just have some faith'.

As we see, the problem with natural selection is the incompatibility of the intermediate forms of an organism with the environment. The answer for Dawkins is this: The spectrum of changes that an organism must go through to get from half an eye to a fully functioning eye must be modified. He agrees that it is highly improbable to go from half an eye to a fully formed eye. These jumps are unreasonable, says Dawkins. This has been a misunderstanding of the mechanism. To raise the probability of half an eye morphing into a fully functioning eye one must envision a spectrum of many intermediate steps between that half-eye and the full eye. So instead of large jumps from half formed eyes to fully formed eyes we have many miniscule alterations that occur that probably involve change on the molecular level, so you can see that the process would be very long indeed and we would have to invoke many millions of years. So the adaptation continuum would range from A to Z instead of A to B, so to speak, because this brings in the idea of many steps and this raises the probability of the organism maturing into the fully adaptable organism that we are used to.

The Dawkins answer to this problem of natural selection is a rather strange doctrine in that it evades the main issue. He calls it 'cumulative natural selection'. This is the proper way to see evolution, according to Dawkins. It has been all misunderstood, mostly by creationists. This move by Dawkins, however, seems only to try to avoid the 'half an eye' criticism and it's improbability. To raise the probability of evolution occurring, he incrementalizes the process into minute steps. As he puts it on page 121 of *The God Delusion*, "The answer is that natural selection is a cumulative process which breaks the improbability up into small pieces. Each of the small pieces is slightly improbable but not prohibitively so." The logic is rather strange, because he seems to avoid the issue as I stated at the outset. The issue is not one of probability but one of *survivability*. The theory says that an adaptation that is favorable becomes a part of the organism— why would the environment favor an adaptation that is *not* favorable? Is Dawkins saying the eye that is incrementally maturing into a functioning eye is better suited to survive than one that makes bigger jumps? What's the difference between an eye half formed (1/2) than one that is 5/8 (in the new cumulative view) formed? Or 7/8? They are both non-functioning as we know the eye to be. *How does an infinitesimal step in evolution, as Dawkins proposes, make an organism more fit for survival when it is still, like the half formed eye, not favorable for the organisms survival?* He does not answer this but side-steps into saying that it becomes more probable. What does probability have to do with function which is a prerequisite for selection? Whether big or small, any increment must be judged on whether it is favorable or not. The question he doesn't ask is what is the probability that an organism with an unformed eye has in surviving. Try to envision an eye that is 3/8, 17/32 or 9/16 etc. of the way to being fully formed— it is still a non-functioning eye. Even though we have adopted his micro-incrementalism the question remains: *How* does an organism survive in a half formed, or with Dawkins' revised theory, a 3/8 state? Instead the question that he asks is : What is the chance of this happening? Well, this seems to be that he is assuming that it happens . . . .

But even this minute incremental-ism is fatal to his cumulative theory. It imposes a huge strain on the already problematic (for the evolutionists) fossil record. If we grant Dawkins his incrementalist approach it seems that there would have to be *many more* intermediate forms between the non-eye to what we would call the fully functioning eye. The evolutionists have difficulty already with the lack of transitional forms in the fossil record. Where are all these micro-mediates? If smaller changes occur between the unformed and fully formed state there would have to be evidence of all these micro-forms. And how many micro-forms are we calling for? Hundreds, thousands or millions? Due to the complexity of the eye there would have to be at least thousands of changes. But this is only digging a bigger ditch for Dawkins and his adherents. Now he has raised the standard of evidence for evolution in his new and revised theory. For now they must go and search for, not only transitional forms but they must look for transitional forms to those transitional forms. This could never end, for these micro-mediates should be more abundant in the fossil record since there are so many steps. We should be seeing creatures with eyes 1/8 formed, 3/16 formed, 1/4 formed, 1/2 formed and so on, in the fossil record. The standard of evidence has just increased exponentially.

THE INCREMENTAL JET

We can understand now why Dawkins calls on us to 'raise our consciousness'. I agree with Dawkins on that point because you must lay logic at the door when crossing the threshold into this theory. It is simply evasive to shunt the problem away from its main critique, the fact that it has a serious internal problem.

An example that Dawkins likes to make light of in his book is the jet plane analogy that was put forth by the astronomer Fred Hoyle. Hoyle likened natural selection in the formation of complex organisms to a cyclone ravaging a junkyard and then as a result forming a massive jet plane. Well, this is absurd claims Dawkins. It shows the misunderstanding the detractors have about natural selection. Natural selection, says Dawkins, is not that drastic. The eye for instance, with its many parts and processes, does not make a leap like Hoyle claims with his massive jet. It is very improbable for *one event* to have this outcome. Instead, as we saw above, it is more probable for a much smaller event to occur and then another ...and then another. Let's see this with a picture by re-imagining Hoyle's massive jet plane.

Let's see if we are misunderstanding Dawkins by utilizing the micro-incrementalist approach regarding the jet plane analogy. Through one event, perhaps a wheel might attach itself to a landing gear assembly. Then through another chance windstorm this assembly attaches itself to a hydraulic line which becomes attached to an electrical assembly that perhaps was assembled by itself incrementally through time. We could go on but I think you get the picture. With the thousands of parts a Boeing jet has, we must postulate thousands of these events occurring to bring these pieces together rather than the hasty one time event that Hoyle chose as an analogy. We can see that there lies an even greater absurdity with this incrementalist approach. The only modification we have brought in is Dawkins' micro-incrementalism. Each change in arranging the jet plane is done one step at a time rather than the big event that Hoyle invoked. It seems that this approach, even more so, calls in the need for an Intelligence to arrange where the individual parts go. Keep in mind the complexity and sophistication of the eye is far greater than a jet plane.

Here is what Dawkins has done. Not only has he evaded the internal error of natural selection but he has also transferred the probability problem. According to Dawkins, because the eye is so complex, it is difficult to envision it as being fully formed and functional through only a few evolutionary steps, so the revised theory of Dawkins has the complexity (many parts) of the organ chopped up into a million 'micro-events' to raise probability. *The problem of a million parts becomes the problem of a million events.* In other words, having understood that the eyeball is extremely complex, Dawkins and his ilk try to make their theory more reasonable by introducing smaller movements in the eyes growth through evolutionary time. But the probability problem is still there with just another name, in this case 'cumulative natural selection'. A million events occurring, to form an eye, is just as improbable as the eye jumping from half formed to fully formed. It is a sleight of hand that probably makes Dawkins feel good. The jet plane analogy above sheds some light on this but perhaps another analogy will help.

Something complex involves more than one part. The best synonym would be the word *intricate*. The other word would be *interrelation*— for the parts, though different, have a connection in their interrelatedness. A complex machine has many parts interrelated, a complex piece of music has parts interrelated, a complex dance move has many moves or events interrelated. The connotations of complexity involve multiple *things* and/or multiple movements or *events* in time as in the dance steps of a dancer. With the multiple events that Dawkins espouses he has just reintroduced that which he was trying to eliminate— complexity and its attendant problem in natural selection, improbability. By diminishing (at least in his mind) the problem of complexity of parts he has brought it back with complexity of events. With increased complexity— many parts or many events–there will always be raised the question of probability.

The question still looms that evolution has not been able to answer— how does a partially formed eye survive? Or in Dawkins case, how does 3/8 of an eye, or an eye changed to a molecular degree, yet still unformed, survive? As in the past, so with the present representative of evolution, it goes unanswered . . . .

ARISTOTLE AT HIGH NOON

But even if we grant the evolutionist his mechanism of natural selection the question must be asked— what is the *ground* of this law? Is this law self explaining or is it grounded or caused by something else? To the theist, laws and all reality for that matter are grounded in a being known as God. Causality lies in a person who is at the same time Creator and Sustainer. To the evolutionist, causality is due to current laws that we are finding more and more about. We are also sustained by these laws. The more we find out about these laws the closer we get to the answer or the secrets to creation, so says the evolutionist. We still have some ignorance on a few thorny issues the creationists raise but that does not mean that sooner or later we will find these things out too. You see, to the evolutionist, everything can be explained by LAWS or PROCESSES.

Like a nervous gunfighter, Richard Dawkins always has his hand twitching for his weapon of choice. In almost any setting, whether through books, lectures or interviews he draws and quips: "We already understand the laws of how that works, therefore we don't need to invoke a deity." This is his handy response to anyone that brings up something that strongly implies design and therefore, Intelligence. According to Dawkins, a law of nature, once found, is explanatory of a process or thing. No need to invoke God for that thing or process because we now *understand* the law or process. Laws, once discovered and understood, explain everything. Our ignorance is blinding us temporarily from discovering ultimate laws but these too will be found out and we'll have an explanation for everything. On the other hand we have the creationist saying that some things can't be explained...that they are Providentially sustained. Little miracles. But what happens from time to time is the evolutionist comes along and discovers a reason for the 'little miracle' happening— so out goes the Creator as explanation for the process. At least this is the commonly held view.

This debate really would be a non-issue if ancient Philosophy were respected for it's insights. In the realm of thought this happens to be most true. Scientists build on knowledge that has been previously discovered; why would anyone be stupid enough to try to re-invent the wheel or the radio? In philosophy we should also build on past thinking but it seems that there is a cloud of conceit that surrounds modern day thinkers in that they are contemptuous toward the ancients. But as we will see throughout these pages and forthcoming volumes, it is the Ancients that hold the key to philosophical conundrums.

Aristotle, the Philosopher, settled the argument of causality over two thousand years ago. He showed that causality is 'multi-phased'. He didn't call it that but we can call it anything—multi-faceted, multi-structured, or even multi-layered. The point is that causality, as we will soon see, has aspects to it that are inherent to the nature of causality. You can not explain causality only in terms of *law or process*. Process is only one aspect of organic causality. Organic causality is causality considered in all of its aspects— in it's fullness. There is an aspect of causality that is non-quantifiable, in other words. An aspect that can't be measured by instruments or constrained by methodology.

Aristotle's key insight was that causality is *compounded*. This is called *organic causality*— if any other type of causality is invoked, it is fractionated and incomplete as we shall see. What he observed is that when anything came to *be*, it always seemed to have multiple factors that brought it into existence. But these multiple factors were inextricable from each other— they couldn't be separated from each other. They had this unique property of absolute unity and distinctiveness at the same time.

First, the thing or event that is caused has an origin. This, Aristotle named the Material Cause and it answers the question, WHAT is the thing made of? The *Material Cause* is *that from which* a thing comes to be.

Second, the raw material must have something or someone to shape it into it's final shape. This, Aristotle named the *Efficient Cause* and it answered the question, HOW does the thing come about? The Efficient Cause is *that by which* the thing comes to be.

Third, the two previous causes work together to Form an object or event. This is the *Formal Cause* and it also answers, What is being made or what is the Form? The Formal Cause is *that into which* the thing takes shape. It is the finished product.

Fourth is the Reason for the something. It is the purpose or end for which the thing was made. It is the Goal or End of the previous three causes. What is the end or goal of making shoes or building that house or going to school? Every activity, every act has an End. This is called the *Final Cause*. It is that for which the thing has come into being. It is the very purpose for the things existence.

To illustrate the four causes in action we'll use the shoemaker analogy— you can plug anything in. The shoemaker takes something, leather, that has no resemblance to the finished product, the shoe. This piece of leather is *that from which (material cause)* the shoemaker will form into a shoe. The shoemaker is *that by which* (efficient cause) the shoe comes into being. He is the director or the agent of change from raw material to finished product or the Efficient Cause. The Formal Cause is the final product, the actual shoe itself. It is *that into which* (formal cause) the leather and labor and knowledge were directed. The Final Cause is the Purpose for the shoe, which I think we all understand. The shoe was INTENDED for something.

If we further distill this analysis of causality by Aristotle we can appreciate that there are really two fundamental aspects to causality:

— a Director or Intelligence and
— the materials which with the Director operates

The important point to bear in mind is that Aristotle is saying that there is another aspect to causality— there is another side to it. It so happens that modern day *complexity theory* bears witness to Aristotle's insight by confirming the compounded nature of causality. And we will show, by further use of analogy in the real world, that if we do not grasp this special dual nature of causality then there will be pain in the world . . .

THE PHILOSOPHY OF EMERGENCE

In Complexity Theory we have two distinct worlds, the micro and the macro. A complex system or thing is one in which *diverse* entities or actors are connected to each other, or *interdependent* that are also *adaptable*. Diversity, interdependence, and adaptability. A complex system like an economy or an ecosystem or corporation, the human body, a city, a painter painting or even a shoemaker shoe-making exhibit all these characteristics of complexity. But here is what is unsettling. Each thing that we just named has two aspects, the micro-level and the macro-level. These two things are aspects of *one thing,* yet the two aspects bear absolutely *no resemblance to each other.*

When two people hug and express feelings for one another what we see is commonly held to be an expression of love. But in complexity theory this is the outer or macro level for there is another aspect that lies hidden to our eyes that is very much unlike what we see on the outside. Inside the individual bodies of these two people hugging, what we see is a whole other world— there are biochemical reactions and hormones releasing and not to mention the multitudes of enzymatic activities occurring at the cellular level and thousands of other reactions all happening at the same time. There is a disjunction between the two aspects that can be difficult to reconcile. These two aspects of the same act, as we said, bear no resemblance to one another. If we were to examine a painting with a low powered microscope we would see all these miniscule dots and lines that are seemingly haphazardly placed. At this micro-level the painting doesn't make much sense. But when we step back we see a picture of a lovely lake with a couple picnicking by the shore. An ecosystem has an incredible diversity of individual entities that do their own thing. The ants know nothing of the birds which know nothing of the bees which know nothing of the soil organisms and so on. Yet out of these layers and layers of activity a system of functional beauty EMERGES. Out of all these micro aspects that have incredible complexity, something emerges which is quite distinct— qualitatively— from the micro-level. Picture again the two people hugging and then remember all the biochemical reactions occurring internally as they hug. There is a discontinuity between the two aspects that is unsettling because of the un-likeness of the aspects. Now, here is an exercise to stretch your brain somewhat. If you were given a picture of the internal reactions of the two people hugging— that is, you do not know they are hugging— all you have is information on biochemical reactions and enzyme activity and blood pressure readings and such— would you be able to deduce from looking at this information or seeing it on some machine that could look into the body— would you be able to deduce that two people were expressing love for one another in the outside world? This aspect bears no relation to the outside yet out of these layers of physiological activity something in the outside world EMERGES. This macro-aspect which emerges does not logically follow from that strange world inside. It is wholly other... It is something more. And it is not quantifiable.

BUT the activity that is going on inside the two individuals has one interesting aspect that the modern age adheres to and worships as it's guiding principle: the activity inside is *measurable or quantifiable*. At the micro-level, law and process, which Dawkins loves to talk about, are king. At the micro-level we have that which can be measured. We have the ability to quantify at this level. We can count the number of dots in the painting. We can classify the species in the ecosystem and measure what they do. We can describe the biochemical reactions in that embrace of two lovers. But is that the whole picture? Does law and process tell us the complete story of reality or is it a disjointed, fractionated picture? Aristotle would say that it is incomplete. It is inorganic. In fact the whole of humankind will stand or fall depending on which view they take. If they take the fractionated view of the modern scientific mind, there will be an incomplete picture of reality and consequences which will result in— pain. In the fractionated view of causality, there is no such thing as art, love, morality. They are all just conventions, made up on a whim which can be explained scientifically.

But the macro level is something more. It is something that can't be measured or fall in the hands of instrumentation. It just is. When you start measuring and quantifying the ecosystem you must focus on a part. These individual parts can never add up to the whole. How does this chaos at the micro-level explain beauty, art and love? It doesn't.

We can see this in Aristotle's shoemaker. The strips of leather, the labor of the man fashioning different parts, the thread lying about, do not make sense at the moment. But something emerges which has purpose. In fact, it is guided by purpose. The only reason something emerges is because of purpose, whether in nature or in the dealings of men. Now, purpose implies MIND.

IN DEFENSE OF MURDER

The following is a true story that has occurred many, many times in real life:

Sound waves, carried through the air due to compression of molecules, reach the auricular cavity of a human being whereby mechanical vibrations are translated into electrical signals which travel to and signal the brain to produce certain neuro-transmitters. These chemical signals then activate the nervous system which through electrical impulses fires certain nerve endings. All these chemical and electrical processes then, in turn, activate mechanical processes that involve musculature and bone. The thousands upon thousands of cellular processes that involve enzymatic reactions, action potentials, cellular receptor binding and formation, are too numerous to mention. The end result of all these reactions is the mobilization of muscles and ligaments which end up, in this case, moving a finger in a precise manner. As Dawkins says, all these actions are understandable and explainable in scientific terms. But all these actions in the interior of the person are *only one side of the story*— they are the micro-level aspect that can be measured but yet does not give the whole picture. What is the whole picture or what is the other aspect to what we have just mentioned?

The other aspect of the story is that of the macro-level. Here is what happened at the macro-level at the very same time as the micro-level processes mentioned above. . .

A member of a gang (an individual human being) heard insults from a member of an opposing gang. These were the sound waves with distinct frequency and amplitude. The gang member receiving the insults then drew his weapon in which he depressed the trigger. A bullet was released, killing the person giving the insults. But, as we demonstrated above, this was also done at a molecular, biological level— the micro-level. If Dawkins was the lawyer, he would be able to defend his client on the basis of law and process, wouldn't he? "Your Honor, this is what really happened. You see, sound waves at a specific frequency traveled through space causing a chain reaction of biochemical reactions in my client which resulted in the bio-mechanical depression of the trigger of a gun which resulted in penetration of the dermal and sub-dermal layers of the . . . ." Even though all these laws and processes occur, which is undeniable, there is a *purposive* macro-action that this world recognizes— it is called Morality. Morality can't be explained in biochemical, acoustic causality— it is something *other*. If that were all to causality, i.e. law and process, then all morality means nothing and Hitler and his henchmen were just so many particular arrangements of atoms that were in a particular place subject to particular laws of physics and chemistry. How could you blame a collection of atoms and the mysterious forces which move them? If we utilize that thinking, we could say with Dawkins in concluding his argument to the jury, "We understand the laws that governed the action of my client, therefore we do not need to invoke purposive behaviour (which implies Mind)."

Purposive behaviour is what governs all of humanity in its dealings and interactions. It is also the other side to causality. As Aristotle intimated there is a Director and there is Matter. The aspect which science focuses on is Matter— to the complete disregard of the other aspect which is Intelligence or Mind. Science uses this fractionated causality regarding nature but there is evidence that this fractionated view of causality has seeped into the thinking and reasoning of society at all levels. There will be certain implications as a result of this 'scientific' way of thinking when applied to all of reality.

First and foremost, as we saw in the above example, there is hardly any blame or guilt that can be attributed to anyone. *It* is nobody's fault. Whatever *it* is, can not be blamed on anyone for *it* is a result of laws and forces at every level.

Secondly, why should I *do* anything? Everything is up to fate (i.e. forces, molecules, atoms etc). Yes, and since everything is determined, why should I act in any capacity at all?

Thirdly, as a corollary of these two, the expressions of

man (art), lose value. How can we judge between molecules and atoms that are configured and act in a certain way (the artists themselves and their work) and say that one is better than the other? After all, they are just atoms and their associated laws and processes. Hence, artistic standards will fall.

So, human thought and action in the moral sphere and in the social sphere and in the artistic sphere are affected.

In the moral sphere the predominant philosophy will be hedonism. After all, each individual's feelings and urges are a result of atomic and molecular laws and biochemical reactions. If these biochemical reactions are all that is, then to call them wrong or right is really just convention or cultural habit. How can a process or a reaction in physiology be wrong? It would be much like attributing moral characterstics to rock and snow when they topple down upon people in a landslide. Can rocks and gravity and the sound spectrum be wrong? We see that this is a silly undertaking. But the same thing should occur in Dawkins' world when we talk about murder. For murder is a physical act that has physiological and cellular origins. How can we call what the cell does as being wrong?

In the social sphere the predominant view will be apathy. This view is really the outcome and the flip side of hedonism. Any injustice that occurs in the world is just a particular arrangement of atoms that is just being moved by mysterious forces. There is no rightness or wrongness in the arrangement and forces of atoms whether they make up human beings or the weather. Hence, there is no injustice *out there* for me to correct or to be active in correcting.

In the sphere of human expression or art there will be

relativism and stupidity on a massive scale— the emperor's clothes will be quite in fashion. If John Cage wants to sit at his piano for four minutes and thirty-three seconds and do absolutely nothing but stare at the piano keyboard while the audience shuffles their feet and makes miscellaneous noises then that is his prerogative. But to call it artistic expression and label it as the artists most important piece? Value will suffer because, again, we are dealing with forces and atoms and molecules that behave a certain way. Just because this arrangement is in a particular form does not give us any justification for declaring it good or beautiful. Beauty truly becomes a subjective form and this allows the likes of a Jackson Pollock work of art to be declared genius rather than laziness.

But the biggest problem may be how we feel inside about life in general. What is the purpose of life if I am just a bundle of atoms prearranged to act in a certain way? We know and feel, intuitively, that there is something more. When we accept a hug from a child or a parent, Dawkins and Science with their fractionated view of causality, would have us believe that that action is just a movement of atoms arranged in a higher order of complexity of organs. This view has saturated our culture and the ramifications are not understood by most for we have only touched on them briefly. But meditating on the principles will hopefully impress upon you the dire consequences of this philosophy.

Realizing this inconsistency of fractionated causality the scientist must come to a conclusion. Is there purpose in man's behaviour or is he just a molecular machine driven by forces above and beyond him? The scientist, in this world, acts in a purposive way but does not believe in purpose or mind regarding nature. But this is really inconsistent. For instance, if a criminal robs Dawkins of his money we can guess some outcomes of this. Firstly, we can guess that Dawkins will be angry. But why? This is completely at odds with his worldview. Why be upset when the man who robbed you is just a collection of atoms and chemicals doing their thing? Secondly, Dawkins' reaction of anger also means nothing— in fact any emotion is just a molecular arrangement anyways. So I think we can see a little bit of how the scientist/atheist, or anyone else who believes this worldview, straddles rather precariously, two worlds at odds with each other. We must recognize the compounded nature of man. Scientists exclude the teleological, purposive aspects of man and adhere to the fractionated view that is one-sided; this does not tell the whole story.

As we have seen, to hold the fractionated view of man is not tenable. Organic causality understands and is inclusive of the intricacy of man and nature. If we adopt this for man then we must also adopt this way of thinking for all of reality which includes physical nature. For nature is part of the order of things and, if man, as Aristotle pointed out, has this multiphased composition, then the *same is true for nature*. The implications of adopting organic rather than fractionated causality is obvious. Nature is composed of this organic causality as is man. We can no longer look at nature in a fractionated way because it is inconsistent when applied even to a small scale, as we have seen. Underneath the laws and processes that scientists observe and measure, there is something else, something more at work . . . . It is purposive . . . . it is Mind.

So as a result of our new understanding of causality let

us breathe in and ponder with all that has been said, the following situation: When a child asks what is causing the wind to blow, the correct answer is GOD.

SELECT BIBLIOGRAPHY

INTRODUCTION _ PARADOX GAINED
–*Language as Ideology*, Gunther Kress and Robert Hodge 1979
–*Syntactic Structures*, Noam Chomsky 1957
–*Grammatical Man*, Jeremy Campbell 1982
–*Tractate Shabbath*, Various authors Internet Version
–*Everyman's Talmud*, Abraham Cohen 1932
FIRST PILLAR _ HISTORY: WE ARE LOSERS
–*The Historian's Craft*, Marc Bloch 1964
–*The Idea of History*, R.G. Collingwood 1994 Revised Edition
–*Mourt's Relation- A Journal of the Pilgrims at Plymouth Plantation*, George Morton; Edition by Applewood Books 1986. Originally Published in 1622
–*Of Plymouth Plantation 1620-1647*, William Bradford; Edition by Alfred Knopf 1952.
–*Good Newes From New England*, Edward Winslow; Internet Version
–*History as Mystery*, Michael Parenti 2001
–*Childhood's End*, Arthur C. Clarke 1953

- *A People's History of the United States*, Howard Zinn 1980
- *WInston Churchill*, Clive Ponting 1994
- *1940: Myth and Reality*, Clive Ponting 1993
- *The Real Lincoln*, Thomas DiLorenzo 2003
- *1421: The Year China Discovered America*, Gavin Menzies 2003
- *When China Ruled the Seas*, Louise Levathes 1997
- *The Origins of Anti-Semitism*, John Gager 1985
- *A Model of Christian Charity*, John Winthrop
- *America's Communal Utopias*, Donald E. Pitzer 1997
- *Visions of Utopia*, Edward Rothstein 2004
- *Republic*, Plato

SECOND PILLAR_ SCIENCE: ET TU, SCIENTIA?

- *The Deep Hot Biosphere*, Thomas Gold 2001
- *Black Gold Stranglehold*, Jerome Corsi 2005
- *Criticism and the Growth of Knowledge*, Imre Lakatos 1970
- *What is This Thing Called Science?*, A.F. Chalmers 1999
- *The Doomsday Myth*, Charles Maurice and Charles Smithson 1984
- *Limits to Growth*, Donella H. Meadows 1972
- *An Essay on the Principle of Population*, Thomas Malthus Internet Edition
- *The Population Bomb*, Paul Erlich 1970
- *Ultimate Resource*, Julian L. Simon 1983
- *The Energy Non-Crisis*, Lindsey Williams 1981
- *Sacred Trust: The Medieval Chuch as an Economic Firm*, Robert B. Ekelund 1996

–*Critical Path*, Buckminster Fuller 1981

THIRD PILLAR_POLITI-NOMICS: THAT WHICH IS UNSEEN

--*I, Pencil*, Leonard Reed
–*That Which is Seen and That Which is Not Seen*, Frederic Bastiat
–*The Law*, Frederic Bastiat
–*Economic Sophisms*, Frederic Bastiat
–*Economics in One Lesson*, Henry Hazlitt 1946
–*Economics For Real People*, Gene Callahan 2004
–*The Wealth of Nations*, Adam Smith
–*Capitalism: The Unknown Ideal*, Ayn Rand
–*The Robber Barons*, Matthew Josephson
–*The Mystery of Capital*, Hernando DeSoto 2003
–*The Roosevelt Myth*, John T. Flynn 1948
--*New Deal or Raw Deal*, Burton W. Folsom Jr. 2009
–*The Myth of the Robber Barrons*, Burton W. Folsom 1991

FOURTH PILLAR_FORTEAN: UFOS ARE SUPPRESSED TECHNOLOGY part 1

–*Timaeus*, Plato
–*Hamlet's Mill*, Georgio deSantillana 1969
–*Worlds in Collision*, Immanuel Velikovsky 1950
–*The Secret Message of Jules Verne*, Michel Lamy 2007
–*Robur the Conqueror*, Jules Verne 1885
–*Master of the World*, Jules Verne 1904
–*Logic and the Art of Memory*, Paolo Rossi 2006
–*The Art of Memory*, Francis Yates 1966
–*The Morning of the Magicians*, Louis Pauwels and Jaques Bergier
--*A Rosicrucian Notebook*, Willy Schrodter 1954

—*Free Energy Pioneer: John Keely*, Theo Paijmans 2004
—*The Secrets of Dellschau*, Dennis Crenshaw 2009
—*Anatomy of a Phenomenon*, Jaques Vallee 1965
—*The Rainbow Conspiracy*, Brad Steiger
—*The UFO Phenomenon*, Time-Life Books 1988
—*The Great Texas Airship Mystery*, Wallace O. Chariton 1991
—*Mystery Airships in the Sky*, Steven A. Arts 2003
—*The Chemical Wedding of Christian Rosenkreutz*, Anonymous
—*The Rosicrucian Mysteries*, Max Heindel 1911

FIFTH PILLAR_GENERAL PHILOSOSPHY: THE POISON FOUNTAIN OF EDUCATION part 1

—*The Underground History of American Education*, John Gatto 2000
—*Building the Educational State 1836-1871*, Bruce Curtis 1988
—*The Graves of Academe*, Richard Mitchell
—*The Irony of Early School Reform*, Michael B. Katz 2001
--*The Poison Fountain*, Zachariah Montgomery 1878
—*Drops From the Poison Fountain*, Zachariah Montgomery 1880
—*History of Education in Virginia*, Cornelius Heatwole 1916
—*Why Johnny Can't Read*, Rudolph Flesch 1955
—*The Psychology and Pedagogy of Reading*, Edmund Burke Huey 1908
—*My Pedagogic Creed*, John Dewey 1910

−*The Primary Education Fetish*, essay by John Dewey 1898
−*Social Control*, Edward Alsworth Ross 1901
−*The Leipzig Connection*, Paolo Lioni 1993
−*Triumphant Democracy*, Andrew Carnegie 1886
−*The Secret of Herbart*, Frank Hayward 1904
−*The Rule of St. Benedict*, St Benedict
−*The History of the Corporation*, Bruce Brown
−*Encyclopedia of Monasticism vol. 1*, William M. Johnston 2000
−*Sacred Trust: The Medieval Church as an Economic Firm* Robert B. Ekelund 1996
−*Your Money or Your Life*, Jaques Le Goff
−*Late Medieval Monasteries and Their Patrons*, Karen Stober 2007

SIXTH PILLAR_HEALTH: FOR THOSE WHO HAVE EYES TO SEE

−*The Bates Method For Better Eyesight Without Glasses*, William Bates
−*Relearning to See*, Thomas R. Quackenbush 2000
−*Take Off Your Glasses and See*, Jacob Liberman 1995
−*Light: Medicine of the Future*, Jacob Liberman 1990
−*Conscious Breathing*, Joy Manne 2004
−*The Molecules of Emotion*, Candace Pert 1999
−*The Art of Seeing*, Aldous Huxley 1952
−*The Relaxation Response*, Herbert Benson 1976
−*Better Eyesight: The Complete Magazines of Willian Bates*, Thomas Quackenbush
−*The Psychology of Attention*, T. Ribot 1911
−*Yoga: Immortality and Freedom*, Mircea Eliade 1970
−*The Wisdom of the Body*, Walter Cannon 1963

−*The Psycho-Biology of Mind-Body Healing*, Ernest Lawrence Rossi 1993

SEVENTH PILLAR_THEOLOGY/METAPHYSICS: A NEW ARGUMENT FOR MURDER

−*PHYSICS*, Aristotle
−*Metaphysics*, Aristotle
−*Summa Theologica*, Thomas Aquinas
−*Aristotle For Everybody*, Mortimer Adler

www.ingramcontent.com/pod-product-compliance
Lightning Source LLC
Chambersburg PA
CBHW070118100426
42744CB00010B/1860